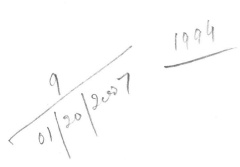

DISCOVERING ANCIENT EGYPT

Discovering Ancient Egypt

ROSALIE DAVID

Facts On File

Discovering Ancient Egypt
First published in the United States by Facts On File, Inc., 1994,
by arrangement with Michael O'Mara Books Limited
9 Lion Yard, Tremadoc Road,
London SW4 7NQ

Facts On File, Inc.
460 Park Avenue South
New York NY 10016-7382

Library of Congress Cataloging-in-Publication Data

David, A. Rosalie (Ann Rosalie)
  Discovering ancient Egypt / Rosalie David.
    p. cm.
  Includes bibliographical references and index.
  ISBN 0-8160-3105-3
    1. Egypt—Antiquities. 2. Egypt—History—640 A.D.
3. Egyptologists. I. Title.
DT56. 9.D39 1994
932—dc20   93-38601

A British CIP catalogue record for this book
is available from the British Library.

Facts On File books are available at special discounts
when purchased in bulk quantities for businesses,
associations, institutions or sales promotions.
Please call our Special Sales Department in
New York at 212/683-2244 or 800/322-8755.

Maps by Peter Funnell
Edited by Serena Dilnot
Designed and typeset by Martin Bristow

Printed in Spain

10 9 8 7 6 5 4 3 2 1

This book is printed on acid-free paper.

Contents

Acknowledgments

I am very grateful to Mr G. Thompson for producing many of the photographs in this book, and also to the Manchester Museum and the John Rylands University Library, Manchester, for permission to use photographic material from their collections.

I should also like to thank Mrs C. Birch for all her help in typing the manuscript, and the publishers for their advice and encouragement in production of the book – particularly Michael O'Mara, Catherine Taylor and Serena Dilnot.

To my husband, as always, I am especially grateful for all his help and support.

Rosalie David
Manchester 1993

Introduction

The aim of this book is to relate how the discoveries of early travellers, archaeologists, and philologists have helped us to understand the ancient Egyptian world and its civilization. Part I is a general introduction to the men and women who travelled to Egypt in order to see the great monuments, to excavate them, and ultimately, to interpret this information into historical facts. These people included early Classical travellers and writers such as Herodotus, Diodorus Siculus and Strabo; the Arab and Medieval scholars and pilgrims; the post-Renaissance explorers; and the early archaeologists for whom Napoleon's military adventure in Egypt opened up many new opportunities. The decipherment of Hieroglyphs, culminating in Champollion's breakthrough, and the work of Mariette, Maspero, and others in founding Egypt's Antiquities Service and National Museum ensured that Egyptology was established as a serious discipline which finally moved away from esoteric theories about hieroglyphs and pyramids. The practices of ransacking the monuments and removing the artifacts, which had previously dominated the subject, were replaced by advances in scientific excavation which were pioneered by Petrie, Reisner and others. They ensured that all archaeological evidence, not simply 'treasure' or inscribed pieces, was saved and studied to assist in reconstructing Egypt's history.

The country has a wealth of monuments – tombs, temples, palaces, domestic dwellings and military sites – which illustrate some six thousand years of civilization. The near-ideal environmental conditions provided by a predominantly stable, warm and dry climate, together with the Egyptians' custom of burying their dead on the edges of the desert surrounded by objects for use in the next life, have ensured that there is an abundance of well-preserved excavated material from these sites. Also, as one of the earliest literate societies with an extensive bureaucracy, the Egyptians kept records of historical events and social, medical and legal matters; they also wrote poetry, composed stories and love songs, and inscribed their tomb and temple walls with texts which provide an insight into their formal religious beliefs and customs. This rich legacy of monuments, objects and texts provides an unsurpassed record of an ancient civilization.

Part II is a survey of the most famous sites which have been explored and excavated, with references to early travellers and to the work of individual excavators and the various learned excavation societies. It is impossible to include here details of all the modern work and studies which are in progress; therefore, most information is provided about the initial discovery and revelation of each site. The epigraphic surveys which have recorded the standing monuments and their inscriptions are another important aspect of Egyptology; the development of these expeditions is traced from the early work of Napoleon's savants, Champollion and Rosellini, Lepsius, and individuals such as Wilkinson, through to the methods and techniques employed in the surveys undertaken at the temples at Medinet Habu, Karnak, Abydos, Esna, Edfu and Denderah.

In addition to excavation of the sites and monuments, and the parallel requirement of copying and recording the scenes and inscriptions, there is also a constant and urgent need to conserve and sometimes restore the ancient buildings and artifacts. Here, in considering individual sites, there are references both to the epigraphic studies and major preservation projects that have been undertaken, as well as to major archaeological discoveries.

Finally, Part III provides an outline history of Egypt which attempts to show how evidence derived from the excavations has helped Egyptologists to reconstruct the main developments and events of the civilization, from predynastic times to the Graeco-Roman Period. It also indicates some of the difficulties involved in providing details for periods of history for which archaeological data is scanty or missing.

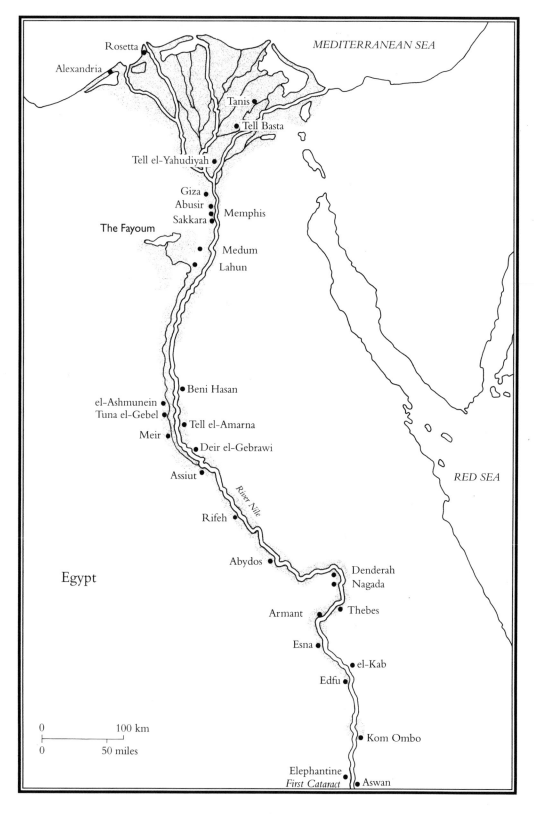

MEDITERRANEAN SEA

Rosetta

Alexandria

Tanis

Tell Basta

Tell el-Yahudiyah

Giza
Abusir
Sakkara • Memphis

The Fayoum

Medum
Lahun

Beni Hasan

el-Ashmunein
Tuna el-Gebel
Meir • Tell el-Amarna

Deir el-Gebrawi

Assiut

River Nile

Rifeh

Abydos

Denderah
Nagada

Armant • Thebes

Egypt

Esna

el-Kab

Edfu

Kom Ombo

0   100 km
0   50 miles

Elephantine
First Cataract • Aswan

RED SEA

PART I

The Discoverers

The modern discovery of ancient Egypt dates from Napoleon's expedition to Egypt in 1798, but researchers, travellers and writers had taken an enthusiastic interest in Egypt since Classical times, and the revelation of this civilization owed much to them as well as to the later scholars. Since Egypt's ancient history stretches back for well over four thousand years, some of the Egyptians were themselves students of their own past, although they were prompted by the desire to discover religious wisdom rather than to reconstruct and understand earlier events. In this sense, the first recorded historian of Egypt was Khaemwese, a son of King Ramesses II, who lived c.1250 BC. He was a High Priest of the god Ptah and a noted magician who devoted much time to seeking out magical texts; a papyrus in the Louvre contains magical formulae which are attributed to him, and his quest led him around the tombs at Sakkara, to study inscriptions on temple walls, and to examine sacred books in the temple libraries. A visit to King Unas' pyramid at Sakkara inspired Khaemwese to record his interest in antiquities in an inscription there, discovered by the archaeologist J. P. Lauer in 1937; it states that Khaemwese has

inscribed the name of the King of Upper and Lower Egypt, Unas, since it was not found on the face of the pyramid, because the priest Prince Khaemwese loved to restore the monuments of the Kings of Upper and Lower Egypt.

The first major source from antiquity, however, is the Classical writer Herodotus (c.484–430 BC), who is regarded as the Father of History. His account – the first attempt to separate fantasy from reality – was based on his firsthand observation of the monuments and on facts and evidence obtained from his discussions with the people, such as the priests, whom he met there. His work certainly contains inaccuracies, but he became one of the few authorities on whom medieval and modern European travellers could rely and was often quoted in their own works.

He was born at Halicarnassus between 490 BC and 480 BC, and his extensive travels took him to Egypt in c.450 BC, during a period when the country was ruled by the Persians. Eventually, in retirement at Thurii in Italy, he added to his work *The Histories* which gave an account of the conflict between Greece and Persia and in Book II (called 'Euterpe') he examined Egypt and its civilization.

His book was mainly an account of the country's history and geography, and his lively mind eagerly grasped the many peculiarities he encountered there: he wrote, 'There is no country that possesses so many wonders, nor any that has such a number of works that defy description.' This is the first factual account written by a foreign observer of Egypt to survive intact. However, some modern scholars have questioned its accuracy, speculating that his visit to Egypt may not have included all the places he mentions; they also doubt that his informants were always truly knowledgeable. It nevertheless formed the basis of all later accounts of Egypt, and was translated by such Classical writers as Diodorus Siculus and Strabo. Some of the facts he gives have been investigated by modern researchers and have been shown to be accurate, although others have not, but for the later periods of Egypt's history, when archaeological evidence is relatively scarce, he remains one of our most important sources.

His travels in Egypt probably took him as far south as the First Cataract, although his omission of Thebes and its monuments is surprising, and the work generally concentrates on the north. He provides his reader with a lively narrative, letting him see these wonders through his own personal and enthusiastic experience. Regarding the features of the landscape, he says: 'My own observation bears out the statement made to me by the priests that the greater part of the country I have described has been built up by silt from the Nile.' He is intrigued by the truth about the source and inundation of the river: 'About why the Nile behaves precisely as it does I could get no information from the priests or anyone else. What I particularly wished to know was why the water begins to rise at the summer solstice, continues to do so for a hundred days, and then falls again at the end of that period, so that it remains low throughout the winter until the summer solstice comes round again in the following year.'

He also shows a lively interest in the flora and fauna; he notes that 'they gather the water-lilies (called lotus by the Egyptians) which grow in great abundance when the river is full and floods the neighbouring flats, and they dry them in the sun; then, from the centre of each flower, they pick out something which looks like a poppy-head, grind it, and make it into loaves which they bake.' Other descriptions provide information about their food:

Some kinds of fish they eat raw, either dried in the sun or salted; they also eat quails raw, as well as ducks and various small birds, after pickling them in brine; other kinds of birds and fish (except those which are considered sacred), they either roast or boil. When the wealthy give a party and the banquet is finished, a man carries round amongst the guests a wooden image of a corpse in a coffin, carved and painted to resemble the real thing as closely as possible…he shows it to each guest in turn, and says: 'Look on this body, as you drink and make merry, since you will be just like it when you are dead!'

Regarding animals, some curious creatures such as the hippopotamus, the ibis, and crocodiles are of particular interest to Herodotus. He says:

The crocodile takes no food during the four winter months…It has eyes like a pig's and great fang-like teeth, and is the only animal to have no tongue and a fixed lower jaw…Some Egyptians reverence the crocodile as a sacred beast; others do not, but treat it as an enemy. There is found in Thebes and around Lake Moeris the strongest belief in its sacredness; in these places, they keep one particular crocodile which they tame, placing rings of glass or gold in its ears and bracelets around its front feet, and giving it special food and ceremonial offerings.

The mythical phoenix is also mentioned:

Another sacred bird is the phoenix; I have not seen a phoenix myself, except in paintings, for it is very rare and visits the country (so they say at Heliopolis) only at intervals of five hundred years, on the occasion of the death of the parent-bird.

His historical details are sometimes correct, such as identifying Menes as the first king who founded Egypt's earliest capital; about him, he says: 'The priests told me it was Men, the first king of Egypt, who raised the dam which protects Memphis from the floods.' However, the characters and actions of kings such as Cheops and Chephren who built their pyramids at Giza are probably based on embellished hearsay. Herodotus' informants (priests who lived some 2,400 years after these kings ruled!) told him that Cheops

closed all the temples, and then, not content with excluding his subjects from the practice of their religion, forced them without exception to work as slaves for his own benefit. The work continued in three-monthly shifts, a hundred thousand men in a shift. It took ten years of this oppressive slave-labour to build the track along which the blocks were dragged. To build the pyramid itself took twenty years.

With kings such as Amasis (Dynasty 26), where Herodotus is the main source, it is difficult to assess the accuracy of information relating to the king's frequent drunkenness.

Herodotus also provides an account of the monuments he visited, including the Giza pyramids (which, unlike some other writers, he identified correctly as royal burial places), the Labyrinth and Lake Moeris in the Fayoum, the city of Memphis and temples at Sais and

Bubastis. He mentions the hieroglyphic system of writing, and gives a description (the first by a foreign writer) of Egyptian religious beliefs and customs. These include festivals, magical rites, dream interpretation and animal cults, but his detailed account of the techniques of mummification is of special importance because, with Diodorus Siculus' later work, it provides our only surviving written source. In this instance, modern scientific investigations have shown that his details are, for the most part, accurate.

He was obviously deeply impressed by this ancient culture and, despite his observations that many customs were the reverse of those found elsewhere, he nevertheless believed that the Egyptians were the most religious of ancient peoples and tried to identify the gods from which the Greek divinities were derived. Herodotus' account provides a stimulating insight by a man who was both a traveller and the world's first historian and is still well worth reading. His genius for experimenting with this new approach – attempting to sift fact from fantasy – and his good fortune in seeing the monuments when they were so much more complete combine to give the modern reader a unique view of Egypt.

Another Greek writer, Diodorus Siculus (late 1st century BC), spent time in Egypt in *c*.59 BC. The first book of twelve volumes of his *Universal History* is devoted to Egypt; although he used his own firsthand experience in this, he also drew heavily on earlier writers such as Hecataeus of Abdera, Agatharchides of Cnidus and most particularly, Herodotus. His compilation of information from other sources is often inaccurate, and it is not a history that can be taken seriously. His subjects include the Osiris myth (documented much more fully by Plutarch), religious customs such as animal worship and funerary beliefs, and administration, law, education and medicine. The plants and animals are discussed, and the possible causes for the inundation of the Nile; some interesting details are given regarding forced labour camps which were brought in as a policy to rehabilitate criminals. The practice of cannibalism – which Diodorus claimed to occur at times of famine – is also mentioned.

He provides information about many of the subjects already dealt with by Herodotus, such as mummification, but as he often gives fresh details, his work, although less interestingly written, supplies some additional facts. For the later periods, when other material is limited, his account is an important source.

Although these remain our major Greek authors, an important historical source, written in Greek, has survived in the work of an Egyptian priest, Manetho (305–285 BC). His *Aegyptiaca* (*History of Egypt*) was written in the reign of Ptolemy II, but no complete copy survives and the text is only preserved in edited extracts in the later writings of Josephus, and in abridged versions in Sextus Africanus, Eusebius and George called Syncellus. Africanus (*c*.AD 220) was a Christian chronographer, who preserved the writings of Josephus and Eusebius; the latter – also a Christian writer (*c*.AD 320) – provides a biased view of Egypt, representing it as a land of superstition, while Syncellus (*c*.AD 880), a Christian monk, provides the latest known version of Manetho's work.

Manetho was a priest who lived at the Temple of Sebennytos in the Delta, and he may also have had some associations with the town of Mendes and the temple at Heliopolis. Knowledge of Greek and Egyptian hieroglyphs, as well as firsthand experience of Egyptian religious beliefs and customs, gave him the background to write eight books of which the most important was *Aegyptiaca*. This chronicle of the kings of Egypt, when complete, included the earliest times when the gods and demi-gods ruled Egypt, followed by the historical dynasties from Narmer (Menes) down to Alexander the Great's conquest of Egypt. Manetho apparently based his record on registers held in the temples to which he, as a priest, had special access. Although the facts of kings' names, year dates and lengths of reigns are often incomplete and inaccurate, and Eusebius and Africanus preserve sometimes divergent accounts, this still remains our basis for Egyptian chronology. However, other anecdotes about the different rulers are not deemed reliable as they were probably derived from popular stories. Manetho's chronology nevertheless helped Champollion in 1828 in his decipherment of Egyptian royal names, because these lists allowed him to see where a particular ruler appeared in the dynastic sequence and thus to confirm his reading of that name.

In later times, the country was firmly administered as part of the Roman Empire, and many tourists, able to move around the country, now visited Egypt's ancient sites. They usually followed a route from Alexandria to Memphis, calling at the Giza pyramids, before moving south to the Valley of the Kings at Thebes and down to the Island of Philae with its wealth of temples. As they travelled, many left behind a record of their journeys in the graffiti they scrawled on the monuments.

This general interest led to further historical accounts. In 25 BC, the geographer Strabo (64 BC–AD 22), accompanied his friend, the Roman prefect Aelius Gallus, on his expedition to Egypt. They probably travelled as far as the First Cataract, a journey which inspired his interest in many aspects of Egypt. The seventeen books of his *Geographia* (written in Greek) contain an enormous compilation of facts about the Roman world, and the last book provides a short account of Egypt's geography. This is primarily a topographical list of towns and resources, although there are references to pyramids, tombs, temples and religious and historical facts within this context; most information is provided about Alexandria and the Delta, and there are interesting comments about his visit to the Theban tombs and the famous Nilometer at Elephantine. He was the first to comment on the 'singing statue' at Thebes (one of the Colossi of Memnon: two great statues that had once flanked the funerary temple of Amenophis III), but he was sceptical about this supposed 'wonder' which first occurred after 27 BC. The phenomenon has since been explained as the result of an earthquake in 27 BC which damaged the statue, so that sudden changes in humidity and temperature at dawn caused an internal vibration, with the result that the statue seemed to 'sing'; when the crack was repaired in AD 199, the singing ceased.

It was Strabo's account which, nearly two thousand years later, provided the French archaeologist Auguste Mariette with a descrip-

tion of the avenue of sphinxes leading to the Serapeum at Sakkara which helped him to discover and correctly identify this site. Strabo says:

One finds also [at Memphis] the temple of Serapis, in a spot so sandy that the wind causes the sand to accumulate in heaps, under which we could see many sphinxes, some of them almost entirely buried and others only partially covered.

Another Roman writer, Pliny the Elder (AD 23–79), gives another account; although much of the information given in his *Historia Naturalis* is drawn from earlier authors, he was one of the first Roman writers to describe the Great Sphinx at Giza; he comments not only on monuments within Egypt but also on those brought out of Egypt and set up in Rome, such as the obelisks. Following the example of Herodotus and Diodorus, he also provides an account of mummification.

In terms of Egyptian religion, a particularly important work is preserved in the *Moralia* of Plutarch (c.AD 50–120) of Chaeronea where the most complete version of the Egyptian myth of Osiris and Isis is given. No extant Egyptian version survives, although there are numerous references and allusions to the myth in Egyptian texts on temple walls and papyri. Although Plutarch's text has been criticized by scholars as a Greek rather than an authentically Egyptian version of the myth, the outline of the story is probably fairly accurate and it does provide the only complete account of Egypt's most important myth. This was one of the few detailed texts relating to Egyptian religion which gave European scholars some accurate insight into these beliefs during the Medieval and Renaissance periods.

The Jewish historian Flavius Josephus (c.AD 70) also supplied much basic information about Egypt for Renaissance researchers. His works include, in addition to edited extracts from Manetho's writings, comments on people and events – such as the Hyksos invasion, Joseph, Moses and the Exodus – which have biblical associations. Particularly for the Hyksos, where other source material is scanty, Josephus' material has to be considered, although it is difficult to ascertain its level of accuracy. He theorized that the invasion into Egypt of the Hyksos (he erroneously interpreted their hieroglyphic name to mean Shepherd Kings or Captive Shepherds, whereas it has since been shown that it should be translated as 'chieftains of foreign lands') was actually the descent into Egypt and sojourn there of the Hebrews in the biblical account. Their later expulsion, he believed, correlated with the Exodus, but there is no alternative evidence to support this theory.

The Classical authors provide a unique view of Egypt and despite their shortcomings, they remained the most reliable source for ancient Egypt until Champollion's decipherment of Hieroglyphs ushered in the modern age of Egyptology.

In the mean time, knowledge of the old civilization made few advances. When Egypt became a Christian country in the early centuries AD, the ancient monuments suffered defacement: the figures of deities and the accompanying inscriptions on the temple walls were destroyed by the people who now believed that they were idolatrous. With the original wall scenes damaged or covered over with plaster, parts of some temples were now turned into churches or filled with houses.

In the next centuries, few travellers visited Egypt, and Christian pilgrims who did reach there almost always interpreted the pyramids and monuments in terms of biblical stories. The earliest account left by a European visiting the ancient sites at this period recalls a journey undertaken between AD 378 and 388 (when Egypt was still a Christian country). The traveller, identified as Lady Etheria, has left a manuscript which was discovered in Tuscany in 1883. She was a nun from Gaul who made the journey to identify sites she had read about in the Bible, and she went to Alexandria, Tanis, and the district around Thebes.

With the arrival of the Arabs under their general Amr in the 7th century AD, the indigenous population was found to have very little memory of their early civilization, and the ability to read the hieroglyphic script had been lost. The new conquerors themselves did not pay much heed to ancient Egypt; there was little to be learnt about it from the native Egyptians, and the Arabs believed that their monuments – massive in concept and scale – had been constructed by giants or magicians.

However, there were still travellers to Egypt who were not Muslim. Bernard the Wise and two monks went there in AD 870, and Rabbi Benjamin ben Jonah of Tudela in Navarre, who made the journey in AD 1165–71, was the first to note that the annual Nile inundation was the result of the rains falling on the Abyssinian highlands. However, the most significant travel account of this period is by an Arab writer. Abd' el-Latif was a doctor from Baghdad who taught medicine and philosophy in Cairo, and around AD 1200, he visited Giza, where he entered the Great Pyramid and viewed the Great Sphinx which was still intact. At Memphis, the one-time capital of Egypt, the ancient buildings were still extensive and he noted, 'It requires a half-day's march in any direction to cross the visible ruins.' His account is particularly interesting since he was in the area at a time when most sites were not visited by European travellers because of the Crusades; and since his observations on the monuments were not taken from a Christian standpoint, they provide a different perspective. However, since his account was not translated from the Arabic until the early 19th century, he had no impact on later European travellers.

When the Crusades ended, interest in the Near East was rekindled; Europeans could travel there more readily and the Crusaders who returned home had aroused interest with their tales of the region. Guidebooks were produced for pilgrims visiting Jerusalem, and the best known of the 14th century accounts was *The Voyage and Travel of Sir John Mandeville, Knight*. It contained quite erroneous information, identifying the pyramids as the biblical granaries of Joseph, for example, but it continued to be used for five hundred years before it was discovered that the author was fictitious and had certainly never visited Egypt. This man – almost certainly Jean d'Outremeuse of Liège – had not ventured out of his own country but had based his work on a compilation of many earlier sources.

In 1517, when Selim I invaded Egypt, it became a Turkish province. He confirmed a treaty signed by the former Sultan which had allowed the French and Catalans to trade there; they were given religious protection, and it now became relatively safe to travel in Egypt. Merchants and diplomats began to arrive from abroad, but pilgrims also came to visit the holy sites, and some travellers also interested themselves in the ancient monuments. This freedom to travel was now coupled with a new interest in the treasures and philosophies of the ancient civilizations, which the free-thinking of the Renaissance encouraged, as rigid medieval attitudes were gradually relaxed. Increasingly, merchants and pilgrims coming to Egypt led the way for antiquarians and collectors who had an avid interest in the ancient treasures.

One of the most curious commodities Europeans sought from Egypt was 'mummy' for use as a medicinal ingredient. In the 16th and 17th centuries, it was one of the most common drugs found in the apothecaries' shops of Europe, and in 1658 the philosopher Sir Thomas Browne commented, 'Mummy is become Merchandise, Mizraim cures wounds, and Pharaoh is sold for Balsams.' However, it seems that from as early as AD 1100, and probably before, mummy was prescribed as a medicinal ingredient.

The word 'mummy', according to Abd' el-Latif, the Arab physician who was writing in the 12th century, was derived from the Persian term mumia which meant pitch or bitumen. In Persia this substance flowed from the mountain tops and, mixed with the waters that carried it down, coagulated like mineral pitch; the resultant liquid was purported to have medicinal properties and indeed may have had some real benefit as an antiseptic. The Mummy Mountain became famed for this healing substance, and even the Queen of England received a gift of mumia from the King of Persia in 1809.

However, the demand rapidly exceeded the natural supply, and so other sources were sought. The blackened appearance of some of the preserved bodies of the ancient Egyptians (particularly those prepared in the later periods) led to the erroneous assumption that this was the result of the bodies being soaked in bitumen, and so it was believed that they would provide an alternative supply of mumia for medicinal use. Indeed, Abd' el-Latif claimed, 'The mummy found in the hollow corpses in Egypt differs but immaterially from the nature of mineral mummy; and where any difficulty arises in procuring, the latter may be substituted in its stead.' The word mumia was consequently applied to these preserved bodies, and they have since continued to be known as 'mummies'.

The history of the trade in mumia thus goes back over several centuries. In the earliest days, a flourishing business was established at Alexandria, and since large profits were to be made, many foreigners began to trade in mumia, exporting complete mummies or packages of fragmented tissue from Cairo and Alexandria. Soon, demand began to exceed supply and in his History of Mummies written in 1834, the surgeon Thomas Pettigrew commented, 'No sooner was it credited that mummy constituted an article of value in the practice of medicine than many speculators embarked in the trade; the tombs were sacked, and as many mummies as could be obtained were broken into pieces for the purpose of sale.'

The Egyptian authorities had to limit the export of mummies, but this only exacerbated the problem and led to fraudulent solutions. Pettigrew explains how Guy de la Fonteine of Navarre investigated the mummy trade in Alexandria in 1564; when he looked into the stock of mummies held by the chief dealer there, he found that the supply was augmented by preparing the bodies of the recently dead, often executed criminals, by treating them with bitumen and exposing them to the sun, to produce mummified tissue which was then sold as authentic mumia. Later in the 18th century, when the nature of such supplies was eventually revealed to the authorities, traders were imprisoned, a tax was levied, and it became illegal to remove mummies from Egypt.

The actual benefits of the ingredient were disputed. On the one hand, it was used to treat, amongst other ailments, abscesses, fractures, concussion, paralysis, epilepsy, coughs, nausea and ulcers. It also received royal approval when King Francis I of France reputedly always carried with him some mumia mixed with pulverized rhubarb to treat his ailments. However, according to the physician Ambrose Paré, writing in 1634, it had no beneficial effects: 'This wicked kinde of

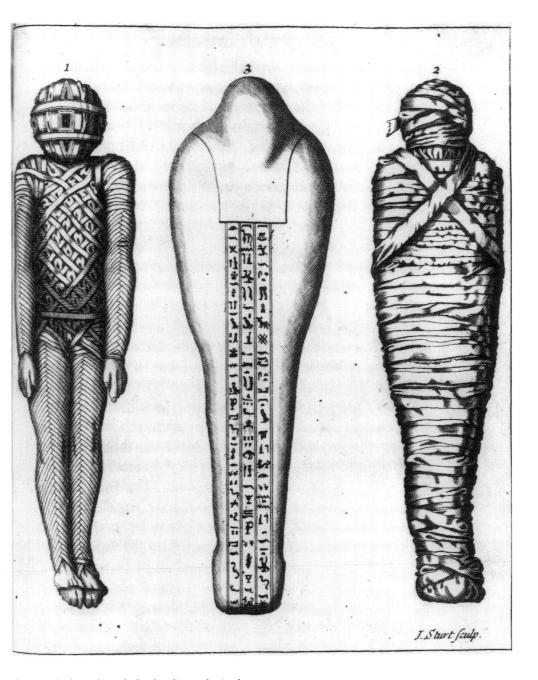

drugge, doth nothing help the diseased…it also inferres many troublesome symptoms, as the paine of the heart or stomacke, vomiting, and stinke of the mouth.' The strict measures introduced to curb the mummy trade did in fact reduce the worst excesses, but the ingredient continued to be in demand, and was still in use in medicines in 19th century Europe.

Increased public interest in Egyptology in the 18th century led to specialist books on the subject. Here, Thomas Greenhill's Nekrokedeia or the Art of Embalming *(1705) shows the usual method of bandaging a mummy. This was based on knowledge gained from contemporary public mummy 'unrollings'.*

17

From the Renaissance until the expedition to Egypt of Napoleon Bonaparte in 1798, an ever-increasing number of people journeyed to Egypt. Some came as travellers who were simply interested to view the ancient monuments and to make a record of the wall scenes, but others were beginning to realize that Egyptian antiquities could be sold to royal or noble patrons in Europe at great profit. The Renaissance had inspired a fashionable interest in knowledge, and from the 17th century scholars were sent to Egypt to search out coins, manuscripts and antiquities for their wealthy European patrons, of whom the French were the most enthusiastic. Indeed, the Kings of France were the most active collectors of these antiquities. Embassies and consulates began to undertake duties additional to diplomacy, and their officials were used as local agents to acquire collections of antiquities. Gradually, foreign collectors also sought permission from the Turkish rulers of Egypt to undertake their own excavations, so that they could acquire and remove inscriptions, statuary and tomb goods. This in turn led to international jealousy and rivalry between the different factions who were all anxious to supply the most desirable antiquities for their wealthy clients.

Some of the great private collections now being compiled eventually became the bases of fine national collections in later centuries. This was particularly the case in Italy and France, and also in England where the British Museum was established by an Act of Parliament in 1756. Here, the Egyptian collection developed from the relatively modest group of artifacts from the collection of the physician, Dr Hans Sloane.

These collections amassed material which would become an invaluable resource for later scholars, but at that time, since the hieroglyphs had not yet been deciphered, the inscriptions added no major contribution to existing knowledge of ancient Egypt. However, Renaissance travellers able to visit the country and explore the sites and monuments left written accounts of their journeys, which supplied firsthand information about Egypt, so that readers were no longer dependent upon accounts derived from Classical sources and from hearsay.

There was a steady stream of such visitors, but some are of particular interest. The French made a major contribution to the field: the first of these 'modern' travellers was Jean de Thévenot whose journey is recorded in his *Voyage au Levant* (1657). Some years later, in 1692, the French Consul in Egypt, Benoit de Maillet, made extensive investigations, entering the Great Pyramid at Giza more than forty times; he also declared the need for scientific exploration – an idea which was eventually realized by Napoleon's expedition. Some men were specially commissioned by the French king to undertake scholarly explorations in Egypt. Paul Lucas, who became the official traveller for Louis XIV in 1716, was instructed to examine antiquities at several sites and to explore a pyramid by excavation, in order to discover its contents. Some forty years before, Louis XIV's chief minister had instructed a German, J. B. Vansleb, to visit Egypt to acquire antiquities for the royal collection and to copy the hieroglyphic inscriptions. He also visited the mummy-pits at Sakkara; many years later, Lucas described his own experience in seeing these pits, believing that he had made a 'new' discovery. One of the most significant of these early French travellers was the Jesuit Father Claude Sicard. He arrived in Cairo as the Supervisor of the Jesuit Mission, but his enquiring mind and ability as an Arabic scholar provided him with the background to respond to the command of the Regent, Philippe of Orléans, to make an exact investigation of Egypt's ancient monuments, and between 1707 and 1726 he travelled widely in Egypt. Essentially, his mission was to visit the Coptic communities, but he also observed the monuments, reaching as far south as Aswan. The information he gathered from twenty-four temples, over fifty decorated tombs and twenty major pyramids was unparalleled at that time. In the Valley of the Kings, he was able to identify ten of the tombs from the total number described in the writings of Diodorus Siculus, but perhaps his most important contribution was to identify Karnak and Luxor temples as part of the site of the ancient capital of Thebes. His significance as an early scholar is partly obscured, however, because information about his discoveries is only preserved in some letters and a map prepared to accompany his own manuscript. This manuscript, which would doubtless provide much valuable information about his explorations, was not published during his lifetime and has subsequently disappeared.

English travellers also left some interesting accounts. George Sandys' journey was published in his *Sundy's Travells* in 1621; it is subtitled 'A Relation of a Journey begun An. Dom. 1610' and the four books tell of his travels in the Mediterranean and in Egypt. However, despite this opportunity to see the monuments at first hand, he adds little that is new, and draws extensively on earlier sources such as Herodotus. Nevertheless, there were accounts that moved knowledge of Egypt forward; the first scientific study that investigated and compared the true facts about one group of Egyptian monuments with the stories that had grown up around them was made by John Greaves. He was Professor of Astronomy at Oxford and his background in mathematics and oriental languages prepared him well for the task. In his *Pyramidographia* (1646), he set out to investigate the true purpose of the pyramids – knowledge which had been lost for centuries; his critical appraisal of the writings of Classical, Arab and later authors on this matter set new standards, and by considering both the literary and archaeological evidence (he published the most accurate survey of the Great Pyramid until then), he was able to draw conclusions about this group of monuments in an innovative way.

Another English traveller, Richard Pococke, visited Egypt in 1737, and reached Aswan; in northern Egypt, he went to Busiris (the ancient centre of the worship of Osiris) and Sakkara, and on his Nile journey he viewed the temples at Denderah, Thebes and Armant. His *Travels in Egypt* was published in 1743, and already comments on the damage to the monuments: 'They are every day destroying these fine morsels of Egyptian Antiquity, and I saw some of the pillars being hewn into mill-stones.'

At the same time as Pococke's journey, a Danish artist and marine engineer, Frederick Lewis Nordern, was also exploring Egypt and attempting to reach the Second Cataract. His expedition, sent by the King of Denmark, Christian VI, only reached Derr in Nubia, but Norden was able to publish in his *Voyage* (1755) a detailed description of Egypt, with excellent and accurate plans and drawings of the monuments. He

This frontispiece is from Sundy's Travells *(1621), an account of George Sandys' journey through the Mediterranean and Egypt. He had the opportunity to observe the monuments at first hand, but his writings rely heavily on earlier Classical sources rather than supplying new information.*

also provided advice to other travellers: 'Begin by dressing yourself in the Turkish manner. A pair of mustachios, with a grave and solemn air, will be very proper companions by which you will have a resemblance to the natives.' For the first time, this kind of information became available to scholars and general readers.

Another interesting narrative is provided by the great 18th century traveller James Bruce, who reached Egypt in 1768 and proceeded to sail up the Nile. In the Valley of the Kings he discovered the tomb of Ramesses III, although it was only years afterwards, when the Hieroglyphs were eventually deciphered, that it could be identified as this king's tomb. It was often referred to as Bruce's Tomb. After he returned to England in 1774, he published his memoirs in five volumes in 1790. They include the description of his travels through Egypt in an attempt to reach the source of the Nile, but this fascinating travel narrative does not make any major contribution to knowledge about ancient Egyptian civilization.

By 1798, when Napoleon Bonaparte went to Egypt in search of an empire, the foundations of the study of Egyptology had already been laid: the extensive journeys throughout the country had enabled travellers to discover all the principal monuments above ground, and in many cases these were already accurately identified with ancient sites. Some excavation had also been carried out, revealing burials at Sakkara and Thebes. The rush to obtain antiquities for great collections abroad had already led to the destruction of monuments and archaeological material, but there were now extensive groups of objects outside Egypt which could be studied by scholars. Interesting and increasingly accurate contemporary written accounts also existed and these augmented the Classical sources and replaced the older, derivative travel books.

However, to carry the study forward, it was now necessary first to develop scientifically organized archaeology, rather than treasurehunting, so that new facts could be derived about Egypt's ancient history and civilization; and secondly, to decipher Hieroglyphs and the related scripts of Hieratic and Demotic to provide the key to understanding the inscriptions which adorned not only the tombs and temples but also many of the artifacts. Napoleon's expedition, which was a military disaster, nevertheless provided the catalyst for the development of Egyptology; one direct result was the production of the first detailed account of ancient Egypt, and indirectly, the expedition also led to the decipherment of Hieroglyphs. It was truly a watershed in the development of Egyptology.

Egypt's geographical position made it important to both England and France. Napoleon Bonaparte persuaded the French Government that control of the country was of great significance, since it lay on the land route to the British possessions in India. The Turkish rule there was weak and the French were fearful that the British might attempt to take Egypt in order to consolidate their lines of communication. Against this background, Napoleon was authorized to proceed to Egypt where, seizing Malta en route, he landed on 1 July 1798.

Under their energetic, twenty-nine-year-old leader, the French soon succeeded in defeating the Mameluke army in the Delta and at the Battle of the Pyramids. They pursued their victory into Upper Egypt, forcing the Egyptian troops to retreat into Nubia. However, it was two peaceful innovations brought in by Napoleon that ultimately had the most profound effect upon Egypt, rather than these initial military successes. He introduced the printing press, and also established a special Scientific and Artistic Commission to accompany the military expedition; this was inaugurated to obtain both cultural and technological information about Egypt which would facilitate Napoleon's plans to colonize the country.

The Commission undertook this research with the aid of a library and scientific apparatus brought from France. It consisted of 167 scientists and technicians, who included mathematicians, astronomers, chemists, engineers, mineralogists, naturalists, botanists, surgeons, physicians, artists, musicians, writers and antiquarians. These savants, recruited by Claude-Louis Berthollet, produced as one of their major achievements the publication in nineteen volumes of the *Description de l'Égypte* (1809–28). The various members of the Commission worked for three years in different parts of Egypt, mapping and gathering information about the natural history and resources, the irrigation system, the customs of the people, and the ancient monuments and antiquities. This provided the basis for the publication; works were also produced independently by members of the Commission, such as Vivant Denon's *Voyage in Lower and Upper Egypt during the campaigns of General Bonaparte* (1801). Denon (who eventually became Director of the Louvre in Paris) was a diplomat and an artist who travelled as an ex officio member of the Commission. These publications, well-researched and beautifully illus-

PL. VI

Tableau des Signes Phonétiques Égyptiens, pour la lecture des noms propres Grecs et Romains.

Lettres Grecques.	Signes Démotiques	Signes Hiéroglyphiques
Α		
Β		
Γ		
Δ		
Ε		
Ζ		
Θ		
Η		
Ι		
Κ		
Λ		
Μ		
Ν		
Ξ		
Ο		
Π		
Ρ		
Σ		
Σ		
Τ		
Υ		
Φ		
Χ		
Ψ		
Ω		
ΤΟ —		

trated, made a great impression in Europe and were the foundation for the serious study of Egyptology which would now emerge. Denon's descriptions capture some of the wonderment he and his colleagues felt when they first encountered Egypt's great monuments. Of the pyramids at Giza, he says: 'The great distance from which

The trilingual inscription on the Rosetta Stone – in Greek, Egyptian Hieroglyphs and Demotic – provided scholars with a new opportunity to decipher the Egyptian scripts. Here, a table in Champollion's Précis du Système Hiéroglyphique *(1824) compares Greek letters with Demotic and Hieroglyphs.*

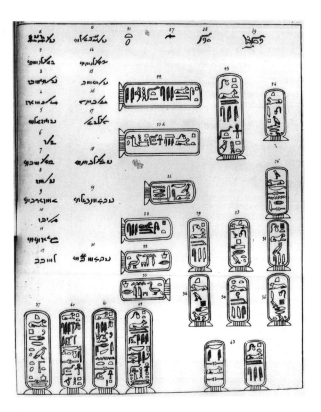

Coptic played an important role in the decipherment of Hieroglyphs. Here, in Champollion's Précis *(1824), royal names are written in Coptic (left) and in Hieroglyphs (as they appeared on the Rosetta Stone). Number 28, for example, reads as* PTOLMIS *(Ptolemy).*

they can be perceived makes them appear diaphanous, tinted with the bluish tone of the sky, and restores to them the perfection and purity of the angles which the centuries have marred.'

At the Temple of Denderah, he is again overwhelmed: 'Pencil in hand, I passed from object to object, drawn away from one thing by the interest of another...I felt ashamed of the inadequacy of the drawings I made of such sublime things.'

He also records the action of the army division to which he was attached when they came in sight of the temples of Luxor and Karnak:

At nine o'clock, turning the end of a chain of mountains which formed a promontory, the French suddenly beheld the seat of the antique Thebes...this exiled city which the mind no longer discovers except

through the mists of time, was still a phantom so gigantic to our imagination that the army, at the sight of its scattered ruins, halted of itself, and, by one spontaneous impulse, grounded its arms, as if the possession of the remains of this capital had been the object of its glorious labours, had completed the conquest of the Egyptian territory.

Napoleon also established and became the vice-president of the Institut d'Égypte in Cairo; this brought together scholars from different disciplines and encouraged an exchange of ideas. Scholars read papers at seminars and generally promoted the concept of research in Egypt. It was these intellectual and academic legacies rather than Napoleon's ephemeral military success which were to produce long-term results. The work of the Commission was a turning point in Europe's perception of Egypt and its ancient civilization; the savants acquired a vast collection of specimens and antiquities from their stay in the country, but more importantly, they amassed knowledge which had not been hitherto available. In political terms, the Egyptian rulers now became aware for the first time of the impact their country had on Europe, both geographically as a corridor to the East and as a source of ancient culture and antiquities.

It was the political dimension, with the French forces ensconced in Egypt, which now led the British to attempt to remove them. Under Nelson, they defeated the French fleet at the Battle of Aboukir, thus cutting off Napoleon's army, and, by enlisting the aid of the Turks, they were able to force the French to leave Egypt. Under the terms of their capitulation, the French had to agree to give the British all the natural history specimens and antiquities that the Commission had collected, but the savants objected so strongly, claiming that they would prefer to burn their collections rather than transfer them to the British, that the British general Hutchinson eventually agreed that they should keep their material, with the exception of a fascinating inscribed stone which had been discovered near the town of Rosetta in the Delta. The Commission finally sailed from Alexandria with their wealth of study-material in 1801, but Britain retained the Rosetta Stone.

The discovery of this stone, which was to prove to be the key to the decipherment of Egyptian Hieroglyphs, was itself a direct result of the war between the French and the British. In 1799, as part of the French attempt to consolidate the coastal defences against the British navy, Lieutenant Pierre François Xavier Bouchard, an officer of the Engineers, was in charge of gathering stone to strengthen the ramparts. At Fort Rachid near Rosetta, one of his men dug up a stone with three horizontal panels of inscription, later identified as Hieroglyphs, Demotic and Greek. Although he recognized that it might be of some importance, the French officer could hardly have foreseen its impact on the development of Egyptology and its crucial role in enabling Champollion (then a child in France) to decipher the script of ancient Egypt. The officer sent the stone to the Institute in Cairo; the Greek was readily translated and the scholars realized that the contents of this inscription were repeated in the other two texts – Hieroglyphs and Demotic – on the stone. This trilingual inscription provided the first real possibility of decipherment.

The study of ancient Egypt had by now reached an impasse; knowledge of the monuments and antiquities, carefully researched, still did not enable scholars to determine the history, with the names and order of the kings, nor understand the religion or many aspects of the lives of the people. An understanding of the way the language worked and the consequent ability to read the texts still eluded them. There had been many attempts to penetrate the hieroglyphic system but most researchers drew wrong conclusions, claiming that the signs were symbols; they did not understand that some signs (we now call these phonograms) were alphabetic, conveying the sounds of a word, whereas others (known today as ideograms) stood at the end of a word to depict its meaning. By attempting to translate the hieroglyphs as individual ideas rather than as the written version of the language of ancient Egypt, these early writers laid a false trail and effectively prevented further investigation.

The Greek writers Horapollon and Chaeremon were amongst the first to produce these erroneous ideas but a Jesuit scholar, Athanasius

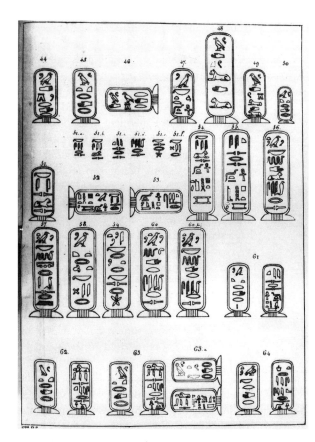

On the Rosetta Stone, Champollion was able to start deciphering Hieroglyphs by using the royal names. Having identified a name in the Greek text (which was easily read), he looked for it in the Hieroglyphs, recognizing that all royal names were enclosed in the cartouches (ovals) shown here.

Kircher (1602–80), became perhaps the best-known exponent of the symbolic theory of Hieroglyphs. He went from his native Germany to Rome where he became Professor of Mathematics of the Roman College (1635–43), subsequently devoting his energies to various research projects. He was intellectually well equipped for this work with wide-ranging interests in philosophy and oriental languages as well as mathematics, and his contribution to the field of Coptic Studies (the last stage of the ancient Egyptian language) was notable. Between 1643 and 1676 he produced at least six works, the largest being his *Oedipus aegyptiacus* (1652–4), and he attempted to read the hieroglyphic inscriptions on the obelisks in Rome. Under the

Romans, a number of these had been removed from Egypt: the granite obelisk now standing before the Aya Sophia Mosque in Istanbul was taken there during this period, and Rome also acquired seven obelisks. However Kircher's attempts with these inscriptions added nothing to knowledge of decipherment, since he continued to regard the individual signs as symbols.

Only one writer discarded the symbolic theory; this was William Warburton (1698–1779) who became Bishop of Gloucester in 1759. A prominent scholar, he recognized that Hieroglyphs were a written language, and believed that a simpler script had evolved from them for everyday use. His essay on the decipherment of Hieroglyphs formed part of his *Legation of Moses,* published in 1738 and translated into French in 1744. It seems that he was the only scholar before Champollion to indicate the correct way in which inscriptions should be read, but his immediate successors reverted to the symbolic interpretation.

William Stukeley, an English physician who founded the first recorded Egyptian Society in London in 1741, presented two papers to the London Society of Antiquaries (of which he was Secretary) in 1762. He claimed that the Egyptian hieroglyphs on a statue in Turin were quite different from Chinese characters (some scholars were now trying to prove that Chinese was derived from Egyptian), but that they were symbolic and therefore impossible to understand completely.

Some progress was made, however, by a Swedish diplomat and orientalist, Johan David Akerblad (1763–1819). While he was at the consulate in Paris, he pursued his studies under Silvestre de Sacy, and his knowledge of Coptic and his attempts to decipher Phoenician and Runic inscriptions provided a good background for his work on the Egyptian scripts. After the discovery of the Rosetta Stone, wax impressions of the inscriptions had been taken and circulated amongst scholars in Europe. Sylvestre de Sacy studied the Greek and Demotic texts on the stone and in 1802 indicated his belief that certain sign-groups in the Demotic corresponded to the names of Ptolemy and Alexander which had been easily identified in the Greek.

Akerblad's own studies had also enabled him, by comparison with the Greek text, to identify these and other proper names in the Demotic, and he also made some other important observations. These significant steps towards the decipherment of the Demotic text were set out in his *Lettre à M. de Sacy* (1802), but he made no further headway.

A major pioneer in the search for a breakthrough in decipherment was the English physician and physicist, Thomas Young (1773–1824). His wide knowledge of many languages was coupled with his pursuit of medicine and scientific studies, where his greatest achievements were made in the field of physiological optics. In mid-life, his interest in Egyptology was kindled and, having obtained copies of the Rosetta Stone, he turned his attention to deciphering the texts. He made several very important discoveries; these included the realization that some of the Demotic characters, as well as linear hieroglyphs and Hieratic, were derived from the Hieroglyphs. The significance of this was that it indicated that Demotic was not entirely an alphabetic script (as Akerblad had claimed), and Young was thus the first to recognize that the Egyptians used both alphabetic and non-alphabetic (ideograms) signs in the texts.

A further important step was his claim (also made independently by other researchers) that the oval cartouches found in the hieroglyphic inscription contained the names of kings and queens. The parallel Greek text provided him with the royal names of Ptolemy and Berenice, and he was able to attribute the sound values of the Greek letters in those names to the hieroglyphic signs within the cartouches. From a list of thirteen signs in the two names, he made correct identifications of six, three were partly right, and four were wrong, but this limited set enabled him to read the name of Ptolemy correctly in the Hieroglyphs. He was also able to propose a close relationship between Hieroglyphs and Coptic, and to identify some other hieroglyphic names.

His work on the translation of the Demotic on the Rosetta Stone was published in his *Remarks on Egyptian Papyri and on the Inscription of Rosetta* (1815), while his other major ideas were advanced in an article entitled 'Egypt' which appeared in the *Supplement to the Encyclopaedia Britannica* (1819). His contributions – to begin a comparison of Greek, Demotic and Hieroglyphs, and to conclude that Demotic was a cursive form of Hieroglyphs – had a major impact on the development of the decipherment process, but financial problems and ill-health prevented further commitment to these studies, and it was the French scholar Champollion who would eventually achieve the breakthrough.

Jean François Champollion (1790–1832) was born on 23 December at Figeac in France, one of five children of Jacques, an impoverished bookseller, and his invalid wife, Jeanne Françoise Gualieu. He was prodigiously talented, teaching himself to read when he was five years old. When he was eleven, he made a visit to the mathematician Jean Baptiste Fournier, who had been one of Napoleon's savants, and this may have inspired his interest in Egyptology and his desire to decipher Hieroglyphs. To prepare himself for this task, he learnt Hebrew, Arabic, Syriac, Chaldean, Sanskrit, Zend, Pali, Parsi and Persian before he was seventeen.

His early education was undertaken by his elder brother, Jacques Joseph Champollion, who was a historian with a great interest in Egyptology and it was probably his influence, at least as much as the visit to Fournier, which led to Jean François' initial enthusiasm for the subject. In later years, the elder brother devoted much of his considerable talent to furthering Champollion's success, contributing to the actual decipherment of the hieroglyphs, and often preparing and editing his works and ensuring that they were published.

The younger Champollion continued his education at the Lyceum in Grenoble, and when he was sixteen, he read a paper to the Grenoble Academy, claiming that Coptic (which he had also learnt) was in fact the same (but written in different characters) as the ancient language of Egypt (which had been written in Hieroglyphs, Hieratic or Demotic). In 1807, he went to Paris to begin his studies with the Orientalist Sylvestre de Sacy. A teaching post in History and Politics took him back to Grenoble in 1809, and after several advancements in his career, he was appointed to a chair in History and Geography at the Royal College at Grenoble in 1818. His

success in deciphering Hieroglyphs ultimately resulted in the creation for him of the first chair in Egyptian history and archaeology at the Collège de France in 1831.

Champollion's self-allotted task – to decipher Egyptian Hieroglyphs – took many years to achieve and was beset by the misconceptions of earlier scholars. The language of the ancient Egyptians had developed through various stages and scripts, and although its origin remains obscure because of its extreme antiquity, the earliest form of the writing is the script we call Hieroglyphs; this was in use at least as early as 3100 BC. Hieroglyphs were developed from pictures and they always retained their pictorial form, but by 3100 BC they were already used as a script to convey a fully developed language, with its own syntax, grammar and vocabulary. The great mistake of most scholars before Champollion was to miss this point and to suggest that Hieroglyphs were merely symbols which represented concepts or ideas.

Hieroglyphs continued to be used for inscriptions on papyrus, wood and stone for more than three thousand years, but even in the earliest historical period, a need arose for a simpler script which could be written down more rapidly. A cursive script – known today as Hieratic – was developed from Hieroglyphs and was widely used until c.800 BC. Each Hieratic character was a simplified version of a hieroglyphic sign and whereas Hieroglyphs were mostly employed for religious or formal inscriptions and were often carved on stone, Hieratic was used for religious, literary and business texts, where speed was required. For these purposes, the cheaper materials of papyrus, wood, leather, or potsherds and limestone flakes (ostraca) were found to be most suitable.

From c.700 BC, another cursive script, Demotic, was evolved from Hieratic, and Thomas Young was able to demonstrate the links between these two writing forms. Demotic, also cursive, became the usual script for business, legal and literary documents for nearly a thousand years, while Hieroglyphs continued to be employed for inscriptions on stone, and religious texts were mainly written in Hieratic.

During the late period of its history, when Egypt was ruled by a line of Macedonian Greeks, the kings and Greek residents who now settled in Egypt introduced Greek as the language for administration throughout the country, although the Egyptian language continued to be widespread amongst the native inhabitants and for religious inscriptions, particularly on walls in the Egyptian temples. The final stage of the Egyptian language, known as Coptic, developed when Egypt became a Christian country. The ancient Egyptian dialects were now written in Greek characters with the addition of a few new signs, taken from Demotic, to express those Egyptian sounds that did not occur in Greek. Coptic played an important role in early Christianity in Egypt: it was the medium for the translation of biblical texts and was still used as the language of the Christian inhabitants of Egypt long after the Arab invasion in the 7th century AD, when Arabic became the official language of the country. It still continues to be the liturgical language of the Coptic Church. Once it was realized that Coptic was the final stage of the ancient Egyptian language, it became an important tool in the decipherment of Hieroglyphs; it threw light on the grammar and the vocabulary, and, since it conveys the vowel sounds through the Greek characters, whereas Hieroglyphs and the other scripts preserve only the consonantal sounds of each word, it has also assisted in understanding something of the pronunciation of the ancient language.

As Christianity grew and spread throughout Egypt, knowledge of ancient Egyptian, written in Hieroglyphs, Hieratic or Demotic, was finally lost, leaving Coptic as the only link with the past. However, Coptic was of little assistance until it was realized that it had developed directly out of the earlier scripts.

It is not surprising that early travellers and scholars, viewing the hieroglyphic signs still visible on the temple and tomb walls, deduced so mistakenly that they were purely symbolic in function, claiming that they hid mystical doctrines rather than expressed the mundane verbs, nouns, adjectives and other grammatical elements of the long-dead language of ancient Egypt.

The Rosetta Stone was to be the key: various scholars had attempted to make sense of the hieroglyphs using the old 'symbolic' theory, but no headway could be made in trying to fit this in with the accompanying Greek inscription. The Rosetta Stone was in fact a decree by the priesthoods of Egypt in honour of King Ptolemy V Epiphanes, which dated to 196 BC. Eventually it would be shown that this same decree was issued here in three scripts: Greek (the current official language), Hieroglyphs (the ancient sacred script of Egypt), and Demotic (the usual legal and business script).

When scholars turned their attention to the Demotic text, they identified it correctly as an alphabetic script representing the language of ancient Egypt, although, as we have seen, Akerblad's conclusion that it was purely alphabetic was soon overturned by Young, who showed that, like the Hieroglyphs from which it was derived, it combined both alphabetic signs (sound values) and ideograms (symbols).

At first, Champollion himself followed the false belief that hieroglyphs were symbolic, setting out this view, which opposed Young, in his *De l'écriture hiératique des anciens Égyptiens* (1821); he concluded that the writing was not alphabetic and that both Demotic and hieroglyphic characters represented 'things' rather than 'sounds'. However, a short time later he adopted the alphabetic approach and soon found that he could make great progress in deciphering names and beginning to compile a hieroglyphic alphabet.

His next major discovery came in September 1822, when he was studying copies of an inscription from the temple at Abu Simbel. Using the established phonetic principles he was able to identify the name of the Egyptian king Ramesses II, and he suddenly realized that the Egyptians used hieroglyphs phonetically not only to write the names of foreign rulers such as Ptolemy and Alexander, but also to render the names of their own kings, such as Ramesses. The truly phonetic nature of many of the hieroglyphs thus became apparent to him, and his conclusions were given in his famous *Lettre à M. Dacier, secrétaire perpétuel de l'Académie royale des Inscriptions et Belles-Lettres, relative à l'alphabet des hiéroglyphes phonetiques* (1822).

Although this marked a turning point in his decipherment, the results received only partial acceptance. At the time, some scholars mistakenly refused to believe that he had succeeded in uncovering the key to Hieroglyphs. Also, there has continued to be dispute about the extent to which Champollion appropriated Young's initial discoveries. He gave Young no credit for his contribution, but Young believed that his own work had laid the foundations for Champollion's major discovery.

In 1824, Champollion was able to publish his *Précis du système hiéroglyphique* in which he showed that the script combined phonetic and ideographic signs – an understanding which eventually allowed the language to be read. In his later works – particularly the *Grammaire* (1836–41) and the *Dictionnaire* (1841–4) – his major discoveries were further formulated, and the true contribution of his work became fully apparent. Nevertheless, his system was only finally accepted in 1837, when Karl Lepsius wrote to Champollion's pupil, Rosellini, stating that he acknowledged it as a true analysis.

Having laid the foundations of reading the inscriptions, Champollion was now anxious to obtain firsthand access to more material. He went to Turin in 1824 to examine the collection built up by Drovetti; he also visited museums in Rome, Naples, Florence, and Leghorn, where he acquired another Drovetti collection which came to form the nucleus of the Musée Égyptien at the Louvre, where he was appointed Conservator in 1826. Champollion's travels around Europe were followed in 1828 by an expedition he led to Egypt. The party numbered fourteen and included his first student, Niccolo Rosellini, as well as architects and artists. Their brief was to conduct the first systematic survey of the monuments, and to copy the inscriptions with the aim of contributing further knowledge about Egypt's history and geography. Altogether, the expedition spent seventeen months in Egypt, travelling as far south as Nubia and copying the scenes and inscriptions from the monuments. Again, as with Denon, their experience of the temple at Denderah was overwhelming: one night they rushed ashore from their boats and, after a two-hour march, they approached the temple, which was bathed in moonlight, in a state of ecstasy. One expedition member wrote that it was

a picture that made us drunk with admiration. On the way, we had sung songs to ease our impatience, but

Young recognized that Demotic was derived from Hieroglyphs; he showed that both scripts combined alphabetic signs and symbols. This table from Champollion's Précis (1824) shows the sound values given to some of the hieroglyphs by Young and Champollion.

here, in front of the propylon, flooded with a heavenly light – what a sensation! Perfect peace and mysterious magic reigned under the portico with its gigantic columns – and outside, the moonlight was blinding! Strange and wonderful contrast!

For the first time, scholars visiting these sites were able to read the inscriptions correctly, and Champollion was able to obtain new material to confirm his theories. Because he could now read the inscriptional evidence, particularly the royal names, he was able to deduce the correct historical context of the monuments.

He returned from Egypt at the end of 1829 with quantities of antiquities and portfolios of drawings, but his recommendations regarding the state of Egypt's heritage were equally important. He was appalled by the destruction he saw and wrote to the Egyptian authorities, condemning the continuing devastation of the monuments and the sale of antiquities. The ruler, Mohammed Ali, responded with his Ordinance of 1835 which was the first attempt to protect the ancient remains; this prohibited the export of antiquities, laid the foundations for the establishment of a national museum in Cairo to house material acquired through excavation, and forbade the destruction of ancient monuments, affirming the Government's duty to conserve them. However, Mohammed Ali also agreed to allow two obelisks to be removed from Luxor to Paris, to act as a memorial to Napoleon's soldiers, but only one was taken and re-erected in the Place de la Concorde in 1836.

Champollion's life was of paramount importance to Egyptology. His decipherment enabled serious study to commence, so that today Egyptian can be read and studied as readily as any other ancient language. Its literature, one of the world's largest and most comprehensive ancient written sources, has opened up to the modern world the ideas and beliefs of a people who lived long before the Greeks and Romans. Doubtless if he had continued with his work, he would have made further advances, but in January 1832 he suffered a stroke and died, aged only forty-two, two months later. His unfinished works, including his Dictionary and Grammar and the volumes of drawings from his Egyptian expedition, were published by his devoted brother. These volumes now inspired others to continue with the arduous task of recording and studying the hieroglyphs, and the German scholars Karl Lepsius and Karl Heinrich Brugsch took up this challenge.

Whilst Champollion had been assiduously pursuing the decipherment of Hieroglyphs, political events in Egypt had ensured that the country became increasingly accessible to foreign travellers, explorers and antiquarians. After the conflict with Napoleon's troops, the British had handed Egypt back to the Turks, and in 1805 the country was taken over by Mohammed Ali, a man of humble origin from Macedonia who rose through the Turkish army in Egypt to become the Pasha or Viceroy. Although he remained nominally subject to the Turks, the force of his character ensured that he became a virtually independent ruler. An ambitious though autocratic leader, he sought to open up his country to foreign merchants, diplomats, tourists and dealers, and to introduce European advances and technology. His modernization programme included the construction of canals, water-wheels and other irrigation devices; he introduced new industries such as cotton, and encouraged small factories to open up. Egyptians were also sent abroad to study medicine, engineering, agriculture and industry.

This openness had a marked effect upon the development of Egyptology. On the one hand, the new freedom to travel coupled with the impetus of Champollion's discoveries inspired serious scholars to visit Egypt; but it also encouraged a rapid increase in the rush to acquire antiquities – an activity now pursued on a hitherto unknown scale.

Treasure seeking had always been an important industry in Egypt. In antiquity, the ransacked burial places and the tomb robbery papyri, giving accounts of trials of the culprits, testify to its widespread occurrence; by the 15th century AD, the Arab writer Ibn Khaldoun recorded that treasure seeking was so commonplace that it was classified as an industry and it was taxed. Books were written in Arabic which purported to give instructions for discovering the places where the treasure was hidden, and these also supplied spells and fumigations to overcome the magical safeguards that were supposed to protect the treasure. The most famous of these was known as the *Book of hidden pearls and precious mystery concerning the indication of hiding-places, findings and treasure*; this was considered valid for centuries, and as late as 1907 the French archaeologist Maspero published it in order that it would receive widespread condemnation because of its ridiculous contents.

With the opening up of Egypt to western ideas and technology under Mohammed Ali, the collectors were able to intensify their search for antiquities; these included not only small objects such as scarabs and papyri but also mummies, coffins and even large inscribed blocks from tombs and temples. Excavation was carried out on behalf of the dealers and collectors and was essentially a treasure-hunt; large and spectacular pieces were required for private collections and museums and little heed was paid to more mundane objects which were nevertheless often vital to the understanding of the archaeology and history of a site. It was argued by the collectors that they were saving the heritage by removing the material from Egypt, since the quarrying of stone from temples and pyramids was causing considerable destruction, and the increasing numbers of tourists, all eager to obtain souvenirs of their visit, were buying many of the smaller items. Since there was no national museum in Cairo where the finds could be placed, the foreign museums argued that they were at least preserving the ancient treasures. Nevertheless, the random excavation techniques, with no systematic rescue scheme, resulted in the loss of material which was of great importance in understanding this ancient civilization. Mohammed Ali realized that the antiquities were assets in gaining the goodwill of countries whose technological expertise he was keen to obtain, and gifts were made to important visitors. Also, the system of issuing firmans (permissions) to allow excavation by foreign collectors or their agents did not sufficiently protect the material. When, for example, the King List was cut from the wall of the Temple of Karnak in 1843 and removed to France the following year, this was done without a firman because the export would have been forbidden under the terms of Mohammed Ali's Ordinance of 1835. Nevertheless, the Ordinance, despite problems in enforcing its conditions, did place some control on the export of antiquities.

Some of the greatest collections were made in this era, and the names of the men associated with them have become famous in Egyptology. Some foreign diplomats of the early 19th century devoted much of their time to collecting antiquities in Egypt. The best known are Bernardino Drovetti (1775–1852) and Henry Salt (1780–1827). Drovetti was an Italian-born diplomat who took French citizenship and fought in Napoleon's Egyptian campaign. He was French Consul-General in Egypt from 1802 to 1814 and again

from 1820 to 1829. Salt was appointed as British Consul-General in Egypt in 1815, and the two men frequently found themselves in conflict in the hunt for antiquities. Since both France and England were politically important to Mohammed Ali, both Drovetti and Salt were granted the necessary firmans to excavate, and they and their agents gained virtual monopoly at this time.

Drovetti's most important acquisition was the Turin Canon of Kings which was taken to Italy; this helped scholars to establish the chronology of Egypt. Other antiquities were obtained by purchase from local diggers and from his agents' excavations, and ultimately his material made a major contribution to three great European museums. The first collection, rejected by the French, was sold to the King of Sardinia and became part of the Turin Museum; the second was bought by France and entered the Louvre; and the third was bought by Karl Lepsius for the Berlin Museum. Drovetti's life ended in a mental asylum in Turin; his methods of dealing with his rivals and acquiring antiquities have been criticized, but his energetic enterprises certainly established the basis of some of the world's major research collections.

Henry Salt similarly enhanced a number of European museums. His main aim was to acquire material for the British Museum, and he also built up his own substantial collection. He used the services of agents to excavate and remove the antiquities. European collectors now frequently employed local agents in Egypt – often Armenians, Greeks or Italians – as dealers and excavators.

One agent was Giovanni Battista Caviglia (1770–1845), an Italian sailor, employed to investigate the Pyramids and Sphinx at Giza, while Giovanni d'Athanasi (1799–1850), a Greek who had settled in Cairo, was taken on to excavate at Thebes (1817–27). Salt encountered many adventures in his quest for antiquities. On one occasion, he had set his sights on acquiring the famous Zodiac ceiling from the Temple of Hathor at Denderah, but a French collector, M. Sebastian Saulnier, decided to obtain it and employed an engineer, Lelorrain, to remove it from the temple and arrange its transportation to France. Under the 'gentleman's agreement' between France and

England, the sites on the west bank of the Nile (including Denderah) were allocated to Britain while the French had the east bank. However, through a series of manoeuvres Lelorrain acquired the Zodiac which eventually entered the Louvre, and Salt was unable to claim his prize.

In Britain, Salt also encountered difficulties. The large collection of antiquities he sent back to the British Museum in 1818 was, in the Trustees' opinion, overvalued, and they ultimately gave him only a modest sum which did not cover the cost of excavation and transport. They refused to buy the fine alabaster sarcophagus of Sethos I which Belzoni had obtained from the king's tomb at Thebes, and this was purchased by Sir John Soane; today it forms the impressive centrepiece of his museum in Lincoln's Inn Fields in London. Salt's second collection was bought by the King of France and entered the Louvre, while the third was sold at Sotheby's in 1835, when many of the objects were purchased by the British Museum.

Salt's successes in building up these collections were helped considerably by the energetic pursuits of his most famous agent in the field, Giovanni Battista Belzoni (1778–1823). Born in Padua, the son of a barber, Belzoni eventually made his way to England where he became a weight-lifter at Sadler's Wells Theatre. During his subsequent travels around Europe, he met an agent of Mohammed Ali in Malta, who arranged for him to visit Egypt in 1815 to build a water-raising machine for the Pasha (he is reputed to have studied hydraulics in Rome earlier in his life). He spent a year in Egypt, working on the design and a model of the wheel, but in the end Mohammed Ali's advisers did not recommend it, and he had to look for other employment.

Travellers such as the Swiss explorer John Lewis Burckhardt (1784–1817) were still able to make spectacular discoveries. He had studied Arabic at Cambridge and, using the name Sheikh Ibrahim and wearing Arab dress, he explored Arabia and Nubia. He found the remarkable ruins of Petra, and he also reported that he had found Abu Simbel in March 1813. From descriptions which he had heard, probably from local inhabitants, he was able to locate the

smaller temple of Nefertari and to see parts of the great statues which flanked the entrance to Ramesses II's own temple, at that time still covered in great drifts of sand. It was his account which later inspired Belzoni to seek out the temple and attempt to enter it.

Salt had become British Consul-General in Egypt, and he took Belzoni on to help him acquire antiquities for the British Museum. His first task was to obtain the colossal head of Ramesses II from the Ramesseum at Thebes. He had been told about this by Burckhardt, as well as about the temples at Abu Simbel. Burckhardt had come upon these monuments from above, descending down the great sand slope which filled the area between the two cliffs. His description captures something of the excitement of this first view:

Having, as I supposed, seen all the antiquities of Ebsambal [Abu Simbel], I was about to ascend the sandy side of the mountain by the same way I had descended when, having luckily turned more to the southward, I fell in with what is yet visible of four immense colossal statues cut out of the rock…now almost entirely buried beneath the sands, which are blown down here in torrents…[Under a hawk-headed figure, surmounted by a sun-disk,] I suspect, could the sand be cleared away, a vast temple would be discovered.

Belzoni says of his discovery of the colossal head of Ramesses II – the inspiration for Shelley's sonnet on Ozymandias (a derivation of User-maat-re, one of the names of Ramesses II): 'I found it near the remains of its body and chair, with its face upwards, and apparently smiling on me, at the thought of being taken to England.' It was eventually moved to the river's edge, using a wooden platform, rollers and manpower, and when the Nile flood made it possible, the colossus was floated downstream and transported to London.

Belzoni's travels took him on to Aswan and Nubia, where he planned to open the entrance to the temple at Abu Simbel, but he could not gather together sufficient manpower to do this. At Luxor he had more success: excavations at the Temple of Mut at Karnak revealed over twenty statues of the goddess Sekhmet; wandering through these temples, he remarked that 'It appeared to me like entering a city of giants who, after a long conflict, were all destroyed, leaving the ruins of their former temples as the only proof of their former existence.'

On the west bank he explored the tombs at Qurna in search of funerary papyri, causing much damage to the mummies buried there. He recalls that, when he first entered the passageway of a tomb, 'Every step I took, I crushed a mummy in some part or other.' Penetrating further into the burial chambers, he says:

a vast quantity of dust rises, so fine that it enters into the throat and nostrils, and chokes the nose and mouth to such a degree that it requires a great power of lungs to resist it and the strong effluvia of the mummies. In some places, there is not more than a vacancy of a foot left, which you must contrive to pass through in a creeping posture like a snail, on pointed and keen stones that cut like glass.

Sometimes, he sought rest, sitting down in the tombs:

But what a place of rest! surrounded by bodies, by heaps of mummies in all directions...the blackness of the wall, the faint light given by the candles or torches for want of air, the different objects that surrounded me, seeming to converge with each other, and the Arabs with their candles or torches in their hands, naked and covered with dust, themselves resembling living mummies, absolutely formed a scene that cannot be described.

He graphically describes one particular occasion when he

sought a resting place, found one, and continued to sit; but when my weight bore on the body of an Egyptian, it crushed like a band-box. I naturally had recourse to my hands to sustain my weight, but they found no better support so that I sunk altogether among the broken mummies with a crash of bones, rags, and wooden cases, which raised such a dust as kept me motionless for a quarter of an hour, waiting till it subsided again.

At Thebes, he discovered six royal tombs, including that of King Ay and – his most famous find – the deep rock-cut tomb of King Sethos I. Here, he lived in the tomb and took wax impressions of the wall scenes and hieroglyphs. When he returned to England in 1821, he held an exhibition in the Egyptian Hall at Piccadilly. This had a large-scale model of the tomb and two full-scale reproductions of its chambers, with their coloured wall scenes, as well as many antiquities, including statues, mummies and papyri. The exhibition, which lasted until 1822, was a great success and established his reputation as a traveller. Immediately prior to its opening, a spectacle had been mounted (popular at that time) at which a mummy was unwrapped before a medical audience.

Belzoni's other important activities in Egypt included the opening of the pyramid of Chephren at Giza and the discovery of the ancient port of Berenice on the Red Sea. His publication, *Narrative of the Operations and Recent Discoveries within the Pyramids, Temples, Tombs, and Excavations in Egypt and Nubia* (1820), further enhanced his reputation and, together with the exhibition, was the culmination of his career. Despite his success, he was unable to obtain funding for further enterprises in Egypt; he left on an expedition to search for the source of the River Niger in Africa, but after beginning his journey, he caught dysentery and died.

As one of the most interesting characters of his time, Belzoni typifies the untrained, aggressive treasure seeker who had an overwhelming desire to seize the prizes for his employers and himself, but little regard for the archaeological context of the material. However, his methods were less disastrous than those of some of his rivals, and his spectacular successes and talent for publicizing his achievements back in England certainly raised the general awareness of Egypt's ancient civilization.

While some archaeologists were pursuing their somewhat dubious ends, other travellers to Egypt were adopting more scholarly attitudes. William John Bankes, an English traveller, collector and antiquarian, had travelled in Egypt and Nubia, and became very interested in the decipherment of Hieroglyphs. A bilingual obelisk from Philae, which was acquired by Belzoni for Salt and eventually came into the possession of Bankes, was transported to England and set up in his park at Kingston Lacy, Wimborne, where it still stands today. Using the key to the hieroglyphs produced by Thomas Young (Bankes disagreed with Champollion's work), and some other material including the Greek inscription on the pedestal of his obelisk, Bankes was able to read the name of Cleopatra in a cartouche.

Mohammed Ali's encouragement of foreign visitors now also brought a number of serious scholars to Egypt to copy and study the inscriptions. These early epigraphers were not affected by the restrictions which the government was beginning to attempt to impose on excavators, and after Champollion's decipherment, there was an urgency to copy more monuments. For the first time, the copyists understood the hieroglyphic signs and their meaning. Champollion's own expedition had pioneered this work, and the results produced by these early scholars are of great importance, because many of the monuments, texts or details have since been destroyed.

One of the most important copyists was Sir John Gardner Wilkinson (1797–1875), who has been described as the founder of Egyptology in Britain. With a small private income, Wilkinson took up the study of the Egyptian language, and arrived in Egypt in 1821, where he spent twelve years recording the archaeological sites and studying Arabic and Coptic to assist him in the decipherment of Hieroglyphs. With no government funding, he was obliged to work in a restricted area, and devoted much of his attention to the tombs at Thebes, where he excavated in 1824 and 1827–8. His travels also took him twice to the Second Cataract.

Amongst his major achievements were the decipherment of dozens of inscriptions, the correct identification for the first time of many royal cartouches, and the first production of a working survey of all the main sites in Egypt and Nubia. He produced the first comprehensive plan of ancient Thebes and made one of the earliest identifications of the Labyrinth at Hawara. His work as a copyist – producing many drawings and coloured reproductions of wall scenes and other material – has probably never been surpassed. It is particularly remarkable that so much was achieved by one man whereas the other great epigraphic expeditions of Napoleon's Commission, and of Champollion and Lepsius had involved teams of experts.

The information he amassed from the archaeological sites, paintings, papyri and inscriptions was used to write the most comprehensive account ever produced about the ancient Egyptian civilization, ranging over many aspects but emphasizing religion, culture and daily life rather than chronology and political history. This was the first serious study to utilize the actual Egyptian evidence rather than Classical accounts as the primary source material; the three volumes of *The Manners and Customs of the Ancient Egyptians* (1835) remain a testimony to his unusual ability to produce an account based on original research which is nevertheless of interest to a general readership. His main ideas were drawn from the tomb scenes which illustrated daily life and these, rather than tomb contents, provided most of his material. Whereas the publications of the great French and German expeditions organized their material according to site, Wilkinson looked at the ancient Egyptians as living people, categorizing his information according to subject matter. Their social classes, buildings, furniture, arts and crafts, and activities such as hunting and fishing were all analysed, providing an extensive and unparalleled account of the civilization.

Another antiquarian who visited Egypt in 1824 was Robert Hay (1799–1863), a Scot of independent means who was able to devote his life to making drawings, plans and copies of the inscriptions on the Egyptian monuments. Between 1828 and 1829, he travelled around the ruins in a systematic manner; an accurate copyist and draughtsman himself, he was also able to employ highly skilled staff, including the artist Joseph Bonomi. The invaluable collection of material he amassed is kept today in the British Museum and consists of some forty-nine volumes of his papers and drawings, as well as his diary and letters. His collection of antiquities was eventually acquired by the British Museum and the Boston Museum of Fine Arts.

Another Scottish antiquarian, Alexander Henry Rhind (1833–63), established new advances in scientific excavation as distinct from treasure hunting. Trained as a lawyer, poor health forced him to abandon his career and travel to southern Europe and Egypt, where he spent two years excavating tombs at Thebes. Here, working on one undisturbed burial, he developed new systematic techniques of excava-

The façade of the Temple of Ramesses II at Abu Simbel, with colossal statues representing the king. Burckhardt was the first modern traveller to discover Abu Simbel and his account inspired Belzoni to attempt excavation there in 1817.

The façade of the Great Temple at Abu Simbel, from the account of Lepsius' expedition, published in *Denkmäler aus Aegypten und Aethiopien* (1849–59). This was the last great epigraphic survey undertaken in Egypt.

The portico of the Temple of Edfu, in a
lithograph from David Roberts' *Egypt and
Nubia* (1846). The sand still partly covered
many monuments when he visited Egypt.

A view of the entrance to the hypostyle hall, Temple of Edfu. Every year the goddess Hathor sailed southwards from Denderah to visit her husband Horus at Edfu and celebrate their sacred marriage.

A view of the hypostyle hall in the Temple of Isis on the island of Philae, from a lithograph in David Roberts' *Egypt and Nubia* (1846). Much of the colour still remained on the columns when he visited Egypt.

A temple colonnade, part of the buildings once situated on the island of Philae. When the High Dam was built at Aswan, a UNESCO project dismantled these and rebuilt them on the neighbouring island, Agilkia.

(Above left) A painted panel portrait of a man, dating to c.200 BC. This was originally placed over the face of his mummy. Petrie discovered many of these portraits when he excavated the Graeco-Roman cemetery at Hawara.

(Left) The painted panel portrait of a woman from the same period shows a hairstyle fashionable at that time.

A colossal stone statue of Ramesses II found at Memphis, discovered by Caviglia and Sloane in 1820 and now housed in a modern building on the site. A similar statue, also mentioned by early travellers, stands in Ramesses Square, Cairo.

The mummy of a six-year-old boy dating to the Graeco-Roman Period. The body is in a good state of preservation and gilding still remains on the face; such mummies were brought back from Egypt as souvenirs in earlier centuries.

tion, for the first time recording the exact location of each object that was found. This approach contrasted sharply with the techniques of Colonel Richard W. Howard-Vyse (1784–1853) who, with the Italian Caviglia, undertook excavations of the pyramids at Giza. With the assistance of the engineer J. S. Perring, a survey of a number of pyramids at Giza and elsewhere was produced. The resulting publication was the most significant on the pyramid fields produced during the 19th century, providing descriptions and measurements of great value. It remains a standard work, but the techniques they used for opening the pyramid of Mycerinus have been described as 'gunpowder' archaeology.

The last great epigraphic survey of the monuments and sites was undertaken by the Prussian expedition (1842–5) which reached Meroë in the Sudan. The best equipped until then, with skilled draughtsmen to survey the monuments, it was led by Karl Lepsius (1810–84), generally regarded as the foremost Egyptologist after Champollion, who carried on the French scholar's pioneering language studies. His expedition to Tanis in 1866 resulted in the discovery of the Decree of Canopus with a bilingual inscription which enabled Champollion's claims regarding the Rosetta Stone to be checked and verified. Lepsius was also mainly responsible for setting up the great Egyptian collection in the Berlin Museum, for which he acquired one of Drovetti's collections, and he also brought back antiquities and casts from the Prussian expedition to Egypt and Nubia. During his time in Egypt, Lepsius excavated the site of the Labyrinth in the Fayoum, where stratigraphic techniques were used well in advance of their employment elsewhere in the Near East. By 1859, the publication of the information gathered on this expedition was completed: the *Denkmäler aus Aegypten und Aethiopien* (1849–59) filled twelve volumes with copies of inscriptions and wall scenes of every major site. Probably the largest Egyptological work ever produced, it included only folio plates but these achieved new levels of accuracy; the accompanying text, published in five later volumes (1897–1913), was compiled from notes after Lepsius' death.

This was the last of the great topographical, comprehensive surveys of the monuments; in future, more specialized accounts of one site or monument would provide the detailed information that was increasingly required. However, these great surveys compiled by the expeditions of Napoleon, Champollion and Rosellini, and Lepsius had given contemporary scholars the basic material from which to study the historical and religious scenes and texts. Their importance to the development of the subject was crucial and even today they preserve some valuable information about the monuments which the intervening years have obliterated.

Thus by the middle of the 19th century great advances had been made in Egyptology: in language studies, the work of Champollion, Lepsius and others now ensured a systematic approach, and scholars such as Heinrich Brugsch (1827–94) continued to build on the existing knowledge of Egyptian grammar by producing a Demotic grammar and a hieroglyphic dictionary. Historical facts gained from literary texts were now based on a firm scientific foundation. The great publications of the monuments and the many accurate books on ancient Egypt, produced to meet a growing popular demand, ensured that in Europe and America there was an increasing awareness of this early civilization. Visits to the great museums also heightened people's interest in the antiquities, and increasing numbers of tourists travelled to Egypt and returned with accounts of the stupendous monuments. However, along with their enthusiasm, people also began to recognize an urgent need to preserve the monuments and antiquities; it was necessary to organize excavation along different lines, and to end the destruction of the sites and the random disposal of the antiquities.

Excavation had remained haphazard: archaeologists sought for objects that would please museums and private collectors and for inscribed pieces that would help language studies. Following Champollion's plea to the Egyptian Government and Mohammed Ali's subsequent Ordinance of 1835, there had been some improvement: an individual could obtain permission from the Pasha to excavate, but there was now no guarantee that he would be allowed to retain the objects. The export of antiquities was prohibited by the Ordinance, and although this was still extremely difficult to enforce, it did have the effect of discouraging collectors from cutting large sections from the walls of monuments, since they would now be difficult to take out of the country. Other appeals and criticisms, including an unfavourable assessment of the consular role in the trade of antiquities, were also made and it was realized that two major developments were urgently required to protect Egypt's heritage. First, it was essential that a national museum to house the antiquities should be established in Cairo. Secondly, there was a crucial need to organize the excavations along scientific lines, introducing procedures to ensure that detailed records were kept, that finds were retained because of their archaeological or historical significance rather than their financial value, and that appropriate conservation measures were carried out in respect of the monuments and the excavated material.

As early as 1821, the traveller Edward de Montule proposed in his *Travels* that a great museum should be established at Cairo or Alexandria. With the proposal for an Antiquities Service in 1835, the Egyptian government had begun to collect antiquities and house them in a small museum in the Ezbekia gardens in Cairo, but this did not long survive Mohammed Ali's rulership. The material was later transferred to another building in the Citadel of Saladin in Cairo, but Abbas Pasha, a later ruler of Egypt, presented the whole collection to the Austrian Archduke Maximilian when he visited Egypt in 1855. It was Ferdinand de Lesseps (1805–94), the originator of the Suez Canal, who used his considerable influence with Egypt's ruler, Said Pasha, to put into action a number of moves to halt the destruction of the ancient monuments, which included the development of the Antiquities Service and the provision of an appropriate national museum. These were to be the major achievements of the French archaeologist Auguste Mariette (1821–81).

Mariette was born at Boulogne in France, and followed a number of careers, including designing models for ribbon manufacturers in Coventry, England, before he returned to France and continued his education, becoming Professor of French at Boulogne in 1843. The previous year,

Mariette had been approached by a relative to organize the papers of his son, Nestor l'Hôte, who had been a member of Champollion's expedition to Egypt. These papers aroused Mariette's interest in Egyptology and he learnt the Egyptian alphabet and studied decipherment, and also pursued studies in Coptic. His first article, a catalogue of the Egyptian objects in the Boulogne Museum, led to his appointment to a minor post at the Louvre, where he assiduously transcribed all the inscriptions then in the collection, from which it was eventually possible to prepare a general inventory of the Egyptian monuments.

Charles Lenormant at the Collège de France was impressed with Mariette's abilities, and in 1850 he instructed him to go to Egypt and collect rare Coptic, Ethiopic and Syriac manuscripts. In Cairo, Mariette contacted the Coptic patriarch, but had little success in his mission, and he turned his attention instead to Pharaonic antiquities. In October 1850, when he was searching the necropolis at Sakkara, he noticed the head of a sphinx protruding from the sands; he recalled the account by the Classical geographer Strabo, describing the avenue of sphinxes leading to the Serapeum where the sacred Apis-bulls were buried. Although he had no official permission to excavate, and funds only to purchase the manuscripts, he followed his hunch and took on thirty workmen to dig for the Serapeum. The avenue of sphinxes was uncovered, and the tombs and two temples of the Apis-bulls were revealed; in one unplundered tomb, he found the intact burial of a bull, with a great granite sarcophagus, the mummified remains of the animal, and the associated jewellery and treasure. This divine animal had been interred during the reign of Ramesses II (*c.*1290 BC), and the footprints of an ancient workman still remained in the sand, undisturbed for over two and a half thousand years. His great discoveries at the Serapeum caused a sensation; further funds were made available by the Louvre and Mariette excavated there for another four years (1850–4). He was promoted to the post of Assistant Keeper at the Louvre, and his reputation as an archaeologist was established; in his *Choix de monuments* (1856), he published a series of plates showing selected objects from his discovery at the Serapeum.

Mariette's true ambition, however, was to develop a service in Egypt to protect the ancient monuments, and he had the opportunity to tell Ferdinand de Lesseps of his proposal. After the assassination of Abbas Pasha in 1854, Said Pasha had become Egypt's ruler and, anxious to please the influential de Lesseps, he agreed to the plan which de Lesseps put before him. It was decided that there should be an organization to look after the standing monuments in Egypt and that a new museum should be established in Cairo. Eventually, in 1858, again on de Lesseps' recommendation, Mariette was appointed as the first director of ancient monuments in Egypt and head of the new museum.

The site chosen for the museum was the small Nile port of Boulaq just north-east of Cairo and although the accommodation was less than ideal, this was the first National Museum to be established in the Near East. Here, Mariette was able to try out new ideas, including an ambitious programme to photograph the treasures of the museum. The larger statuary was photographed inside the building, whereas displays of the smaller pieces were recorded outside. Unfortunately, a disastrous flood occurred in 1878, when many of the objects were washed away or stolen, and in 1890 the remaining collections were moved to an old palace belonging to Ismail Pasha at Giza. Eventually, they were transferred to the Cairo Museum which was built in 1902; designed by the French architect Marcel Dourgnon, this followed the neo-classical style, with two main floors devoted to exhibition galleries. Here the world's largest collection of Egyptian material, totalling some 120,000 objects, is housed. Mariette's ambition was achieved and his foresight rewarded, but his plans were strongly opposed by the dealers, since their activities would be directly affected. Mariette was also dependent upon the financial support of the ruler for the future development of the museum, but its international significance as the finest museum of ancient art and history persuaded the Pasha to continue his aid. When he died at Boulaq, Mariette was given a state funeral and was buried outside the museum there; later, his sarcophagus was moved to the forecourt of the new Cairo Museum, where it was surmounted by a bronze statue by Xavier Barthe, unveiled in 1904.

In his other great ambition – the development of the world's first National Antiquities Service – Mariette was equally energetic. He inaugurated excavations at many sites, including Sakkara, Giza, Thebes, Abydos, Tuna, Esna, Sais, Mendes, Bubastis and Elephantine. Altogether, over thirty years, digs at thirty-five different locations stretching from the Delta to the First Cataract involved thousands of workmen. Many important discoveries were made, including the monuments of Tanis and the famous treasure of Queen Ah-hotep at Thebes, and Mariette started workshops at various sites where the objects could be dealt with appropriately. The sand and rubbish and modern dwellings were now cleared from some of the temple sites, such as Deir el-Bahri and Karnak at Thebes; at Edfu (the most complete temple), a modern village was removed from the roof enabling the temple to be fully visible for the first time. Newly exposed wall scenes and texts greatly added to knowledge of these buildings, which – even a short time before, as in the works of such artists as David Roberts (*Egypt and Nubia,* 1842–9) – had appeared partially submerged by desert sands.

Nevertheless, although Mariette's discoveries were remarkable, he was later criticized for his secretiveness in keeping his schemes from others and for his attempts to forbid any excavations in Egypt other than his own. Most particularly, his excavation methods were censured by later archaeologists. It was essential that he retained the interest and support of the Pasha by continuing to make spectacular finds, and this was a major incentive in his work. However, because of the large number of sites being excavated simultaneously, there was no proper site supervision, and no adequate recording of finds. The urgency to find treasure even led to the use of dynamite as an excavation tool, but in general Mariette's attempts, if somewhat extrovert, still compared well with those of contemporary excavators.

Mariette also played a useful diplomatic role between France and Egypt; in 1867 he was sent to Paris to oversee a major display at the International Exhibition which set out to reconstruct the life of ancient Egypt. The centrepiece was the famous jewellery of Queen Ah-hotep. When Mariette's workmen at Thebes found this queen's tomb and its elaborate sarcophagus, the local governor of Qena, in Mariette's absence, hurried to Thebes and possessed the treasure in the name of the government, proceeding to rip open the coffin and take out the jewellery. He then sent the coffin to Cairo as a gift to the ruler and retained the jewellery for himself. Hearing of this adventure, Mariette pursued the governor, gained access to his boat and forced him to hand over the treasure. Mariette then went to Cairo and related his actions to the Pasha, taking care to present him with a couple of pieces of the jewellery for one of his wives. Much impressed, the ruler commended his actions; this event also helped Said Pasha to decide that a national museum should be built.

The Suez Canal was finally opened on 17 November 1869; to mark the event, Verdi composed the three-act opera *Aida* which was first performed in Cairo in 1871, and Mariette was asked to co-operate in writing the libretto for this.

In his last ten years, Mariette saw his own life undergo some dramatic changes. In the flood at Boulaq, he lost most of his papers in his house which adjoined the museum. Cholera claimed his wife's life in 1865, and because of his own ill-health, the doctors in Paris recommended that he should not travel, but Mariette nevertheless returned to Cairo and died there in 1881.

His achievements were considerable: a permanent museum and an established Antiquities Service ensured that the export of antiquities from Egypt was slowed down, and his excavations, if lacking a proper methodology, at least terminated the treasure seeking that Salt, Drovetti and Belzoni had pursued. In addition, Mariette was the first to raise public awareness concerning the need to clean and conserve the monuments, and he promoted a worldwide interest in saving Egypt's heritage. In the year of his death, there was a military revolt in Egypt, which alarmed Britain and France because their major investments in the Suez Canal and in industrial development in Egypt would be threatened by political instability. The British sent a fleet and an expeditionary force to Egypt in 1882, with the result that order was restored under a nominal Egyptian ruler (the Khedive). A British agent and consul-general (who actually had no formal authority over the Khedive) was installed, and through the British officials who were now introduced into defence, the police force, foreign affairs, finance and public works, the British exerted considerable influence for many years. The French, however, continued to dominate the areas of education, archaeology and the arts, and their government was anxious to see another Frenchman succeed Mariette as head of the Museum and the Antiquities Service.

Gaston Maspero (1846–1916) had first met Mariette in Paris in 1867, when he was still a young student. Although of Italian parentage, Maspero was born in Paris, and became interested in Egyptology while still a schoolboy. He was appointed Professor of Egyptian Philology and Archaeology at the Collège de France in 1874, and first went out to Egypt in 1880, to lead an archaeological mission. When Mariette died, he was ready to inherit his post; at the museum he continued Mariette's work, organizing and cataloguing the ever-increasing collections and rearranging the displays. As Director of the Antiquities Service, he regulated excavation throughout Egypt and with the support of the British Consul-General Lord Cromer, he developed the Service's work, so that it functioned under five regional inspectors. He continued Mariette's work in opening some of the smaller pyramids and copying the Pyramid Texts, and eventually produced the first edition of these very important inscriptions. His achievements were extensive and included a scheme to systematically clear and preserve the great temple complex at Karnak. Although he retained Mariette's general principles for authorizing excavations, he relaxed some of the restrictions so that a controlled, moderate flow of antiquities was now allowed to go to museums in Europe and America. He also initiated the important Archaeological Survey of Nubia which the American archaeologist George A. Reisner undertook in 1907–9. A prolific writer whose publications exceeded in number those of any other Egyptologist, Maspero not only edited the *Catalogue* of material in the Cairo Museum which then filled fifty volumes, but also produced popular works such as his *Histoire ancienne des peuples de l'orient classique* (1895–9).

Perhaps, however, he is best remembered for his crucial role in rescuing the mummified remains of some of the kings and queens of the New Kingdom.

Until 1870 the modern world remained unaware of the royal mummies, but in 1871 Ahmed Abd er-Rasul, who lived in the village of Qurna near the Theban necropolis, stumbled across the ancient communal burial place of a number of the rulers when he was searching for a goat. In antiquity, the kings of a later dynasty had ordered the reburial of these mummies in two caches, removing them from their original plundered tombs, so that they might achieve a second chance of eternity. This first cache at Deir el-Bahri supplied Abd er-Rasul and his relatives with a supply of small objects, including ushabtis (model figures of agricultural workers), canopic jars, papyri and scarabs, which could readily be sold to the many dealers and tourists who now visited the area.

When material bearing the royal insignia gradually began to appear on the international market, the news reached Maspero who began an investigation at Luxor. Suspicion fell on the er-Rasul brothers and eventually, as the result of a family quarrel, the police were able to undertake enquiries. One brother – Mohammed – confessed and as a result apparently obtained immunity from punishment, received a reward, and was even appointed head workman over the excavations at Thebes. He led the archaeologist Brugsch, who was acting on behalf of the Antiquities Service, to the cache. Maspero inspected the find in January 1882, and eventually the mummies were transported by river to Cairo, where many of them were later unwrapped and autopsied, providing basic information for our knowledge of mummification techniques in the New Kingdom.

From the middle of the 19th century, tourism had become increasingly popular in Egypt. The publications of David Roberts with their magnificent lithographs of the drawings he had made of the monuments in the Holy Land, Egypt and Nubia had inspired widespread interest in visiting these sites, and photography now added another dimension. F. Frith's *Egypt and Palestine* (1858–63) captured something of the romance of the ancient buildings with his photographs and accompanying text, although, as in this description of the temple at Luxor, he noted their deterioration: 'Around many of the stupendous ruins of Old Egypt are now heaped mountains of the debris of deserted towns, or else modern Arab hovels of mud cluster round the columns.'

Many visitors came to Egypt from England, America, Germany, France and Belgium. Some wished to spend the winter in a country where the warm, dry climate was particularly beneficial to their health. With the construction of the Suez Canal, many people en route to India now stopped in Egypt and made a detour to Cairo, often staying at Shepheard's Hotel, so that they could visit the Giza pyramids. Some tourists made more extensive journeys: pioneering travel agencies such as Thomas Cook enabled groups of tourists to make the Nile journey, and some went overland, travelling by train to the major sites which could be viewed in a three-week visit. The most leisurely tour, however, was enjoyed by people who could afford to charter a *dahabeah* (sailing vessel) and travel from Cairo to the Second Cataract. This Nile journey took about three months, and combined the advantages of privacy and the company of friends with the delights of watching the timeless river scenery and stopping off at will to explore the archaeological sites and monuments, or the bazaars with their wealth of colour and frenzied activity.

Amelia B. Edwards is a good example of a tourist whose visit to Egypt had a profound effect on the development of Egyptology. A successful popular novelist, she travelled to Syria and Egypt in 1873–4, and made the typical Nile journey to the Second Cataract in a *dahabeah*. This inspired her best-known book, an account of her travels entitled *A Thousand Miles Up the Nile* (1877); it provides a delightful view of the land and customs she saw and had a marked influence on her readership. Here she describes the delights of sailing along the Nile:

Thus the morning passes. We sit on deck writing letters; reading; watching the sunny river-side pictures that glide by at a foot's pace and are so long in sight. Palm-groves, sand-banks, patches of fuzzy-headed dura (a kind of sorghum) and fields of some

Some tourists made extensive tours in Egypt in the 19th and early 20th centuries, sailing from Cairo to the Second Cataract and visiting the ancient monuments en route. Here, a passenger on a Nile boat negotiates a purchase with local vendors at Esna.

yellow-flowering herb, succeeded each other. A boy plods along the bank, leading a camel. They go slowly; but they soon leave us behind. A native boat meets us, floating down side-wise with the current. A girl comes to the water's edge with a great empty jar on her head, and waits to fill it till the trackers have gone by. The pigeon-towers of a mud-village peep above a clump of lebbek trees, a quarter of a mile inland. Here a solitary brown man, with only a felt skull-cap on his head and a slip of scanty tunic fastened about his loins, works a shaduf, stooping and rising, stooping and rising, with the regularity of a pendulum. It is the same machine which we shall see by and by depicted in the tombs at Thebes.

The great monuments had a dramatic effect upon Amelia Edwards; of the pyramids at Giza she says:

But when at last the edge of the desert is reached, and the long sand-slope climbed, and the rocky platform gained, and the Great Pyramid in all its unexpected bulk and majesty towers close above one's head, the effect is as sudden as it is overwhelming. It shuts out the sky and the horizon. It shuts out all the other pyramids. It shuts out everything but the sense of awe and wonder.

When her party arrived at the island of Philae, she describes the delights of the scene before them:

The approach by water is quite the most beautiful. Seen from the level of a small boat, the island with its palms, its colonnades, its pylons, seems to rise out of the river like a mirage. Piled rocks frame it on either side, and purple mountains close up the distance. As the boat glides nearer between glistening boulders, those sculptured towers rise higher and ever higher against the sky. They show no sign of ruin or age. All looks solid, stately, perfect. One forgets for the moment that anything is changed. If a sound of antique chanting were to be borne along the quiet air – if a procession of white-robed priests bearing aloft the veiled ark of the God, were to come sweeping round between the palms and the pylons – we should not think it strange.

Another highlight of the tour was the experience of the sunrise at Abu Simbel:

Every morning I waked in time to witness that daily miracle. Every morning I saw those awful brethren pass from death to life, from life to sculptured stone. I brought myself almost to believe that there must sooner or later come some one sunrise when the ancient charm would snap asunder, and the giants must arise and speak. It is fine to see the sunrise on the front of the Great Temple; but something still finer takes place on certain mornings of the year, in the very heart of the mountain. As the sun comes up above the eastern hill-tops, one long, level beam strikes through the doorway, pierces the inner darkness like an arrow, penetrates to the sanctuary, and falls like fire from heaven upon the altar at the feet of the Gods.

No one who has watched for the coming of that shaft of sunlight can doubt that it was a calculated effect, and that the excavation was directed at one especial angle in order to produce it. In this way Ra, to whom the temple was dedicated, may be said to have entered in daily, and by a direct manifestation of his presence to have approved the sacrifices of his worshippers.

Amelia Edwards' personal experience of Egypt profoundly affected the rest of her life.

The Scientific and Artistic Commission that accompanied Napoleon's military expedition produced the Description de l'Égypte *(1809–28). This plate shows the obelisk known as Cleopatra's Needle. It was brought from Alexandria to London in 1877 and set up on the Embankment.*

Aware of the rapid deterioration of the ancient monuments, she now set herself the task of raising public awareness in England and America of the need to establish scientific excavation in Egypt, together with systematic recording of the standing monuments. Through her writing, she sought to spread this message and to stem the destruction of Egypt's heritage; realizing the need for a society which could promote, encourage and act upon these ideas, she was instrumental in founding the Egypt Exploration Fund in London in 1882, with the help of the Orientalist Reginald Stuart Poole and the famous surgeon Sir Erasmus Wilson who had supplied the finance to bring Cleopatra's Needle to London. Amelia Edwards became the society's Secretary and devoted her talents to promoting the work of the Fund and its excavators, giving talks and writing many popular articles for journals and newspapers. In 1889–90 she visited the USA to give a series of lectures and to inspire popular interest in the American section of the Egypt Exploration Fund. The Fund was one of the first organizations to apply for excavation permits in Egypt; its aims of undertaking scientific excavation and publishing its results, and of fostering interest in Egyptology amongst its

largely lay membership still continue today (it is now known as the Egypt Exploration Society).

Amelia Edwards' other great service to Egyptology was to found, under the terms of her will, the first chair of Egyptology in Britain, at University College London, which also received her library and collection of Egyptian antiquities. It was her wish that William Flinders Petrie, who had excavated for the Fund, should be appointed to this post, and it was his methodology of scientific excavation in Egypt which would pioneer a whole new approach to archaeology. Unlike earlier archaeologists, he did not seek large and impressive finds (although he made many of those), but he concentrated instead on the careful examination of each site and its contents, however mundane they might appear. He was rightly convinced that it was these insignificant objects that held the key to understanding the civilization of ancient Egypt, and his techniques were ultimately adopted in many fields of archaeology.

William Matthew Flinders Petrie (1853–1942) received no formal education, but gained a practical knowledge of surveying and geometry from his father. When he was thirteen, Petrie read Charles Piazzi Smyth's book *Our Inheritance in the Great Pyramid* which proposed that divine prophecies were enshrined in the structure of Cheops' pyramid. This inspired his interest in Egyptology, and he and his father planned an expedition to Egypt in 1880–2, to make a detailed survey of the pyramids. In later years, in his book *Seventy Years in Archaeology,* he describes his early working methods:

Usually, measurements inside the pyramid were begun after the tourists had left at sunset, and continued till midnight, so as to be undisturbed. It was often most convenient to strip entirely for work, owing to the heat and absence of any current of air, in the interior. For outside work in the hot weather, vest and pants were suitable, and if pink, they kept the tourist at bay, as the creature seemed to him too queer for inspection. After rigging up the rock-tomb with shelves, and remaking the old shutters and door...I found the place comfortable. The petroleum stove by the door cooked my meals, which I prepared at any time required by the irregular hours of work.

However, his interest in small objects (as a boy he had collected coins) and an acute awareness of the destruction facing many monuments in Egypt led him to take up excavation. He criticized earlier archaeological attempts, saying:

Nothing seems to be done with any uniform and regular plan, work is begun and left unfinished; no regard is paid to future requirements of exploration, and no civilized or labour-saving devices are used. It is sickening to see the rate at which everything is being destroyed, and the little regard paid to preservation.

He obtained financial support from the Egypt Exploration Fund and excavated for them in 1884–6, but a quarrel with the Committee brought the funding to an end. However, through the good offices of Amelia Edwards, he obtained financial support from a Manchester businessman, Jesse Haworth, and from Martyn Kennard who had family interests in Egypt. This enabled him to excavate the sites of Illahun, Kahun and Gurob; recalling his working days at Kahun, Petrie shows a marked sympathy with the site:

...having examined hundreds of the rooms, and having discovered all the ordinary objects of daily life as they were last handled by their owners, I seem to have touched and realised much of the civilisation of that remote age, so that it is hard to realise that over four thousand years have glided by since those houses last echoed to the voices of their occupants.

Haworth's support continued for several years, providing a firm foundation for future excavation at various sites. In return, Haworth received a substantial share of the antiquities found by Petrie, and these came to form the nucleus of the Manchester University Museum collection.

To ensure his independence, Petrie founded his own archaeological organization – the Egyptian Research Account – in 1894; later this became the British School of Archaeology in Egypt, and had the important aim of raising funds from the public to support Petrie's excavations. In 1892, he became the first Edwards Professor of Egyptology at University College London, a chair he held until 1933, and he excavated again for the Egypt Exploration Fund in

Flinders Petrie pioneered many techniques in Egyptology. This photograph was taken by C. T. Campion (right) in 1914 at Kahun when he visited Petrie (centre) and his wife Hilda (left). Petrie had just finished clearing the enclosure around the nearby Lahun pyramid.

1896–1906. Eventually, he moved his activities to Palestine in 1926, working there at Hyksos and other sites until 1938.

In over forty years of excavation, he dug as many sites as Mariette, and his major archaeological discoveries were more numerous than those of any other Egyptologist. Among the most significant was the discovery of Naucratis (in 1884–5), the city of Greek residents in Egypt. Here he introduced the use of stratigraphy for the first time, fixing the dates of the different layers of the buildings by referring to the small objects he found there, such as coins or inscribed pieces which could be specifically dated. In the Fayoum he discovered remarkable royal treasure in a tomb near the Lahun pyramid, but he also excavated the town sites of Kahun and Gurob (1889–90). These were very important because they pro-

vided evidence of everyday living conditions rather than funerary customs. Kahun – a purpose-built town which housed the families of pyramid workers – was the first example of town planning ever uncovered in Egypt. Foreign pottery at both sites led Petrie to speculate about connections between Egypt and Greece; because the inscriptional evidence at the Egyptian sites enabled them to be firmly dated, a chronological framework could be proposed for sites in Greece where similar pottery was found. Thus, the foreign imports found in Egypt helped Sir Arthur Evans to establish the basis of a chronology for the discoveries he made at the palace of Knossos in Crete a short time later. The presence of foreign material at the Egyptian sites enabled Petrie to demonstrate that there had been commercial connections between Egypt and her neighbours and that it was not an isolated civilization.

At Amarna, his excavations (1891–2) revealed the famous Amarna letters and new information about the heretic pharaoh Akhenaten; he surveyed Sinai (1904–5) and discovered the first texts in the Sinaitic script; at Tanis, he uncovered

At Kahun, a pyramid workmen's town excavated in the 1890s, Petrie found a great variety of pottery made for domestic use. Dishes of this type – oval, made of coarse red pottery, and decorated with incised patterns and designs – were probably used for serving food.

part of the temple; and in the Fayoum at Hawara, he discovered the superb painted mummy portraits dating to the Graeco-Roman Period.

Perhap his greatest achievements focused on the earliest years of Egypt's history. At Abydos, the concession to excavate the royal tombs of the Archaic Period had been granted to Émile Amélineau (1850–1916), a French cleric who had studied under Maspero. In his excavations there (1894–8), he had searched only for decorated or inscribed pieces and had discarded the other material he uncovered. When, in 1899, Petrie obtained the concession from Maspero, he reworked the site, finding several royal and many non-royal tombs of Dynasty I and carefully mapping, recording and photographing the remains. The material that Amélineau had ordered to be broken up was now taken and studied, and with his painstaking approach, Petrie was able to throw new light on this early period.

However, an even earlier phase – the so-called Predynastic Period – awaited discovery. Excavation of graves in southern Egypt had revealed material which was unusual and did not con-

form to the types and styles found elsewhere. This led to speculation that a New Race of outsiders had entered Egypt bringing this culture with them, although the French archaeologist De Morgan disagreed with this and claimed that the material was Egyptian but prehistoric. It was indeed difficult to understand why no evidence had until then appeared to show development prior to the establishment of the historical kingdom *c*.3100 BC, and this material was thus particularly important.

In 1895, in the great cemetery near the modern town of Nagada, Petrie discovered over two thousand graves. He was able to use the material from these graves to test whether such items did indeed belong to a New Race or whether a direct development could be traced between later dynastic objects and these pieces. Since there were no inscriptions to provide the basis for dating, Petrie developed his own system, known as Sequence Dating. This used the stylistic changes seen in the extensive supplies of pottery found in the graves as the basis for dating and arranging sequentially all the other associated material, including ivories, slate palettes, stone vessels, tools and weapons. Although Sequence Dating had its limitations, it could be used to place material which could not be dated otherwise, and it has evolved and been employed to great effect by later

Egyptologists. Together with Petrie's discovery of the Predynastic and Early Dynastic Periods, it remains his greatest single contribution.

Until Petrie appeared, the aims of scientific archaeology, although outlined by Rhind in 1862, had not been effectively achieved. Petrie had scant regard for earlier archaeologists such as Mariette, or for his own contemporaries, particularly Amélineau. He exerted a profound effect not just on Egyptology but also on the general development of archaeology, establishing a methodology for excavation, recognizing the importance of all objects and retaining everything that might be of academic value to himself and others. On the ethics of archaeology and the archaeologist, he said:

Conservation must be his first duty, and where needful even destruction of the less important in order to conserve the more important. To uncover a monument, and leave it to perish by exposure or by plun-

dering, to destroy thus what had lasted for thousands of years, and might last for thousands to come, is a crime.

He was able to use his excavated material and the evidence from the systems he had devised to propose and test new theories. Unlike many earlier excavators, he promptly published his results and opinions in over a thousand books, articles and reviews, and in museums where his excavated material came to be housed, his suggestions on the conservation and display of the objects were of great influence. He said:

To undertake excavating and so take the responsibilities for preserving a multitude of delicate and valuable things, unless one is prepared to deal with them efficiently, both mechanically and chemically, is like undertaking a surgical operation in ignorance of anatomy.

Petrie was also responsible for an innovative approach to his excavation workforce: whereas Mariette had been able to provide only minimal personal supervision for his labourers, Petrie employed his men directly and was frequently at the site himself. They were housed, and paid a fixed price for discovery of different categories of objects, so that their loyalty could be ensured in

Cosmetic jars of stone and faience held perfumed oils and ointments, and kohl which was used to outline the eyes. This selection from Kahun (a pyramid workmen's town, c.1890 BC) shows that craftsmen's wives had elegant toilet equipment in a variety of materials.

the face of competition from the dealers. The labourers were organized into groups, each undertaking specific work, and in the excavations at Quft (Koptos), Petrie began to train the diggers so that they could progress to become foremen at other sites in later seasons. Today, the Quftis still provide the trained and experienced overseers for many excavations in Egypt.

Petrie also trained many assistants in Egyptology, including Griffith, Newberry, Quibell, Carter, Mace, Davies, Engelbach, Brunton and Caton-Thompson; they carried on the principles of his scientific approach and made their own substantial contributions to the subject. There are various accounts of his camps; the published letters of the American Egyptologist Charles E. Wilbour describe his visit to Petrie's camp at Medum:

He has a cot bed in the tomb of Nefer-maat, whither he retires at dusk to write and read, for he has a few miscellaneous books, 'a pinch of books', he said, and two tents, one a kitchen with a petroleum stove. He lives mainly on London food, sent out to him from Civil Service Stores in boxes, each holding three weeks' rations, does his own cooking, lives with Arabs only and pays the men who dig for him by the cubic metre, they trusting to his fairness both for the measurement and the rate.

A controversial character, Petrie's one failing was perhaps his inability to change and develop his own methods, which had advanced the subject so much, and it was left to later excavators such as the American George Reisner to introduce new ideas and techniques.

The end of the 19th century witnessed several major developments and discoveries, and an intensification of archaeological work in Egypt. The century had been a time of virtually continual exploration, with great advances in methodology. The discovery of the first cache of royal mummies at Deir el-Bahri in the 1870s was followed by Victor Loret's excavation of the tomb of Amenophis II in the Valley of the Kings in 1898, where nine more royal mummies were found. An American businessman, Theodore M. Davis, financed several excavations, including further exploration of the Valley of the Kings (1903–12), and several

Englishmen worked for him, including Carter, Weigall and Ayrton, since it was now a condition of the Egyptian government that excavation could only be carried out by an experienced archaeologist. Davis' expeditions produced spectacular results: the royal tombs of Hatshepsut, Horemheb, Siptah and Prince Montu-her-khepshef were found, as well as the tomb in the Valley of the Kings of Yuya and Thuya, the non-royal parents of Tiye, the wife of Amenophis III. Working for Davis, Howard Carter also found the tomb of Tuthmosis IV which still contained some goods, including a decorated chariot. The burial of Yuya and Thuya, with its golden treasure, was particularly fine, although it had been entered by robbers in antiquity. In 1907, Davis also discovered Tomb 55 in the Valley of the Kings, with its mysterious occupant who, at the time, was identified as Queen Tiye, although subsequent examinations of the mummy have led to suggestions that it was Akhenaten or, more recently, Smenkhkare. The tomb contents continue to arouse controversy.

The most spectacular discovery in the Valley of the Kings (and indeed in Egypt) was made by Howard Carter (1874–1939), when he uncovered the tomb of Tutankhamun in November 1922. Despite fears that the area was exhausted, Carter had persuaded his patron, Lord Carnarvon, to continue the search for a royal tomb. Carter later recounted his emotions when the passage beyond the entrance door to the tomb was first discovered:

It was a thrilling moment for an excavator. Alone, save for my native workmen, I found myself, after years of comparatively unproductive labour, on the threshold of what might prove to be a magnificent discovery. Anything, literally anything, might be beyond that passage, and it needed all my self-control to keep from breaking down the doorway, and investigating there and then…could it be the tomb of a noble buried here by royal consent? was it a royal cache, a hiding-place to which a mummy and its equipment had been removed for safety? or was it actually the tomb of the king for whom I had spent so many years in search?

On 26 November 1922, Carter finally peered into the antechamber and saw the treasure; his excitement at this great discovery is evident in his later account:

As my eyes grew accustomed to the light, details of the room within emerged slowly from the mist, strange animals, statues, and gold – everywhere the glint of gold. For the moment – an eternity it must have seemed to the others standing by – I was struck dumb with amazement, and when Lord Carnarvon, unable to stand the suspense any longer, inquired anxiously, 'Can you see anything?' it was all I could do to get out the words, 'Yes, wonderful things.'

For a further ten years, Carter and his staff devoted themselves to the task of excavating the tomb, and cleaning, packing and transporting the treasure to Cairo. It was an enormous undertaking, carried out with great care and patience; here, Carter describes the opening of the sarcophagus in their second excavation season, over a year after the tomb was first discovered:

The tackle for raising the lid was in position. I gave the word. Amid intense silence the huge slab, broken in two, weighing over a ton and a quarter, rose from its bed. The light shone into the sarcophagus.

At first sight, the contents were disappointing, since the coffin inside was covered with linen shrouds, but once these were removed the archaeologists gazed on the outermost of the three golden coffins that enclosed the king's mummy:

Upon the forehead of this recumbent figure of the young boy king were two emblems delicately worked in brilliant inlay – the Cobra and the Vulture – symbols of Upper and Lower Egypt, but perhaps the most touching by its human simplicity was the tiny wreath of flowers around these symbols, as it pleased us to think, the last farewell offering of the widowed girl queen to her husband, the youthful representative of the 'Two Kingdoms'.

Although a definitive publication is still awaited, Carter left detailed records of the objects and his work. This discovery was only the most dramatic of a series of finds he made, including five other royal tombs, Hatshepsut's Valley Temple and many non-royal tombs.

Also on the Theban west bank, Herbert Winlock (1884–1950), excavating at Deir el-Bahri for the Metropolitan Museum of New York, made several important discoveries. At the temples of Mentuhotep (Dynasty 11) and Hatshepsut (Dynasty 18), he continued the work of Édouard Naville, one of the early excavators for the Egypt Exploration Fund. Clearing this area, he found two intact royal burials at Mentuhotep's temple, and a mass burial of sixty soldiers interred in the royal precinct. These were Mentuhotep's victorious soldiers who had died in battle and been brought to the king's own temple complex. In 1919–20, in the tomb of the chancellor Meket-Re, Winlock found the models of this man's house, estate, and workshops, providing a unique glimpse of life at that period. In the next season, the archive of family letters of Hekanakhte was discovered, again adding a wealth of information to existing knowledge of the First Intermediate Period. Winlock also excavated the Theban palace of Amenophis III at Malkata.

Another American, George A. Reisner (1867–1942), who became Professor of Egyptology at Harvard, also made significant contributions, taking Petrie's regard for detailed recording to new lengths. Reisner aimed to provide records, including his diary, object register and photographs of each object, which would enable later scholars to reconstruct every detail of the conditions found by the excavator. His most important discovery was the tomb of Queen Hetepheres at Giza, complete with its furniture, but he also undertook other important work at Giza, particularly at the nobles' mastaba (bench-shaped) tombs, and the Valley Temple of Mycerinus.

The construction of the Aswan Dam at the First Cataract in 1899–1902 and the subsequent raising of its height had made the archaeological survey of Nubia, parts of which would now be inundated, a most urgent task. Different techniques were needed for surveying a wide area rather than excavating a single site, and Reisner developed a methodology which has since continued to be used. For many years he also worked further south in the Sudan, exploring the pyramids and sites at Kummeh, Kerma, Napata (Gebel Barkal), el-Kurru, Nuri and Meroë. He provided evidence for much of our understanding of this Kushite kingdom which reversed the pattern and conquered Egypt in Dynasty 25.

Another spectacular discovery which illuminated one of the less well-documented periods – Dynasty 21 and 22 in this case – was the excavation of the royal tombs at Tanis by Pierre Montet (1887–1966) just before the Second World War. The treasure found there almost equalled that of Tutankhamun, but in this instance it came from the burials of several kings and princes.

These are merely a selection of highlights from a succession of discoveries made in the 20th century. The royal workmen's village at Deir el-Medina, the human and animal cemeteries at Tuna el-Gebel, the funerary barque buried alongside the Great Pyramid, Emery's spectacular finds at Sakkara, and many other excavations have all contributed to a vastly expanded knowledge of Egyptian civilization.

However, Egypt's unique heritage also offers the possibility of reading the thoughts and ideas of men and women who lived thousands of years ago, and the archaeological discoveries have been matched by advances in language studies and literary interpretation provided by many scholars. Amongst these should be mentioned the pioneering work of Francis Llewellyn Griffith whose publication of Demotic papyri and work on Meroitic writing was significant, and the contributions made to our understanding of the grammar of Hieroglyphs by Adolf Erman, Kurt Sethe and Alan Gardiner. Erman and Sethe were responsible for the overall compilation of material for the *Worterbuch,* the historical dictionary of the ancient Egyptian language based on all the inscriptions available at the time of its publication.

Advances in understanding the language and literature have relied to a considerable extent on the copying and validating of inscriptions found on monuments. The recording and publishing of standing buildings has proceeded apace since around 1900, when production techniques became adequate. Although this work is less exciting than excavation, it is complementary and also essential, since so much of the detail on the monuments continues to be lost. In Nubia, because of the raising of the first Aswan Dam and the construction of the High Dam in the 1970s, there has been great urgency to record the monuments which would be entirely submerged as the result of this work.

There have been a number of major epigraphic studies, starting with the attempts by Maxence de Rochemonteix (1849–91) and Johannes Dümichen (1833–94) to produce a complete record of Egypt's monuments. Under the editorship of Francis Llewellyn Griffith, the Egypt Exploration Fund long ago began an Archaeological Survey of Egypt, for which the artists Norman and Nina de Garis Davies produced many copies of tomb scenes, which were unequalled in excellence for many years. This survey produced more than twenty-five volumes on tombs at sites including Beni Hasan, el-Bersha, Deir el-Gebrawi, Amarna and Meir.

In 1924, Chicago House was established in Luxor as the field-station of the Oriental Institute of the University of Chicago. The Institute had been created by James H. Breasted, with the financial support of John D. Rockefeller. A major epigraphic survey of the temples of Medinet Habu (from 1930 to 1970) was launched by Chicago, and experiments were undertaken to produce an exact system to copy a large area of wall-surface at the temple, preserving as accurately as possible the detail of the scenes and texts. Rockefeller also funded another survey, that of the Temple of Sethos I at Abydos, where Amice Calverley recorded and published the magnificent wall scenes. These projects have set demanding standards in epigraphic work.

By 1960, the governments of Egypt and the Sudan had decided to embark on a major engineering project. This entailed building a new dam at Aswan behind which a vast lake would be created. Despite the benefits this would give the modern populations of these countries, the increased area of land which would now become submerged included some three hundred miles containing major archaeological sites, particularly the famous temples at Philae and Abu Simbel. Through UNESCO, an appeal was made to the world to save the Nubian monuments, and money and expertise came from many sources so that, with international goodwill and co-operation, it was possible to relocate some of the most important monuments to safe sites in Egypt. In other cases, temples were donated to other countries where they now form spectacular features in museum settings.

*Egypt became increasingly popular with European travellers in the
19th and 20th centuries. Their journey often included a stay in Cairo
to visit nearby monuments. Here, a visitor poses in front of the Great
Pyramid at Giza, emphasizing the magnitude of the stone blocks.*

Today, there is a constant battle to save the antiquities from deterioration; many nations are involved in excavating a variety of sites in Egypt, but there is also emphasis on the continuing need to conserve the monuments and antiquities, in the field and in museums, and to protect them from pollution and destruction. As well as high-profile projects such as saving the Nubian temples, restoring the tomb of Nefertari in the Valley of the Queens, and attempting to arrest the Great Sphinx's deterioration, there is also the low-key but essential continuous monitoring of buildings and wall scenes along the Nile and of objects in museum galleries and reserve collections. Egyptology is a young subject (it is usually defined as dating from Napoleon's expedition), and much undoubtedly remains to be discovered which will redefine some of our currently held opinions. Hopefully, new information will also be forthcoming about the least well-documented periods of the country's history. However, despite the search for new material, constant vigilance is also required to protect and preserve the monuments and artifacts we already possess.

PART II

The Sites

This is by no means intended as a comprehensive list of all the archaeological sites in Egypt, but it attempts to show how excavation of important monuments and artifacts has provided the basis of our understanding of Egyptian history.

The selection has been limited to the major sites found along a route from north to south, somewhat similar to the journeys undertaken by the early travellers. It concentrates on the Delta and Nile Valley, and therefore excludes peripheral areas such as the oases in the Western Desert, and Sinai. Since sites have been chosen which primarily illuminate our knowledge of predynastic and dynastic Egypt, later foundations such as Alexandria and the Fayoum towns of the Graeco-Roman Period are not described in detail here.

The sites are arranged under broad headings: the relatively little-known centres of the Delta in Lower Egypt which, although important in antiquity, have not enjoyed the ideal environmental conditions found in the south; the vast cemeteries of the north, including Giza and Sakkara, which served the Old Kingdom capital of Memphis and are dominated by the pyramids; the Fayoum area on the left-hand side of the Nile Valley with the important Middle Kingdom and other sites; the area of Middle Egypt which includes the magnificent rock-cut tombs of the First Intermediate Period and the Middle Kingdom, and the site of Akhenaten's city at Tell el-Amarna; the northern region of Upper Egypt, with its great religious centres at Abydos and Thebes (the political capital of Egypt and its empire in Dynasty 18); the southern part of Upper Egypt with sites that range from the predynastic settlements at Hieraconpolis and el-Kab to the Egyptian temples of the Graeco-Roman period at Esna and Kom Ombo; and finally, the monuments of Nubia, straddling Egypt and the Sudan, which include the temples built by Egyptian rulers (such as Abu Simbel), now moved to new locations following the construction of the High Dam at Aswan, and the towns and pyramids constructed by rulers of the 'Ethiopian Dynasty' and of the Napatan and Meroitic kingdoms.

Lower Egypt: Delta Sites

Tell el-Yahudiyah

This site (the Mound of the Jews) had the ancient Greek name of Leontopolis. A major feature is the partly preserved rectangular earthwork enclosure which, it has been suggested, is a defensive enclosure wall dating to the late Middle Kingdom or early Second Intermediate Period. Termed the Hyksos Camp, it may have been constructed by these infiltrators, although other opinions regard it as a religious building rather than a fortification.

Statues of Ramesses II found inside the wall indicate that he may have built a temple here, and to the west was the temple of Ramesses III which was decorated with glazed tiles representing rosettes, cartouches and foreign captives (most of the tiles are now in the Cairo Museum).

Outside the enclosure are remains of a temple and town built (c.170 BC) by Onias, a Jewish priest who was helped by Ptolemy VI Philometor to build a temple modelled on Solomon's Temple in Jerusalem. This was for the benefit of Onias and other exiles who had been expelled from Jerusalem, and the community continued until Vespasian closed the temple in AD 71. The

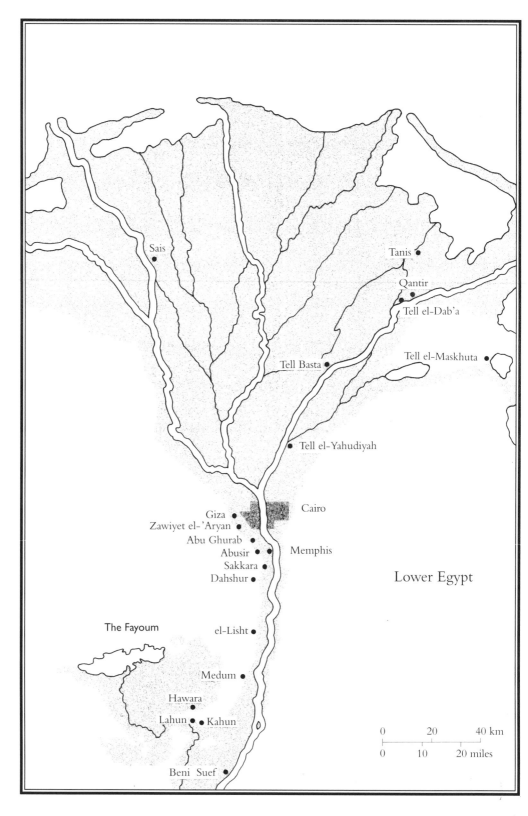

Sais

Tanis

Qantir

Tell el-Dab'a

Tell el-Maskhuta

Tell Basta

Tell el-Yahudiyah

Cairo

Giza
Zawiyet el-'Aryan
Abu Ghurab
Abusir   Memphis
Sakkara
Dahshur

Lower Egypt

The Fayoum

el-Lisht

Medum

Hawara
Lahun ● Kahun

0	20	40 km
0	10	20 miles

Beni Suef

site was investigated and published by Naville, Griffith and Petrie, and by Du Buisson for the French Archaeological Institute.

Tell Basta

The extensive ruins of Tell Basta represent the city which was known to the Egyptians as Per-Bastet (The House of Bastet), and which occurs in the Greek form as Bubastis and in the Bible as Pi-beseth. It was an important centre in early times when a temple was begun by Cheops and Chephren for the cult of the local cat-goddess, Bastet. In the later periods, it became the capital of the Bubastite nome (an administrative district), and in Dynasty 22 reached its zenith as the original home and residence of the kings.

Various temples and chapels were built there by rulers of the Old, Middle and early New Kingdoms as well as of the Third Intermediate Period, and some important officials were buried at Bubastis in the New Kingdom. However, the most important structure was the main temple dedicated to Bastet which incorporated halls built by Osorken II and III of Dynasty 22, and Nectanebo II of Dynasty 30; these were built on top of earlier additions made by Ramesses II to the first temple started by Cheops and Chephren.

According to Herodotus, the temple stood on an island with water channels on two sides, and was situated at a lower level in the middle of the city. Excavation has shown that this statement was correct, although the building itself is very ruined. When Naville explored it for the Egypt Exploration Fund (1887–9), it was not possible to determine the plan of the building but granite blocks, columns and a few statues were recovered. The temple was apparently used for the great festival of Bastet, and Herodotus supplies a vivid account of this event:

When the Egyptians travel to Bubastis, they do so in this manner: men and women sail together, and in each boat there are many persons of both sexes. Some of the women shake their rattles and some of the men blow their pipes during the whole journey, while others sing and clap their hands. If they pass a town on the way, some of the women land and shout and jeer at the local women, while others dance and create a distur-

bance. They do this at every town on the Nile. When they arrive at Bubastis, they begin the festival with great sacrifices, and on this occasion, more wine is consumed than during the whole of the rest of the year.

He goes on to relate that the Egyptians estimated that 700,000 adults plus their children used to make the annual pilgrimage to Bubastis.

Other discoveries at the site include the extensive animal cemeteries, particularly for the cats which the pilgrims purchased as an offering to Bastet, and two gold and silver hoards of the Third Intermediate Period which were found in a railway cutting near the temples. The second group of objects can be seen in the Cairo Museum.

The site is described by the early traveller Nestor l'Hôte.

Qantir

Not far from the modern village of Qantir, this site was excavated by Naville for the Egypt Exploration Fund; he found the ruins of a large town, and buildings and other material that could be dated to the Middle Kingdom and to the Ramesside Period.

It has been suggested that Qantir could be the ancient Hyksos capital of Avaris, but recent evidence indicates that it is more likely to be the site of Pi-Ramesse, the Delta residence of the Ramesside kings and the town of Ramses mentioned in the biblical account of the Exodus.

Tell el-Dab'a

Recent excavations carried out by Bietak have revealed that a large influx of foreigners arrived here in the Second Intermediate Period. This would correlate with the rise of Dynasty 15 when the Hyksos ruled Egypt, and there is a strong probability that this, rather than Tanis or Qantir, was the site of their ancient capital of Avaris.

Building activity was resumed here at the end of Dynasty 18 under Horemheb, and the Ramesside rulers made further additions, including a temple to Seth.

Tanis

This extensive and impressive site, the ancient Egyptian town of Dja'net and the biblical Zoan, is usually known by the Greek name of

Tanis. It lies near the modern village of San el-Hagar, and was first identified by the early traveller, Lady Etheria. Other visitors included Burton, Nestor l'Hôte, Denon, Rifaud, and Wilkinson. Lepsius discovered the Decree of Canopus here.

Tanis became the capital city, royal residence and burial place of the kings of Dynasties 21 and 22 when they abandoned Thebes in favour of a northern centre. The most important excavations were carried out by Mariette (in the late 19th century), Petrie (1883–6), and Montet (1921–51). The central area features a large, mudbrick enclosure with an inner enclosure containing the great Temple of Amun. Much of the inscribed material here dates to the reign of Ramesses II, and Montet therefore speculated that this was the Ramesside Delta town of Pi-Ramesse. However, it is now known that the inscribed pieces of Ramesside date were probably all introduced from other sites for use as building material. The earliest buildings excavated so far do not predate the reign of Psusennes I of Dynasty 21, although several later rulers made additions to the monuments. Speculation that Tanis was the Hyksos capital of Avaris has been discounted.

A most spectacular discovery was made by Montet in 1939 when he found the location of the royal tombs of Dynasties 21 and 22 within the temple precinct. The tombs of Psusennes I, Amenemope, Osorkon III and Shoshenk III, as well as two unnamed ones, were revealed; the sarcophagus of Takelot II was also discovered in a room in Osorkon III's tomb, and the silver, falcon-headed coffin of Shoshenk III was recovered from the tomb of Psusennes I.

The tombs had no superstructures and were so well concealed that they remained undisturbed. The burials, placed in underground chambers constructed of stone or mudbrick, were approached down a shaft; the walls of some of the tombs were decorated with scenes and inscriptions, but most of the emphasis had been placed on the magnificent funerary treasure. The environmental conditions of the Delta are less ideal than those in the Theban area, and the mummies and any organic material did not survive, but these intact burials with their silver, gold and jewelled treasure provide a unique opportunity to study the royal funerary customs of the later period. Coffins, face masks, jewellery and other equipment demonstrate the skills of the craftsmen, although the heavier style and execution of many of the pieces cannot rival the skills displayed in some earlier examples.

Tell el-Maskhuta

This is probably the ancient Egyptian Tjeku and the biblical Pithom, although not everyone accepts this identification. The site was explored by Naville for the Egypt Exploration Fund in 1883, and he found a large mudbrick enclosure with the remains of temple buildings and several deep, rectangular chambers without doors which he believed were grain stores. He suggested that they dated to the reign of Ramesses II and perhaps represented the 'storehouses' mentioned in the Bible; he entitled his publication *The Store-City of Pithom*. Other information about the temple is provided by Prisse, Wilkinson and Petrie. Naville was very interested in the site because he believed that it had strong biblical associations.

Lower Egypt: The Pyramid Area

Memphis

Little remains today of Memphis, the ancient Egyptian 'White Wall' which was probably founded by Menes as the country's first capital. During the early dynastic period and the Old Kingdom it remained the capital and main royal residence, and was also important in later times as a religious and commercial centre with a good harbour and well-established workforce expert in various skills and crafts. In the Old Kingdom, it was the focus for artisans engaged in producing the art and sculpture for royal and private burials.

The cemeteries that served Memphis were extensive and included the sites known today as Sakkara, Dahshur, Abusir, Zawiyet el-'Aryan, Giza and Abu Roash. Its importance gradually disappeared with the rise of Alexandria in the Graeco-Roman Period; finally, with the Edict of Theodosius I (AD 379–95) which established Christianity as the religion of the Roman Empire, the Temple of Ptah was destroyed and the religious significance of Memphis was eclipsed. When Egypt was conquered by the Arabs in AD 641, they established a new capital at el-Fustat at the south end of modern Cairo.

Over the centuries, blocks of stone from Memphis were used in the construction of Cairo, but even in Abd'el-Latif's time it was still an impressive site and he recounted that it contained many wonders that were beyond description. However, after his visit the destruction continued and its location appears to have been lost until it was accurately identified in 1590 by the European traveller Sieur Villamont.

It had, of course, been a place on the itinerary of Classical tourists and Herodotus mentions it, referring to Menes' action in raising a dyke to protect the city from the inundation. Undoubtedly the strategic location of Memphis at the apex of the Delta, giving control over north and south Egypt, ensured its political and administrative importance for so long.

The chief god of Memphis was Ptah, and his temple, once one of the most extensive in Egypt, is still the largest building which can be seen at the site. Although it contained elements of earlier periods, it was essentially the work of Ramesses II. Part of it has been excavated, mainly by Petrie (1908–13), who also investigated the palace of Apries and the smaller temple of Merneptah, whose palace was excavated by the University Museum of Pennsylvania expedition.

The colossal statues of Ramesses II are mentioned by various travellers; one now stands in Ramesses Square in Cairo, and the other, discovered by Caviglia and Sloane in 1820, remains at Memphis. The colossal alabaster sphinx of New Kingdom date, excavated in 1912, can also be seen at the site. Currently, the Egypt Exploration Society is undertaking extensive excavations at Memphis.

Giza

The Pyramids

The Pyramids have been the centre of tourist interest since earliest times. When Herodotus visited them in the 5th century BC he mentioned that the blocks of the outer casing were covered with inscriptions, and these were probably graffiti left by earlier tourists. Later, Romans travelled to wonder at these monuments, and the writer Pliny was one of the first to describe the Great Sphinx. Over the centuries, men have pondered their true purpose: Pliny believed that they were designed as royal burial places, but also to provide employment for the workforce and to prevent them becoming rebellious. Another legend, quoted by Julius Honorius (pre-5th century AD), was that they were granaries built by Joseph, and most medieval travellers accepted this idea.

Arab writers were also fascinated with them: the physician Abd' el-Latif entered the Great Pyramid and so did Caliph Ma'mun, son of Harun al-Rashid (of the *Arabian Nights*), in search of treasure in the 9th century AD. His account of what he saw is probably fanciful, but he mentions a green stone statue of a man (perhaps a coffin) in which lay a body with a gold breastplate, a magnificent sword, and a ruby of great size and beauty. It is most unlikely that such treasure survived the attentions of the tomb-robbers who probably ransacked the pyramid soon after the king's burial. Some Arab writers also suggested that the pyramids were built as places of refuge against natural disasters.

Other early authors credited the ancient Egyptians with a profound knowledge of astronomy, and suggested that the pyramids were observatories or, according to Paul Lucas in 1714, perhaps sundials which marked the sun's changes at the solstices. Later investigators have tried to attribute a mystical significance to them; perhaps the most famous of these is Charles Piazzi Smyth, the Astronomer Royal of Scotland, who resigned from the Royal Society in 1879 because he was denied the opportunity to read a paper which dealt with the design of the Great Pyramid. He believed that God's great plan for the universe was enshrined in the measurements of the Great Pyramid, and that correct interpretation of these would reveal this profound knowledge. The idea that the pyramids were designed as repositories of arcane wisdom has continued until today and is known as pyramidology.

It is difficult for some people to accept that so much effort was expended on a monument that would merely act as a burial place for one man. However, this was the true purpose of the pyramid (accurately identified by Herodotus), and although modern explorers have found that the pyramids are empty, sarcophagi remaining in the burial chambers were clearly intended for the royal burials. According to the ancient Egyptian belief, the labour and expense devoted to such a massive construction were quite appropriate, since it protected the king's body and was probably intended as a magical means of access to the heavens. The pyramid was vital to help the king gain immortality, and his subjects could only hope to achieve some kind of eternal life through him.

The Giza area has probably been more systematically excavated than any other site in Egypt, although important work still continues there today. There are several major monuments and features.

The Pyramid Complex of Cheops

This would have consisted of the pyramid, mortuary temple, causeway and valley temple, but although new excavations are revealing information about some of these features, modern building has obscured the Valley Temple and the Causeway, which was apparently visible on old maps of the site in the last century. The Great Pyramid was probably structurally intact until Caliph Ma'mun caused the large opening to be made in the stone just below the original entrance, but from then on the outer limestone casing was stripped off and used for building the walls, houses, bridges and other constructions in Cairo and Giza.

Herodotus repeated a story which described a subterranean part of the pyramid, although he made no claim to have seen this himself. This account indicated that Cheops (Khufu) had designed a burial chamber for himself below the pyramid, which was built on an island of some sort, surrounded by water brought by canal from the Nile. However, no evidence of the island or canal has ever been discovered, and it is quite possible that Herodotus never entered the pyramid himself, as it was probably resealed in Dynasty 26 as part of an ancient restoration project.

The Great Pyramid has been surveyed and measured more times than any other Egyptian monument. The first truly scientific account was given in John Greaves' *Pyramidographia* (1646) which provided the most accurate survey until that date. The pyramids were also carefully surveyed by Nicholas Shaw in 1721 (although he believed that a subterranean connection existed between the Sphinx and the Great Pyramid); other accounts include those of Prisse, Burton, Bruce, Hay, Wilkinson, Norden, Pococke, and Lepsius, who provided various sketches, plans and measurements. One of the savants on Napoleon's expedition, Edmé-François Jomard, also produced relatively accurate measurements. Caviglia, employed by Henry Salt, found new information when he entered the Great Pyramid, and he excavated for a time with Colonel Howard-Vyse. With the engineer Perring, Vyse undertook a major survey of the pyramids, and although he used violent methods to gain entry to the pyramid of Mycerinus, this survey and subsequent publication of the pyramid fields was the most significant account in the 19th century until Petrie's work in 1880–2. Originally drawn to Egypt because of his interest in Piazzi Smyth's theories about the Great Pyramid, Petrie soon began to establish his scientific methodology at Giza. He produced the first exhaustive survey of the pyramid, which remained the standard work until J. H. Cole of the Survey Department of the Egyptian government provided new measurements with more modern instruments in 1925. The plan of the pyramid mortuary temple was traced by Lauer in 1946.

Two important chambers in the Great Pyramid are the Queen's Chamber and the King's Chamber. The Queen's Chamber is a misnomer for the intended burial place of the king which was abandoned in favour of adding another room (the King's Chamber) and the Grand Gallery. The King's Chamber is built of granite and contains the royal sarcophagus which, according to Petrie, must have been placed there during construction as its dimensions are wider than those of the ascending corridor. Above the flat ceiling of the chamber is a series of five compartments; the first four have flat ceilings but the top one has a pointed roof, and the four uppermost compartments were only discovered by Vyse and Perring in 1837–8, when they hol-

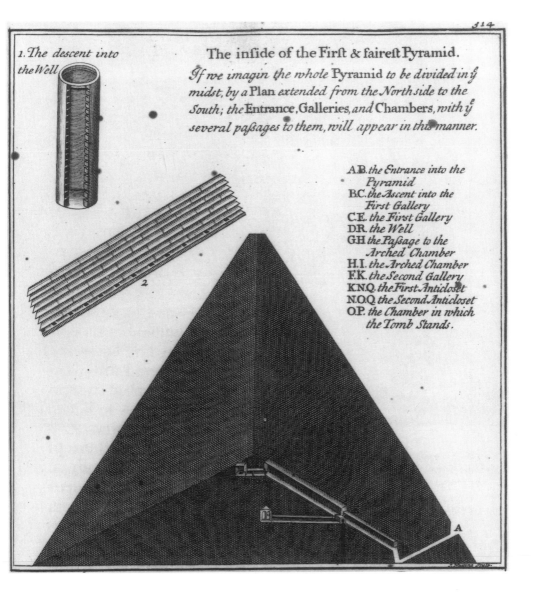

1. The descent into the Well

The inside of the First & fairest Pyramid.

If we imagin the whole Pyramid to be divided in ÿ midst, by a Plan extended from the North side to the South; the Entrance, Galleries, and Chambers, with ÿ several passages to them, will appear in this manner.

AB. the Entrance into the Pyramid
BC. the Ascent into the First Gallery
CE. the First Gallery
DR. the Well
GH the Passage to the Arched Chamber
HI. the Arched Chamber
FK. the Second Gallery
KNQ. the First Anticloset
NOQ. the Second Anticloset
OP. the Chamber in which the Tomb stands.

The Great Pyramid, built by Cheops at Giza, was the subject of much speculation by early travellers, including John Greaves (1646) who tried to investigate the true purpose of the pyramids. This plan of the Great Pyramid from Greenhill's Nekrokedeia *(1705) shows some of the internal features.*

lowed out a shaft from below. This structure was designed to prevent the weight of the masonry from collapsing into the burial chamber.

The Royal Boat: In 1954, Kamal el-Mallakh found a pit on the south side of the Great Pyramid, below the temenos wall. Reisner had previously cleared three boat-shaped pits cut in the rock in other parts of the same complex but they had provided little information. However, the fourth pit, which is rectangular, over 31 metres in length, and was covered with forty-one limestone blocks cemented together with plaster, still held an undisturbed burial. The archaeologists found a dismantled, flat-bottomed boat built largely of cedarwood; there were over a thousand pieces, arranged in thirteen layers which, according to quarry markings on the pit blocks, had been sealed in during the reign of Cheops' successor.

The best-preserved example of an Old Kingdom pyramid complex can be seen at Giza; built for Chephren, the main elements of pyramid, mortuary temple, causeway and valley temple still survive. Mastery of building techniques using large masonry blocks is evident here in the temple.

The boat was reassembled by Ahmed Youssef over a period of fourteen years and is now displayed at Giza in the Boat Museum. In almost perfect condition, the boat has nevertheless posed many problems regarding its reconstruction and preservation. There were marks on the main timbers to indicate their correct position in the vessel so that it could be reassembled by the ancient builders. Ropes of halfa grass or pegs of sycamore were supplied to make the joins, and the overall length of the boat is 43.5 metres; six pairs of oars were also included.

The purpose of the boat remains uncertain. Boat burials occur in the enclosures of some mastaba tombs of Dynasty 1, but they have only been found in association with royal burials in the Old Kingdom. Ahmed Youssef's opinion was that the boat had probably only been used once, perhaps to bring the king's body from Memphis to Giza for burial. However, according to other theories, it either belonged to the royal flotilla and took part in religious festivals, or was never used in the king's lifetime but was intended for his afterlife when he would sail with the sun-god in the heavens.

A fifth boat-pit lies to the west of the Boat Museum; scientific probes, used to look beneath the forty limestone blocks that cover it, have indicated that it contains the remains of another boat which is less well preserved than the one already excavated.

The Pyramid Complex of Chephren

The second pyramid was built for Cheops' son Chephren, and it retains at the apex the remnants of the original limestone casing and, at the base, some of the red granite course which once supported the limestone mantle. Herodotus refers to this, saying, 'The lowest layer is of variegated Ethiopian stone.'

Belzoni was the first European to enter the pyramid, on 2 March 1818; although he found no human body, he discovered the fine granite sarcophagus (with cattle bones inside) in the burial chamber with the lid, broken in two pieces, lying beside it. He also discovered the Mortuary Temple.

The Valley Temple (originally wrongly thought to be associated with the Great Sphinx) was discovered by Mariette in 1853 and, cleared of sand then and again in 1869, it became a prime site for visitors. It is the best-preserved monument of this dynasty, and was the place where the king's embalming ceremonies were re-enacted (although the actual mummification process may have happened elsewhere), and

Because of their vicinity to Cairo, the pyramids and Great Sphinx at Giza have been visited and studied by countless travellers, archaeologists and scholars over the centuries. This early 20th-century photograph clearly shows the face of the sphinx, which may reflect King Chephren's own features.

where the Ceremony of Opening the Mouth was performed on twenty-three statues of the king now in the Cairo Museum (Mariette found the superb diorite statue of Chephren in a deep pit in the antechamber). In 1909–10, the von Sieglin expedition, led by Hölscher and Steindorff, excavated the whole complex, including the Mortuary Temple. This complex is the first to preserve all the architectural features that became standard in later examples.

The Great Sphinx: Near the Valley Temple of Chephren's pyramid lies one of the most visual symbols of ancient Egypt. This natural knoll of rock was probably too friable to be used by the workmen quarrying blocks for Cheops' pyramid, and so in Chephren's reign it was turned into a lion-bodied, human-headed figure that probably portrayed Chephren's own face. It may have been plastered and painted to hide the defects in the stone, and although its original religious significance (if any) remains obscure, it came to be regarded as the guardian of the Giza necropolis.

The Sphinx was first excavated and restored by King Tuthmosis IV (*c.*1420 BC), as he recorded in the Dream Stela which Vyse discovered between the paws of the statue. In Graeco-Roman times there were further attempts to clear away the sand, and an altar was constructed in front of it, but, as it was not mentioned by Herodotus, Diodorus or Strabo (although Pliny did describe it), it was probably covered by the sand for long periods. In later times, the face was mutilated as a symbol of idolatry, and it was used as a target by the Mamelukes for their shooting practice.

The first modern excavation was undertaken by Caviglia in 1817; he found the flight of steps that ascend to the Sphinx and the pavement between the paws, as well as fragments of the beard and uraeus (the snake on the forehead). Smaller clearances of the sand were carried out by Mariette (1853) and Maspero and Brugsch (1886); a new excavation and restoration was undertaken by Baraize in 1923–36 for the Egyptian Department of Antiquities. Pieces which had fallen off the Sphinx were now cemented back in place, and while clearing the figure Baraize also uncovered the small Sphinx Temple immediately in front. Further exploration was carried out by Selim Hassan in 1936–7, and in 1965 Ricke and Schott produced a detailed study of this Temple of Harmachis ('Horus on the Horizon') for the Swiss Institute of Archaeology in Cairo.

The Pyramid Complex of Mycerinus

Mycerinus, the grandson of Cheops, built the smallest of the kings' pyramids at Giza. It was hastily finished in brick, and was probably restored in Dynasty 26 when interest in the Old Kingdom was revived and a cult of the early rulers flourished again at Giza.

Herodotus preserves some interesting traditions about Mycerinus. Unlike the tyrannical Cheops and Chephren, Mycerinus was pious and just, but his beneficent actions flouted a divine oracle which stated that the Egyptians would suffer for 150 years. Because of his disobedience, the gods decided that he would only reign for six years, so he lived night and day to extend his time on earth to twelve years.

Vyse used gunpowder to gain access to the pyramid in 1837–8; when he found the king's name written on the roof of the burial chamber in one of the subsidiary pyramids of the complex, he was able to confirm the ownership that Herodotus and Diodorus had attributed to it.

In the second burial chamber of Mycerinus' pyramid, Vyse found a basalt sarcophagus without a lid. While it was being transported to England in October 1838, the ship sank in the Mediterranean, and therefore only the drawings made at the time of its discovery have survived. The lid of a wooden body coffin found by Vyse in the original burial chamber (and now in the British Museum) is inscribed with the name of Mycerinus, but stylistically it cannot be dated earlier than Dynasty 24; human bones he discovered there have been submitted to carbon-dating tests and consequently placed in the Christian era.

The excavations undertaken in 1905–27 by Reisner for the Boston-Harvard expedition revealed the Valley and Mortuary Temples and showed that the complex had been hastily completed by Shepseskaf, Mycerinus' successor. Repairs and slight modifications to the temples were attributed by Reisner to the actions of mortuary priests of Dynasties 5 and 6 who were responsible for the upkeep of the complex.

In the Valley Temple, Reisner discovered the superb slate triads, each showing the king with the goddess Hathor and one of the nome deities; other statues included the outstanding group of Mycerinus and his queen, Khamerernebty II. These can be seen in the Cairo and Boston Museums, and have provided Egyptologists with a unique opportunity to study the development of Old Kingdom royal sculpture.

Queens' Burial Places

Pyramids

Reisner also excavated three subsidiary pyramids which were associated with Mycerinus' pyramid, but found no proof of ownership. It is possible that they housed the burials of royal women, although not all scholars accept this suggested use of the subsidiary pyramids at Giza; they may have been intended to hold the king's own viscera, or built for some other purpose. If they are queens' burial places, one probably belonged to Khamerernebty II, the chief wife of Mycerinus. Vyse discovered a small granite sarcophagus in the second pyramid, and also human bones which perhaps belonged to a younger queen or princess.

South of the causeway and on the east side of Cheops' pyramid there are three subsidiary pyramids. It is possible that the northernmost was for the chief wife Mertiotes, the central one for the mother of Cheops' successor Radjedef, and the third for Queen Henutsen. Two of these pyramids also had boat-pits.

Herodotus again had a story to relate about one of these monuments: he said that the middle pyramid was built for a Great Royal Wife, and that Cheops had been able to build it because he forced his daughter to become a prostitute. Each client, in addition to payment of a fee which Cheops took to assist him with his economic problems, also gave her a stone which was used to construct this pyramid. However, tombs at Giza which have been clearly identified as queens' burial places have not incorporated pyramids. Some, such as the beautifully decorated tomb of Queen Meresankh discovered by Reisner during the Boston-Harvard expedition of 1927, are situated amongst the mastaba tombs near the kings' pyramid complexes. However, the tomb of her relative Queen Hetepheres was not indicated by any kind of superstructure.

Tomb of Hetepheres

In 1925, to the south of the causeway of Cheops' pyramid, George Reisner, the director of the Boston-Harvard expedition, discovered the previously undisturbed tomb of Queen Hetepheres, the wife of Sneferu who founded Dynasty 4, and the mother of Cheops. The tomb had no superstructure, and limestone gravel had been placed over the entrance hole so that it lay hidden for nearly five thousand years. The burial was equipped with superb treasure, providing a unique glimpse of the elegant world of the early Old Kingdom. There were gold vessels, razors, knives and a manicure instrument; a toilet box containing eight alabaster vases which had held kohl and perfumes; exquisite jewellery inlaid with malachite, lapis-lazuli and turquoise; and

fine furniture, including a wooden canopy-frame covered with gold, armchairs, a bed, and a carrying-chair also partly cased in sheet gold. Although the wood had suffered over the centuries, it was possible for the expedition experts to reconstruct the furniture, and this can now be seen in Cairo Museum (a replica set is in the Boston Museum).

However, when Reisner and his colleagues opened the sarcophagus it was found to be empty, although the viscera removed from the body during mummification were discovered in an alabaster chest. To explain the lack of a body in the tomb, Reisner suggested that the queen had originally been buried at Dahshur near to the pyramid which is ascribed to her husband Sneferu, but that when this tomb was plundered the queen's body and jewellery were removed. Her son Cheops perhaps then ordered that the remnants of the burial, including the queen's viscera, should be brought and reburied with another set of funerary equipment in the shadow of his own pyramid at Giza.

Apart from the magnificence of the treasure and the information it provides about Old Kingdom burial customs, Hetepheres' physical remains are of great importance in reconstructing the history of mummification. The discovery of the viscera clearly indicates that, early in Dynasty 4, the complete process involving evisceration of the body and dehydration of the bodily tissues with natron was already in use, at least for members of the royal family.

The Giza Necropolis

The families, priests and officials of the kings buried at Giza were interred in the extensive cemeteries surrounding the royal pyramids. The largest fields lie to the west, south and east of Cheops' pyramid, where mastaba tombs were built in regular rows. Constructed with a rectangular superstructure of stone blocks and a shaft cut into the rock substratum, which ended in a burial chamber, the mastaba tomb was designed both to accommodate the burial and to provide a place where offerings could continue to be presented to the deceased. This took place in an offering chapel situated either in a couple of brick-built rooms attached to the east face of the mastaba, or in the superstructure of the mastaba itself. In later periods, other tombs were built between the rows of mastabas.

Another type of Old Kingdom non-royal tomb has also been found at Giza, south-east of the pyramids of Chephren and Mycerinus, where quarries provided rock faces which could easily be used for rock-cut tombs.

In the Old Kingdom, the tombs were built and decorated by the royal craftsmen at the king's expense; he also provided the tomb goods and the perpetual supply of food offerings. The Giza tombs, with their fine wall reliefs and sculptures, provide an excellent picture of funerary ceremonies, tomb equipment, and daily life.

The cemeteries have been extensively excavated, and scenes in some of the tombs have been copied. The main necropolis has been worked by Ballard (1902), Schiaparelli for the Turin Museum (1903), Reisner for the Hearst Expedition of the University of California (1903–5), and Steindorff for the University of Leipzig and Pelizaeus Expedition (1903–7) and the von Sieglin expedition (1909). Junker excavated many tombs for the Akademie der Wissenschaften in Vienna, Pelizaeus, and the University of Leipzig expeditions (1912–28), and Reisner and Fisher led the Boston-Harvard expeditions (1905–33). Abu Bakr excavated for the University of Alexandria (1949–53), Fakhry for the Egyptian Service of Antiquities (1932–4), and Selim Hassan for Cairo University (1929–37). Some of the mastabas were also excavated and copied by earlier explorers, including Lepsius, Nestor l'Hôte, Wilkinson, Burton, Rosellini, Champollion, Cailliaud, Mariette and Brugsch. To the west of Chephren's pyramid, Lepsius, Wilkinson and Mariette recorded the rock-cut tombs, and to the east, the Saite tombs of Dynasty 26. Amongst these (near Mycerinus' pyramid), Vyse in 1837 discovered a family tomb which belonged to an Overseer of the Royal Scribes; he named it Campbell's Tomb after Colonel Campbell who was then the British Consul-General in Egypt. These Saite and later tombs were explored by Petrie who, in 1906–7, also excavated tombs dating to the earliest dynasties.

Zawiyet el-'Aryan

This is the site of two unfinished pyramids: the earlier one, known as the Layer Pyramid and probably started by Kha'ba of Dynasty 3 as a step pyramid, was excavated by Barsanti and later examined by Reisner. The second, known as the Unfinished Pyramid, is very similar but dates to Dynasty 4 and was also excavated by Barsanti (1904–5).

Abu Ghurab

Six sun-temples are known to have been built by the rulers of Dynasty 5, but only two – those of Userkaf and Niuserre – have so far been found.

Sun-Temple of Userkaf

Situated halfway between Abusir and Abu Ghurab, this was a new type of monument introduced by Userkaf; it emphasized the close association between the rulers of Dynasty 5 and the cult of the sun-god, Re. It followed the layout of a pyramid complex, with a valley building, causeway, and the equivalent of a mortuary temple and pyramid, but the pyramid was replaced by an open court in which stood a squat stone obelisk mounted on a platform. This was the god's cult-symbol and imitated the Benben stone which was the central feature in the sun-god's first temple at Heliopolis.

This site was visited by Lepsius, and located and partly explored by Borchadt at the beginning of this century; it was systematically excavated by Ricke and Haeny for the joint expedition of the Swiss and German Institutes (1955–7).

Sun-Temple of Niuserre

One mile north of Abusir, at Abu Ghurab, Niuserre built a temple similar to Userkaf's monument which incorporated a valley temple near the canal, a causeway linking this area to the upper temple, and the upper temple itself which included a large, open-air court with an altar and squat obelisk. There were also large stone basins here, probably to receive the blood of animals sacrificed as part of the temple ritual.

Magnificent reliefs discovered in this building (and taken to the Cairo and Berlin Museums) depict the animals and plants created by the sun's life force. Particularly noticeable amongst these

are the scenes showing the personifications of
the three seasons and of the Nile, the Sea, Grain
and Nourishment, who all bring their offerings
to the sun-god.

Early travellers referred to this temple as the
Pyramid of Righa. With the patronage of Baron
von Bissing, it was excavated by Borchadt and
Schäfer for the Deutsche Orient-Gesellschaft in
1898–1901, and revealed much information
about the layout of sun-temples which have a
different tradition from the Egyptian cultus and
mortuary temples.

Abusir

The pyramids of Dynasty 5 were of inferior construction, and incorporated a core of small stones
enclosed within a limestone casing. Userkaf built
his pyramid at Sakkara, but his son Sahure inaugurated the royal cemetery at Abusir, where his
successors Neferirkare and Niuserre also built
pyramids. These were visited by Lepsius, examined by Perring and Vyse, and excavated by Borchadt for the Deutsche Orient-Gesellschaft
(1902–8).

Pyramid of Sahure

This pyramid, the most complete example of
Dynasty 5 to be excavated and published, displays a high level of artistic achievement. A variety of materials was used: local limestone and
rubble formed the basic core, but fine limestone
from Tura was employed for the reliefs, granite
from Aswan was used for the columns (which
represent bound papyrus stems), door jambs and
lintels, and black basalt was introduced for the
pavements. Fragments of the sculptured wall
reliefs that have survived illustrate a range of subjects centred around the king's relationship with
the gods and his public duties. They include
scenes of hunting, baiting hippopotamuses, and
campaigns against the Libyans, as well as a trading expedition in sea-going boats which probably went to Byblos on the coast of Syria.

Pyramid of Neferirkare

This pyramid complex, although planned to be
larger than that of Sahure, was never completed;
the valley temple was taken over by Niuserre
and incorporated in his own funerary complex.

In 1893, important papyrus fragments were discovered which have provided information about
the accounts and administration of Neferirkare's
funerary temple.

Pyramid of Niuserre

This pyramid, less well preserved than the
Sahure monument, has interesting reliefs which
were found in the causeway corridor, showing
the king as a lion or griffin trampling his enemies
underfoot. The reliefs in the pyramid and temple show the excellent standard achieved at this
period; names of some of the king's important
courtiers are also preserved here, including Ti
who owned an impressive mastaba at Sakkara.

In recent years, Verner (working for the
Czechoslovakian Institute of Egyptology) has
discovered the remains of another pyramid, situated between the pyramid of Sahure and the
sun-temple of Userkaf. The owner remains
unidentified and the pyramid was never finished,
but it was planned on a larger scale than any
other found so far at Abusir.

Mastaba of Ptahshepses

The most important tomb at this site belonged to
the vizier and son-in-law of Niuserre. It was
examined by Lepsius (who wrongly identified it
as a pyramid) and excavated by De Morgan
(1893); it has recently been re-examined by the
Czechoslovakian Institute of Egyptology.

Sakkara

Sakkara, the extensive necropolis of the ancient
capital Memphis, was accessible to writers such
as Strabo and later travellers including Vansleb
and Lucas (who 'discovered' pits containing
mummified birds), Pococke, Nestor l'Hôte, Hay
and Burton. Lepsius and Mariette worked at the
site, and excavations have been undertaken for
the Egyptian Antiquities Service by Firth,
Quibell and Lauer. Major discoveries have also
been made by the Egypt Exploration Society.

The Pyramids
The Step Pyramid

The world's first great stone monument was
reputedly built by Imhotep for King Zoser
c. 2630 BC and, with its surrounding complex,

displayed many unique and innovative features. Described by various early writers, it was later investigated by Vyse, and by Firth and Lauer; the latter spent more than fifty years at the site where he undertook extensive restoration, reassembling the entrance colonnade, part of the enclosure wall, and several other buildings. Before these excavations, only the Step Pyramid was visible.

In the Step Pyramid enclosure, the unfinished pyramid of one of Zoser's successors, Sekhemkhet, was discovered and excavated by Goneim for the Egyptian Antiquities Service (1951–5) but his death in 1959 prevented completion of the task. The work was continued by Lauer (1963–76).

Pyramid of Userkaf

The first king of Dynasty 5 built his pyramid at Sakkara although several of his successors went to a new site at Abusir. This pyramid was explored by Lepsius, Vyse and Perring, and Lauer and Firth who also excavated the associated mortuary temple in 1928.

Pyramid of Isesi

Also belonging to Dynasty 5, this pyramid was explored by Lepsius, and Vyse and Perring; the associated mortuary temple was investigated by Leclant.

Pyramid of Unas

Built for the last king of Dynasty 5, this is the earliest pyramid to be inscribed with the Pyramid Texts which are to be found on its interior walls. Opened by Maspero in 1881, the pyramid was later excavated for the Antiquities Service by Hassan (1937–8) and Hussein. A causeway decorated with interesting scenes links the mortuary temple to the valley building. The mortuary temple was excavated in 1900 by Barsanti, and then more completely by Firth (1929), Lauer (1936–7 and 1939), Hassan and Hussein (1937–49), and the French Archaeological Mission at Sakkara (1974–6). An inscription on the south side of the pyramid records that Prince Khaemwese, son of Ramesses II, restored this monument.

Pyramid of Teti

This belonged to the founder of Dynasty 6. It was explored by Vyse and Perring, Maspero, Firth, Gunn and Quibell. The internal walls are decorated with Pyramid Texts; since 1965, Lauer and Leclant have cleared the interior passages and chambers of this and other Dynasty 6 pyramids and have copied the Pyramid Texts.

Pyramid of Pepy I

This Dynasty 6 pyramid was explored by Lepsius, Perring and Vyse, Petrie and Lauer. It was here that the inscriptions known as the Pyramid Texts were first discovered by Brugsch in 1880–1.

Pyramid of Pepy II

Discovered and excavated by Jéquier (1926–7), this also contained Pyramid Texts, and represents the standard pyramid complex in its most developed form. Jéquier also excavated the pyramids of two queens, Neit and Iput, which contained Pyramid Texts, and in 1924 he explored the Mastabat el-Fara'un, the burial complex of Shepseskaf which had been previously examined by Mariette in 1858. This belonged to a ruler of Dynasty 4 who broke the tradition of pyramid-building and constructed instead this huge sarcophagus-shaped structure. The only known parallel for this monument is the tomb at Giza of Khentkaus, the mother of the founder of Dynasty 5.

Tombs

Early Dynastic

The mastaba tombs of the first two dynasties were excavated by Emery for the Egypt Exploration Society (1936–56); there has been much debate as to whether these (as opposed to the Abydos monuments) were used for the royal burials or whether they belonged to high officials.

Old Kingdom

Mariette excavated many of these tombs and others were explored by Lepsius, Firth and Gunn, Quibell, Lythgoe and Ransome Williams.

Particularly famous tombs belonged to Ti, the Overseer of pyramids and sun temples, which was studied by Mariette and by Steindorff, and to the vizier Mereruka, which was discovered in 1893 and studied by Daressy, Firth and Gunn, and Duell.

New Kingdom

Few tombs before the reign of Amenophis III have been found at Sakkara, probably due to chance of discovery, but large stone structures were built in his reign, and when Tutankhamun returned from Amarna and established his political capital at Memphis, Sakkara again became the main cemetery until the reign of Ramesses II. These tombs, plundered or excavated with insufficient control, were often dismantled and the stone blocks, decorated with scenes and inscriptions, were subsequently removed to many museums. Reworking this area in recent years, the Anglo-Dutch expedition of the Egypt Exploration Society

From Maspero's Histoire Ancienne des Peuples de l'Oriente Classique *(1899), this drawing shows the main gallery of the Serapeum at Sakkara. Discovered by Mariette in 1850, the Serapeum housed the burials of Apis-bulls which were associated with the worship of Ptah-Osiris at Memphis.*

and the National Museum of Antiquities in Leiden, led by Martin, has discovered the tombs of Horemheb (as army commander – his royal tomb was subsequently built at Thebes), Tia and Tiu, and Maya (the Overseer of the Treasury under Tutankhamun and Horemheb).

Sacred Animal Complexes

A number of animal cemeteries were located at Sakkara which was a place of pilgrimage for many centuries. Animal worship was always a major element of Egyptian religion and many species of animals were regarded as the earthly forms of the various gods.

The northern group of complexes include hawk, ibis and baboon galleries which have been excavated by Emery, Smith and Martin for the Egypt Exploration Society. The eastern group has been studied by Quibell, and Smith and Jeffreys, and the jackal galleries were published by Gaillard and Daressy as a Catalogue in the Cairo Museum series.

However, the most famous animal complex is the Serapeum or Apis-bull enclosure. From the reign of Amenophis III, the sacred Apis-bulls

This drawing is based on an engraving published by Mariette in his Choix de Monuments de Sérapéum, *produced after he discovered the Serapeum. It shows the burial chamber and enormous sarcophagus of an Apis-bull. The bulls were regarded as earthly images of Osiris.*

teen years, the burials were quite infrequent, and the priests would then search for a new sacred bull; in this quest, they sought an animal which would be identified by the presence of certain markings on its body.

Above the galleries, there were various chapels and a temple for the dead god's cult. The complex remained in use in the Ptolemaic Period, and the name Serapeum comes from the Greek word Osorapis, meaning the deceased Apis-bull; this cult was eventually identified with the worship of Serapis, a new supreme state deity introduced by the Ptolemies.

In Dynasty 30 various additions were made to the complex including an avenue of human-headed sphinxes which Nectanebo I caused to be built between the Serapeum and the city of Memphis. When Mariette was searching the area in 1850, he saw one of these sphinxes partially uncovered from the sand and recalled Strabo's reference to the Serapeum at Memphis, with the avenue of sphinxes leading to the burial place of the Apis. This inspired him to gather together a group of workmen and begin searching for the Serapeum; he soon made his great discovery of the avenue of sphinxes, the underground galleries, and the chambers and temples dedicated to the Apis.

Dahshur

This southernmost area of the Memphis necropolis contains several important pyramids.

The Bent Pyramid

This pyramid, conspicuous because of its unique blunted appearance (the result of a decision to change the angle of incline of its sides during the course of construction), was built during the reigns of Huni, the last king of Dynasty 3, and Sneferu, the first king of Dynasty 4. The interior was explored by the English traveller Edward Melton in 1660, and it was described by many travellers including Burton, Hay, and Lepsius; in 1860, Le Brun found a small chamber inside. It was examined by Perring, and the valley building was excavated by Fakhry for the Egyptian Antiquities Service in 1951–5. In 1964 Maragioglio and Rinaldi published a survey of the pyramid.

were buried in tombs at Sakkara, but in the reign of Ramesses II an underground burial ground was started which consisted of a rock-cut gallery (a second one, at right angles, was added later) from which the individual burial chambers led off. After they received the bull burials, these chambers were walled up. The cult of the bulls was closely associated with the worship of Ptah at Memphis, but it also came to be linked with the worship of Osiris, god of the dead, and it was believed that at death each bull was united with Osiris. The Apis-bull was regarded as the god's earthly image and was treated with great reverence in life; when it died, the bull was mummified and buried in wooden coffins and a great sarcophagus inside the Serapeum burial chamber. Since each animal's lifespan was about four-

The Northern Stone Pyramid (the Red Pyramid)
This pyramid was also built for Sneferu and is the earliest known example of a true pyramid, conceived and executed as such. It was built after the Bent Pyramid, and the architects used the same angle of incline (43°) which had been employed on the upper part of the Bent Pyramid. It was described by Pococke, Burton, and Lepsius, and investigated by Perring and Vyse, and Fakhry; in 1982, the joint expedition of the Egyptian Antiquities Organisation and the German Institute of Archaeology excavated the mortuary temple and found evidence that Sneferu was the owner of this pyramid. It is possible therefore that Sneferu had three pyramids – two at Dahshur and one at Medum – but the reason for this is unclear.

Dahshur was also used as a burial place by Middle Kingdom rulers:

Pyramid of Ammenemes II (the White Pyramid)
Described by Lepsius, this pyramid was excavated by De Morgan (1894–5); in the royal burials on the west side of the pyramid he found the treasure – jewellery and personal possessions – of two princesses.

Pyramid of Sesostris III
Investigated by Vyse and Perring, this pyramid and its enclosure were excavated by De Morgan (1894–5). In the royal tombs in the vicinity, he found the jewellery of Sit-hathor (daughter of Sesostris II) and of Mereret (daughter of Sesostris III). In each case, the treasure was concealed within the tomb rather than being placed on the mummy. With the jewellery found at Lahun by Petrie, this discovery provides evidence of the exquisite craftsmanship of the Middle Kingdom. Six boat burials have also been found in association with this pyramid.

Pyramid of Ammenemes III (the Black Pyramid)
This complex was visited by Burton and others, and investigated by Vyse and Perring, Firth, and De Morgan. Arnold, excavating for the German Institute of Archaeology from 1976, found human remains and associated objects in the pyramid which indicated that members of the royal family had been buried here. He also discovered evidence of subsidence, and it was possibly structural problems in this pyramid which persuaded the king to build another pyramid for himself at Hawara; the Dahshur pyramid was ultimately used for burial of the queens.

el-Lisht
Although the capital city of It-towy, established by Ammenemes I at the beginning of Dynasty 12, has not been located, its main necropolis has been identified at el-Lisht.

Pyramid of Ammenemes I
This complex continued the features found in the Old Kingdom, and included provision for the associated burials of the royal family and officials. It was explored by Perring and Vyse, by Gauthier and Jéquier for the Institut Français d'Archéologie Orientale (1894–5), and by Lythgoe and Mace for the Metropolitan Museum, New York. All the contents had been robbed in antiquity.

Pyramid of Sesostris I
The ownership of this southern pyramid was identified by Maspero in 1882 when he found fragments of inscribed alabaster objects inside. It was extensively explored by Gauthier and Jéquier in 1894 when they discovered the cachette containing the well-known statue of Sesostris I; successive expeditions of the Metropolitan Museum, New York (1906–34), directed by Lythgoe, Mace, and Lansing, completed the work on the pyramid and the surrounding area. This included the Old Kingdom rock-tombs, and the Middle Kingdom mastabas where, in 1907, coffins and jewellery were discovered.

Medum
This pyramid demonstrates the first attempt to construct a true pyramid, although the original design had started as a seven-stepped and then an eight-stepped structure. By filling in the steps and adding an outer casing, the builders attempted to change the plan, but because of several architectural errors, the outer walls collapsed and the building was abandoned. It is

possible that the disaster at Medum persuaded the builders of the Bent Pyramid at Dahshur to adjust the angle of its sides.

It is probable that this pyramid was built for Sneferu, although it may have been started by his predecessor, Huni. The site was visited by several early travellers including Denon, Burton and Wilkinson. Maspero was the first archaeologist to enter it in modern times, and it was subsequently excavated and investigated by Petrie in 1891 (and again with Wainwright 1910–12), by Borchadt, and by Rowe for the Eckley B. Coxe Expedition of the University Museum of Pennsylvania (1929–30).

Petrie wished to gain exact information about the construction of the pyramid and to see if there was a mastaba or small stepped pyramid in the interior; his assistant, Wainwright, therefore entered the pyramid by means of a tunnel bored from the east face of the pyramid, at its base, almost through to the burial chamber.

The cemeteries associated with the pyramid date from early Dynasty 4, and contain the mastabas of Sneferu's courtiers. Three famous tombs belonged to Ra-hotep and Nefert (whose well-known pair-statue is in the Cairo Museum), Nefermaat, and Itet. Wall reliefs were removed from these to Cairo and other museums; perhaps the most famous is the representation of Egyptian geese from the tomb of Itet. Mariette, Petrie, and Rowe excavated the tombs at Medum.

The Fayoum

This large fertile depression lies to the west of the Nile Valley and is linked to the Nile by a tributary known as Bahr Yusef (Joseph's river). In the north-west is the lake known today as Birket Qarun; this was the Lake Moeris of antiquity, when it covered a much larger area.

The abundant vegetation and wild life attracted the Egyptians and, later, the Greeks and Romans, to visit and settle here, and it was an important centre during Dynasty 12 and in the Graeco-Roman Period. When Ammenemes I relocated his capital to It-towy in the vicinity of the Fayoum, the area became economically

important and royal cemeteries were established at Lahun and Hawara. A successor, Ammenemes III, was credited by the Classical writers with the construction of Lake Moeris (as well as the Labyrinth, his mortuary temple), but he probably actually undertook reclamation schemes, reducing the amount of water that entered the lake and building up the land. In Graeco-Roman times, the Fayoum attracted new residents when the Ptolemies established settlements there for the Greek and Macedonian immigrants. The lake was again reduced in size to gain new land. Excavation of these Fayoum towns has revealed numerous Demotic and Greek papyri which illuminate our understanding of this later period.

The geographer Strabo praises the Fayoum highly:

The Arsinoite Nome is the most remarkable of all, both on account of its scenery and its fertility and cultivation. It is planted with large and richly productive olive trees, and the oil is good when the olives are carefully gathered. In the rest of Egypt, the olive tree is never seen, except in the gardens of Alexandria where, under favourable circumstances, it yields olives but no oil.

Strabo also describes the lake:

Owing to its size and depth, Lake Moeris is capable of receiving the superabundance of water during the inundation without overflowing the habitations and crops, but later, when the water subsides, and after the lake has given up its excesses through the same canal, both it and the canal retain water enough for the purposes of irrigation. At both ends of the canal, there are lock-gates by which the engineers can regulate the influx and efflux of the water.

Herodotus, however, says that the lake was an artificial construction, and also mentions 'two pyramids'. The early traveller Sandys did not visit Lake Moeris, but he quotes Herodotus' story that the lake was dug by hand, and also mentions the two pyramids in the lake, 'each on a colossus of stone, the sepulchres of King Moeris and his wife'. In 1672, Vansleb saw the lower portion of one of two colossal statues at Biahmu, and Lepsius and then Petrie (1888) investigated the pedestals on which these figures had once stood. These large piles of stones which once supported the two statues were almost certainly the 'pyramids' which Herodotus described as standing in Lake Moeris.

Hawara

The brick-built pyramid of Hawara belonged to Ammenemes III of Dynasty 12 (his other pyramid was at Dahshur). It was visited by Burton and Lepsius, and investigated by Perring, and by Petrie who, in 1889, discovered the entrance on the south side and the intricate passages leading to the burial chamber.

The mortuary temple was the 'Labyrinth' described by Herodotus and Strabo. The latter's account is of particular interest:

There is also the Labyrinth here, a work as important as the pyramids, adjoining which is the tomb of the king who built the Labyrinth...At the end of this structure, which is more than a stadium in length, is the tomb, consisting of a square pyramid...It is asserted that so many palaces were built because it was the custom for all the nomes, represented by their leaders, with their priests and victims, to assemble here to offer sacrifice and gifts to the gods, and to deliberate on the most important concerns. Each nome then took possession of the hall destined for it.

Today, very little remains of the 'Labyrinth' but its site at Hawara was identified by Wilkinson and it was explored by Lepsius in 1843. Further excavation was carried out by Petrie in 1888–9.

The cemeteries near by were used in the Middle Kingdom and in the Late and Graeco-Roman Periods; the tombs were explored by Lepsius, and here Petrie discovered the famous painted panel portraits associated with the mummies of the Graeco-Roman Period.

Lahun

Pyramid of Sesostris II

This pyramid, built for a Middle Kingdom ruler, incorporated several interesting architectural features. Constructed of mudbrick, the architect had utilized a natural knoll of rock as the nucleus of the pyramid; it also incorporated a star-shaped framework of limestone retaining walls which radiated out from the centre. The stone casing which originally covered the pyramid has long since disappeared, and today only

the mudbrick internal structure is visible. It was excavated by Petrie (1889), who spent months looking for the entrance; it was located in the south face instead of the north, and a shaft then descended vertically to a passage cut deep below ground which led eventually to the burial chamber. Here, Petrie found a fine red granite sarcophagus, but no treasure.

However, in 1914, when he and Brunton excavated four shaft tombs on the south side of the pyramid, belonging to the royal family, they discovered the treasure of Princess Sit-Hathor-Iunut in the easternmost shaft. This included superb jewellery and personal possessions – a gold diadem, gold pectorals with the names of Sesostris II and Ammenemes III, necklaces, a collar, girdles, rings, bracelets and toilet equipment. It was similar to the treasure found at Dahshur, and exhibited the superb quality of craftsmanship of the Middle Kingdom. The treasure is in the Cairo Museum and the Metropolitan Museum, New York.

To the north of the pyramid are another eight rock-cut tombs. The site was visited by various travellers including Burton, Denon and Lepsius.

Kahun

Less than a mile away from the pyramid of Sesostris II at Lahun lies the town known as Kahun, originally built to house the families of the workers engaged in constructing the pyramid and associated temple (which was actually situated in the town). Surrounded by a thick mudbrick wall, it included terraced houses for the workforce and larger villas for the officials, and was similar in design to the other towns at Deir el-Medina and Amarna, also purpose-built to accommodate the royal necropolis workforce.

Excavated by Petrie in 1889, Kahun was extremely important as the first example of town planning to be uncovered in Egypt; also, the inhabitants had apparently deserted the town and left their possessions behind, and these provided unique evidence of living conditions at that time. Famous Hieratic papyri were found here; these included literary, mathematical, medical, veterinary, legal and administrative documents, and reveal something of the organization and composition of the workforce.

67

Middle Egypt
·················

Oxyrhynchus

This site, near the modern village of el-Bahnasa, was the ancient Egyptian town of Per-medjet which was once the capital of the 19th Upper Egyptian nome. Only heaps of debris now survive, but the town was also important in the Graeco-Roman Period when it was named Oxyrhynchus after the species of mormyrus fish that was worshipped there. The neighbouring town of Cynopolis had a dog-cult, and Plutarch recounts the dispute which broke out between the two communities because they had killed and eaten each other's sacred animals.

Remains of the Graeco-Roman Period have been revealed, including part of a colonnade and a substantial Roman theatre. The town retained importance in Christian times when it had twelve churches and many convents. The site was visited by Denon, Prisse, Wilkinson and Nestor l'Hôte, and Petrie dug there in 1896 for the Egypt Exploration Fund. However, it is probably best known for its wealth of Greek, Coptic and Arabic papyri. The Greek papyri were as numerous as those found in towns in the Fayoum, and provided a wealth of information. These were discovered by Grenfell and Hunt (1896–1907) who began excavating for papyri when the Graeco-Roman Branch of the Egypt Exploration Fund was formed; they subsequently edited many volumes of the *Oxyrhynchus Papyri* for the Branch.

Beni Hasan

On the east bank of the river, some distance south of the modern city of Minya, there are thirty-nine tombs cut into the cliff side; the most important of these belonged to the great provincial rulers of the 16th nome of Upper Egypt (the Oryx Nome) who lived at the town of Monet-Khufu during the later years of Dynasty 11 and the beginning of Dynasty 12. They have very interesting architectural and decorative features, and represent the most significant tomb-group between Memphis and Assiut. Only when the kings of Dynasty 12 finally curtailed the power of the provincial

governors did this necropolis and other similar centres cease to flourish. The tombs developed a distinctive architectural style, and their interesting wall scenes represent aspects of daily life, food production, and military training.

The most important tombs belonged to Khety and his father Bakhet, Khnumhotep I and II, and Amenemhet. As well as these tombs of Dynasties 11 and 12, there were less elaborate ones dating to Dynasty 6 when the provincial governors had begun to establish their power bases along the Nile. In 1902–4, Garstang excavated tombs dating from Dynasty 6 to Dynasty 12. The most significant rock-tombs had been visited and recorded by Nestor l'Hôte, Rosellini and Champollion, Bonomi, Burton, Hay, Napoleon's expedition, Lepsius and Wilkinson.

Newberry was in charge of the Archaeological Survey of the Egypt Exploration Fund to Beni Hasan (1890–4); this was his first independent work, and the publication, undertaken with Griffith and others, produced excellent results. Carter produced drawings for the survey at Beni Hasan as one of his earliest pieces of work in Egypt, and Nina de Garis Davies copied scenes in the tombs in 1931–2.

Speos Artemidos

This rock-cut temple, dedicated to the local lioness-goddess Pakhet, is situated just south of the tombs. It was built by Hatshepsut, with additions by Tuthmosis III and Sethos I. It was visited by Champollion, Nestor l'Hôte, Bonomi, Burton, Wilkinson, and Lepsius. The long text (placed on the architrave during Hatshepsut's reign) which denounces the Hyksos has been published by Maspero, Sethe, and Golénischeff. Near by is the cat cemetery where animals were buried in honour of Pakhet.

el-Ashmunein

This site was once the ancient Egyptian town Khnumu, a religious centre of great importance in the Old Kingdom where the god Thoth was worshipped; however, no remains of this early development have been recovered. It became the capital of the 15th Upper Egyptian nome whose rulers were buried at Deir el-Bersha.

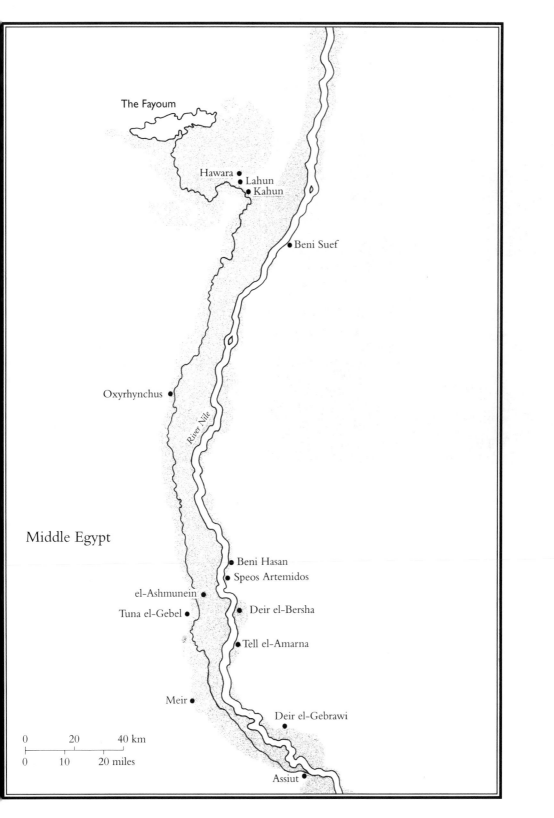

The Fayoum

Hawara ●
● Lahun
● Kahun

● Beni Suef

Oxyrhynchus ●

River Nile

Middle Egypt

● Beni Hasan
● Speos Artemidos

el-Ashmunein ●
Tuna el-Gebel ●
● Deir el-Bersha

● Tell el-Amarna

Meir ●

Deir el-Gebrawi
●

0   20   40 km

0   10   20 miles

Assiut ●

Animal cults were widespread throughout Egypt at all periods. Cats represented the goddess Bast and were worshipped as protectors of the home. Many were buried in large cemeteries, and some were mummified and placed in shaped wooden coffins. This is a particularly fine example (c.900 BC).

Part of a temple built by Ammenemes II was also found, as well as the pylon of a Dynasty 19 temple decorated with scenes of Sethos II. The German expedition under Roeder (1929–39) excavated the pylon of a temple built by Ramesses II which contained over fifteen hundred blocks brought from the dismantled temples dedicated to the Aten at Amarna.

Today, Ashmunein is badly ruined, with only part of the agora and the Christian basilica still preserved, but many Roman and Byzantine Period papyri have been recovered from the site.

Tuna el-Gebel

This desert area west of Ashmunein was used as the extensive necropolis of Hermopolis Magna; it is also the location of the stela marking the north-western boundary of Akhenaten's city and environs which were centred at Amarna.

The most important feature of the Ashmunein necropolis are the catacombs containing the burials of ibis and baboon, animals sacred to Thoth, god of Hermopolis. Here, in addition to the mummified animal remains, pottery, bronze statuettes, and Aramaic papyri of the 5th century BC were found.

The important and unique tomb of the family of Petosiris, built c.300 BC, can also be seen at Tuna el-Gebel. It is a rare example of the mixed Egyptian-Greek style. Petosiris, his wife, and one of their sons were buried in the underground chambers. South of this are other tombs and mortuary houses dating to the first centuries AD, which represent both Greek and Egyptian styles; the tomb of Isidora is of particular interest.

Excavation of the necropolis was undertaken by Chassinat (1903–4) and Weill (1912), and Lefebvre cleared the tomb of Petosiris in 1920; Gabra's expeditions for Cairo University uncovered the galleries and the city of the dead in the 1920s and 1930s.

Deir el-Bersha

A desert ravine called Wadi el-Nakhla, situated almost opposite the modern town of Mallawi, has many quarries and groups of rock-cut tombs. Deir el-Bersha, a modern village to the west of this wadi, has given its name to this site.

Known to the Greeks as Hermopolis Magna, this was derived from Hermes, the Greek name for Thoth, who was worshipped as Hermes Trismegistos by both Greeks and Egyptians, and was attributed with secret knowledge preserved in a corpus of writings. Hermopolis became a centre of pilgrimage for both Greeks and Egyptians and flourished as a Greek town. The Temple of Thoth which was built by Alexander the Great and Philip Arrhidaeus was visited and described by Pococke, Nestor l'Hôte, Bonomi, Minutoli, Wilkinson, Denon and Burton, and in the early 19th century some columns in the hypostyle hall were still standing.

The most important tombs, dating to Dynasty 12, belonged to the nomarchs (local rulers) of the 15th Upper Egyptian nome (the Hare Nome) who lived at Khnumu (Ashmunein). They are similar to those found at Beni Hasan. The most impressive was built for Djehutihotep (reigns of Ammenemes II, Sesostris II and III) and has a columned chapel and an inner chamber with a statue niche; the scene on the west wall of this room, showing the transportation of a colossal statue from the alabaster quarries at Hatnub, was copied by Wilkinson before 1856. There are also Old Kingdom and Ptolemaic Period tombs at this site.

Apart from Wilkinson, the Middle Kingdom tombs were recorded by Bonomi, Nestor l'Hôte, Bankes, Rosellini, Cailliaud, Hay, Burton, Prisse and Lepsius. They were excavated (1891–3) and published (1894–5) for the Egypt Exploration Fund by Newberry, Griffith and others, and by Reisner, Dunham and others for the Boston-Harvard expedition (1915). Daressy and Kamal also produced studies on the tombs and the Coffin Texts were included by Lacau in the Catalogue Series of the Cairo Museum.

Tell el-Amarna

Tell el-Amarna is the modern name used for the ancient city of Akhetaten ('Horizon of the Sun'), which was built and briefly occupied by the heretic pharaoh Akhenaten towards the end of Dynasty 18. His reasons for this choice for a capital city remain obscure, but it had the advantage of being a virgin site, free from associations with the traditional gods, where the worship of the Aten could be vigorously pursued.

Situated in the Hermopolitan nome, it was built on both banks of the river and its boundaries were marked by a series of stelae with inscriptions that gave Akhenaten's conditions for establishing the city. On the west bank it extends northwards as far as Tuna el-Gebel, and this cultivated land was probably used mainly to supply food for the city. The main buildings – temples, palaces, administrative quarters, houses – were on the east bank, stretching along the river for a distance of some thirteen kilometres; they formed the three main districts – northern, central and southern – of the city. To the east, the city was encircled by cliffs which were interspersed with wadis (desert valleys); the tombs of the courtiers and officials were cut into these cliffs (a break with the tradition of locating the cemeteries on the west bank), and the royal tomb lies at the end of one of the wadis.

The site was abandoned at the end of the Amarna period and never reoccupied; desecration of the buildings by the counter-revolutionaries and removal of the stone to other sites, especially Ashmunein, caused damage to the city. However, because there are no later layers of occupation, it has been possible for archaeologists to determine its layout, and it is one of only a few towns in Egypt to be extensively excavated and studied.

It was mentioned by early travellers such as Prisse, Champollion, Wilkinson, Burton, Lepsius, Hay, Burton and Bonomi, and it has been excavated by Petrie, Borchadt for the Berlin Museum, and the Egypt Exploration Fund; currently, an expedition directed by Kemp is working at Amarna for the Egypt Exploration Society.

The Central City

This was excavated by Petrie (1891–2), by the Egypt Exploration Fund (1920s and 1930s), and by Borchadt (1907–16) for the Deutsche Orient-Gesellschaft. Pendlebury cleared and examined much of this area for the Egypt Exploration Fund in 1928–31; other members of the expedition included Frankfort, Peet (who inaugurated this excavation), Woolley and Griffith; Nina de Garis Davies copied the mural paintings here in 1925–6.

The Great Temple

Petrie excavated here, and later Pendlebury and Lavers were able to reconstruct the layout and much of the plan of this building.

The Smaller Temple

This was excavated by Petrie and Pendlebury.

The Great Palace

This was the official state building, and included several courts and halls with columns; there were state apartments, the harem (living area) with attached servants' quarters, and a coronation hall. Akhenaten's residence was situated across the city's main road, connected by a bridge to the Great Palace. Petrie, Steindorff, Borchadt and Griffith worked here; Petrie found a fine stucco pavement but this was destroyed in 1912 (the fragments were then removed to the Cairo Museum for restoration). Pendlebury and Lavers were also able to reconstruct the layout and plan of this building.

The Records Office

Petrie had first visited Amarna briefly with Griffith in 1886, and his interest in the site was immediately aroused; a few months later, a peasant woman was digging in the mudbrick remains to obtain soil (sebakh) which was used as fertilizer for the fields, when she found a number of inscribed clay tablets. These were sold on through a chain of agents and dealers; when Petrie came to excavate Amarna, he found the source for these tablets when another eighteen fragments turned up in several rubbish holes under the floor of a room which Petrie called the Foreign Office. All the tablets were inscribed in cuneiform, and amongst Petrie's find was part of a large dictionary or vocabulary of Akkadian and Sumerian words which would have been used by Babylonian scribes. Sayce, a scholar working in cuneiform, visited Amarna and made copies of the tablets which he later published. This extremely important archive was demonstrated to be the correspondence between the Egyptian rulers (Amenophis III, Akhenaten and Tutankhamun) and the leaders of states in Palestine, Syria, Mesopotamia and Asia Minor; it provides a unique insight into Egypt's foreign relations at that time. Today, the tablets are in museums in Cairo, Berlin, London, Paris, Oxford, Brussels, New York and Chicago, and also in private collections.

Budge, Keeper at the British Museum, had visited Egypt in 1887 and viewed some of the tablets from the peasant woman's find; although others were sceptical, he believed that they were genuine, and when another group was brought to him in Luxor, he decided that they were authentic and purchased them for the London collection.

The Surrounding Central Area

The nucleus of state buildings was surrounded to the north and south by houses, workshops, sculptors' studios and so forth; the ownership of some houses, such as those of Nakht and Ramose, could be identified by inscriptions found *in situ*. Borchadt excavated these houses in 1911–14 and also discovered the workshop of Thutmose, the Master Sculptor, where he found many of the fine sculptures and plaster masks of royalty and nobility which were used for teaching students. These are now in the Cairo and Berlin Museums.

The Northern City

The major building here was the North Palace.

The Southern City

The Italian archaeologist Barsanti excavated (but never properly published) the Maruaten in the Southern City. Later, Borchadt, and Woolley and Gunn made further explorations here. Sometimes called the Summer Palace, the Maruaten was a group of buildings, decorated with painted scenes and pavements, which also incorporated a lake, a kiosk on an island, and flower gardens.

Workmen's village

Lying halfway between the northern and southern tombs, this was built to house the workforce and their families who were engaged in constructing Akhetaten. The village has many features in common with the other purpose-built villages of Kahun and Deir el-Medina. It was excavated by Peet and Woolley, and has also been extensively studied by the current Egypt Exploration Society expedition.

Tombs

Officials' tombs

Cut into the eastern cliffs encircling the town, these were arranged in two main groups in the north and the south. They continue the tradition of earlier Dynasty 18 tombs at Thebes, and have a forecourt leading through a door to a long hall and then a broad hall (both sometimes have columns), with a niche for a statue. The wall scenes, executed in sunk relief, provide much information about the cult of the Aten and the Royal Court at Amarna, and include very different subject matter from the traditional tombs. Inscriptions on the walls preserve the hymns to the Aten which are our main literary source for this cult.

Many of the tombs were unfinished or unused because the owners returned to Thebes when Akhetaten was deserted, and some of them had prepared tombs elsewhere before or after the Amarna period. In the northern group, the tombs of Huya (Superintendent of the royal harem and Chamberlain to Queen Tiye), Merye II (Superintendent of the royal harem), Ahmose (Fan-bearer) and Pentu (Physician) are particularly important.

Early travellers who visited this area included Prisse, Nestor l'Hôte, Hay, Burton, Wilkinson and Lepsius. Norman de Garis Davies recorded the scenes and inscriptions for the Egypt Exploration Fund in 1903–8 in the tombs here and in the southern group, where the most important included those of Mahu (Officer of Police), Maya (Military Commander), Suti, and Ay (who later became king and was buried in the Valley of the Kings at Thebes). Bouriant, Legrain and Jéquier published a study of the southern tombs in 1884.

The Royal Tomb
The tomb built for Akhenaten and his family (but probably never used) lies over nine kilometres away from the city, in a remote mountain valley. It was published by Newberry in 1893 and by Barsanti in 1894; it was subsequently studied by Bouriant and his colleagues, and cleared again by Pendlebury. In recent years, it has been studied and published by Martin.

Boundary Stela at Tuna el-Gebel
Situated on the west bank and delineating the boundary of the city and its environs, this was recorded by Hay, Bonomi, Prisse, Nestor l'Hôte and Lepsius, and the inscription copied by Daressy and Davies.

Hat-nub Quarries
Quarries are situated in the hills enclosing the plain where the city was built. The most

important, the alabaster quarries of Hat-nub, were discovered by Newberry in 1891. Rock inscriptions found there show that the quarries were in use during the Old and Middle Kingdoms. They have been published by Petrie, Anthes, Moller and Fraser.

Meir
Meir is the name of the modern village near which archaeologists found the rock-cut tombs of the local rulers of the 14th Upper Egyptian nome, which date from Dynasties 6 and 12. These were family tombs and they provide some of the most naturalistic wall scenes of the Middle Kingdom; the most interesting are those of Senbi (reign of Ammenemes I) and his son Ukh-hotep (reign of Sesostris I).

The most important archaeological work was undertaken here by Blackman (1914–53). The model boats found here were described by Reisner, Daressy produced a study of the coffins, and Kamal and Lacau published the Coffin Texts in the Catalogue Series of the Cairo Museum.

Deir el-Gebrawi
Near the modern village of Deir el-Gebrawi are the rock-cut tombs which belonged to the provincial governors of the 12th Upper Egyptian nome during Dynasty 6, when the local rulers were establishing their power bases away from the Old Kingdom capital of Memphis.

The tombs are arranged in two main groups (north and south) and, like the more famous tombs at Beni Hasan, their wall scenes represent various crafts, harvesting, fishing and hunting.

Wilkinson visited and recorded some of the details of these scenes, and Newberry's expedition for the Archaeological Survey of the Egypt Exploration Fund visited the site in 1892–3; Norman de Garis Davies copied and published the tombs for the Survey in 1902.

Assiut
This town had commercial importance in antiquity because it was at the start of the caravan route leading to the oases in the Libyan desert. It was the capital of the 13th nome of Upper Egypt, and the cult-centre of the god Wepwawet; in Greek times, it was known as

Lycopolis, and the great neo-Platonic philosopher Plotinus (AD 205–270) was born there.

However, although it marked the boundary between the northern and southern administrative districts of Egypt until the end of the New Kingdom, it only really politically important in its own right during the First Intermediate Period and Middle Kingdom, when the great provincial governors ruled here almost independently. They supported the Heracleopolitan kings of Dynasties 9 and 10, and continued to build large tombs in Dynasty 12.

It is these rock-cut tombs that have survived and are of particular interest: the provincial governors Khety I, Itefibi and Khety II were important allies of the Heracleopolitan rulers, and these tombs preserve biographical texts which throw light on the poorly documented conflict between the Heracleopolitans and the Thebans of Dynasty 11.

One of the main aims of the Egypt Exploration Fund was to record the details of standing monuments, and the Archaeological Survey was established under Griffith's editorship. It produced a series of volumes, including Griffith's study of these Middle Kingdom rock-tombs, which were also described by Hay, Bonomi and Montet.

Further up the cliff, the large tomb of Hepzefa I, a local prince in the reign of Sesostris I, was discovered; it was recorded by Hay, Denon, De Rouge and Wilkinson, and studies have been produced by Griffith, Reisner and Montet. In keeping with the times of military conflict between the districts, local tombs were equipped with wall scenes and models of soldiers to protect the owner in eternity, and particularly fine sets of soldier models were found at Assiut in the tomb of Mesehti.

Some of the tombs were reused in the Saite and Graeco-Roman Periods, and these have been studied by Chassinat and Palanque for the Mission Archéologique Française au Caire.

Upper Egypt (North)

Abydos

The name Abydos is derived from the Egyptian Abedju and the Coptic word Ebot, and this was one of the most important religious centres in Egypt. At first, it was the site of the royal tombs (or cenotaphs) of the Early Dynastic Period, and the last rulers of predynastic Egypt may also have been buried here. The town and necropolis were originally dedicated to Khentiamentiu, but by the late Old Kingdom this god had become identified with Osiris. During the Middle Kingdom, Abydos became the centre of Osiris' cult, where the Mysteries were performed annually to ensure the god's resurrection and where many pilgrims came to participate in the religious festival and to set up stelae so that their chance of eternity, through the beneficence of Osiris, would be greatly enhanced. The kings also wished to be identified with Osiris in the afterlife, and began to build secondary mortuary temples here, as well as at their burial sites.

Abydos was visited during the Roman Period; Ammianus Marcellinus, who came in the 4th century AD, spoke of an oracle of Bes that flourished there, and Strabo provides an account of the Temple of Sethos I:

Above it [Ptolemais] lies Abydos, the site of the Memnonium, a wonderful palace of stone, built in the manner of the Labyrinth, only somewhat less elaborate in its complexity. Below the Memnonium is a spring, reached by passages with low vaults consisting of a single stone and remarkable for their extent and mode of construction. This spring is connected with the Nile by a canal, which flows through a grove of Egyptian acacias, sacred to Apollo. Abydos seems once to have been a large city, second only to Thebes, but now it is a small place.

Sicard visited Abydos between 1707 and 1726, and when Granger came to Egypt from Dijon in 1731 at the request of Pignon, the French consul, his travels took him to Abydos, where he found the Sethos Temple almost intact.

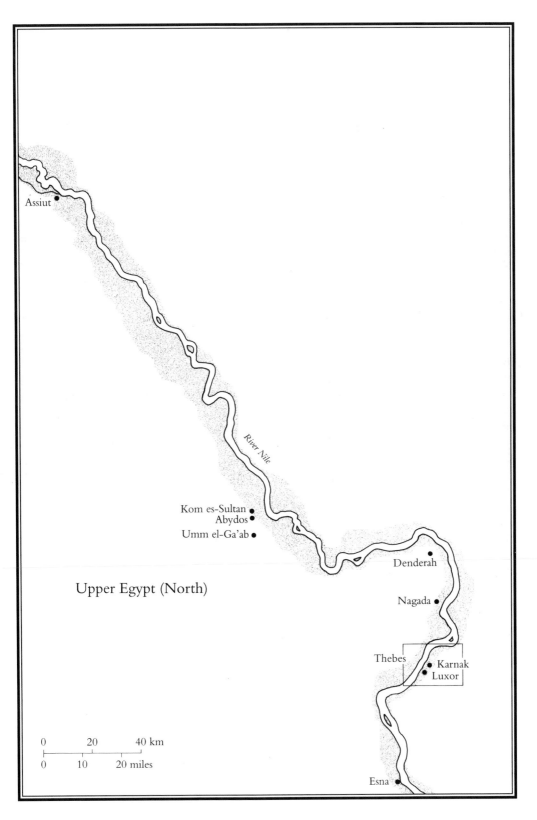

Assiut

River Nile

Kom es-Sultan
Abydos
Umm el-Ga'ab

Denderah

Nagada

Upper Egypt (North)

Thebes
Karnak
Luxor

0   20   40 km

0   10   20 miles

Esna

Cemetries

Umm el-Ga'ab

Here, in 1895–6, Amélineau had the concession to excavate the royal cemeteries of the earliest dynasties, but his techniques were disastrous. Searching only for decorated or inscribed pieces, he disposed of much of the material and the situation had to be rectified by Petrie, who reworked the site (1899–1901). He not only found the remains of the monuments (whether tombs or cenotaphs) of many of the rulers of Dynasties 1 and 2, with their subsidiary burials for women and servants, but also royal stelae and other objects. It was one of his most important archaeological discoveries. The tomb of King Djer was later regarded as the sacred grave of Osiris and undoubtedly these early monuments established the reputation of Abydos as a place of great sanctity. The area was also excavated by Naville and Legge.

Shunet el-Zebib

This large mudbrick ruin, surrounded by two walls, has the appearance of a fortress, although it may be an early monumental grave. It has been investigated by Mariette, Ayrton and Petrie.

Kom es-Sultan

This mound, at the centre of the ancient walled town of Abydos, dates back to the beginning of Egyptian history; objects found here show that the site was in use from Dynasty 1 until the Graeco-Roman Period. The enclosure walls, built in the Middle Kingdom, still remain and there are traces of the temple dedicated to Khentiamentiu and subsequently to Osiris. The site was excavated by Mariette and Amélineau.

Between Kom es-Sultan and Shunet el-Zebib are the Middle Kingdom tombs, some with small brick pyramids, and graves of the New Kingdom and later periods. In the southern part of the area, near the modern village of el-Araba, are the tombs dating to the New Kingdom, and north of this is situated the Old Kingdom cemetery.

Several archaeologists worked in these areas, including Mariette, Amélineau, Petrie, Garstang, Ayrton, Currelly, Weigall, Peet, Loat, Frankfort, Randall-McIver and Mace.

Mortuary Temples

Several rulers chose to build secondary mortuary temples here, and the New Kingdom examples are relatively well preserved:

Temple of Sethos I

Started in the reign of Sethos I, the temple was completed by Ramesses II and Merneptah. Built to a unique design, it is L-shaped rather than rectangular; it has seven chapels in the sanctuary area which are dedicated to six gods and to the dead, deified Sethos, instead of only one main sanctuary; and at the rear of the temple there is a special set of chambers dedicated to the Osiris Mysteries.

The wall scenes in the sanctuary preserve a more complete version of the Daily Temple Ritual than those found in any other temple, and the quality of the reliefs throughout the parts of the building completed during Sethos I's reign probably surpasses anything found at any other New Kingdom site.

After Granger's visit in the 18th century, the temple remained full of sand until Mariette cleared and excavated it in 1857–9 at the expense of the Khedive Said. Various travellers record knowledge of Abydos, including Nestor l'Hôte, Bonomi, Hay and Lepsius, and studies were also made by Capart and Caulfield, but the definitive publication of most of the temple was produced by Amice Calverley (1896–1959). She was a Canadian artist who, in 1927–49, undertook the task of copying the scenes on the walls and columns for a series of volumes produced by the Egypt Exploration Society, with funds provided by Rockefeller.

The Osireion

This unique building, lying at the rear of the Temple of Sethos, was discovered by Margaret Murray in 1903, and was excavated and examined further by Naville and Frankfort for the Egypt Exploration Fund in 1911–26. It was designed as the cenotaph of Osiris, and imitated a royal tomb; it incorporates an island surrounded by water, symbolizing the primeval mound where creation was believed to have taken place. This building is closely associated with the main temple, and there have been different opinions

regarding its date. It has been suggested that it was built during the reign of Sethos I but completed under Merneptah (the reliefs decorating some of the chambers date to his reign), although others would date it completely to Merneptah's period. In style, it reflects the simplicity of the Old Kingdom pyramid temples at Giza.

The columns in temples symbolized the verdant plant growth of the original Island of Creation. Here, in the hypostyle hall of the Temple of Sethos I at Abydos, the capitals represent the closed lotus-bud form. Scenes on the columns show the king making offerings to the gods.

Temple of Ramesses II

A short distance north-west of Sethos I's building is the Temple of Ramesses II, which is also dedicated to Osiris and the cult of the deceased king. It is only partly preserved, but the general plan of the building can be seen and the remains of the coloured scenes on the bases of the walls indicate that this would also have been a magnificent monument.

It was recorded and studied by Nestor l'Hôte, Hay, Mariette and Murray, and the famous Abydos King List was removed from here by the French consul, Mimaut (1774–1837), and obtained by the British Museum after his death.

Temple of Ramesses I

This small temple, situated close to Ramesses II's monument, was built by Sethos I for his father. It is recorded by Nestor l'Hôte, and was published by Winlock in 1937.

Denderah

This was the site of the Egyptian city of Iunet (Greek Tentyris), the capital of the 6th nome of Upper Egypt where Hathor, goddess of love, joy and beauty, was worshipped together with her husband, Horus of Edfu, and her son Ihy (who, according to mythology, was born at Denderah).

Today, very little remains of the ancient town although the cemetery includes tombs from the earliest dynasties, the Old Kingdom and the First Intermediate Period. However, much of the magnificent temple remains, situated to the west of the old town. It probably occupies the site of an older temple of the Old Kingdom, but the building visible today dates mainly to the Ptolemaic Period, with some decoration carried out under the Romans.

There are several features of interest: crypts set on three levels in the thicknesses of the outside wall are decorated with the best-preserved reliefs in the temple, and were used for the storage of cultic equipment and archives; staircases within the wall thicknesses ascend to and return from the roof, and these are decorated with reliefs showing the ceremonial procession of priests carrying images of Hathor and other deities for the celebration of the New Year's Festival. On the roof there is a kiosk in which Hathor was ritually united with the sun's rays, and two shrines dedicated to Osiris, one of which contained the famous Zodiac which was removed to the Louvre in Paris. On the south rear outer wall of the temple is the scene showing Cleopatra VII in the presence of the gods of Denderah.

Other buildings in the temple enclosure include a birth house (Mammisi) which was decorated in Augustus' time, and a second Birth House begun by Nectanebo I and completed under the Ptolemies, where the scenes show the birth of the divine child Ihy. South of this birth house is the sanatorium where the sick were received and housed in cubicles; they could bathe and enter the state known as the Therapeutic Dream, when they returned to Nun, the void which had existed before creation took place, in the hope of being healed by the goddess.

The early tombs were excavated by Petrie (1897–8) and by Fisher for the Eckley B. Coxe Jr Expedition of the University of Pennsylvania (1912). The temple was visited and recorded by Napoleon's savants, Bruce, Pococke, Champollion, Nestor l'Hôte, Prisse, and Wilkinson. It was cleared by Mariette, and has been extensively studied and published by Chassinat and Daumas (1934–65).

Nagada

The Nagada cemeteries excavated by Petrie (1894–5) lay in the vicinity of the modern village of Nagada, between Tukh and El-Ballas. These cemeteries represented the last two cultures of the predynastic era (now known by the terms of Nagada I and Nagada II), and accommodated the burials of the inhabitants of the nearby town of Nubt (Greek Ombos). This, as an early capital of Upper Egypt, was a place of considerable importance in the later Predynastic Period, perhaps partly because of the accessibility of the gold workings in the Eastern Desert. Nubt was also the cult-centre of Seth, the god who later became the personification of evil. The earliest history of the town remains obscure but it obviously continued to have some importance, because a New Kingdom temple dedicated to Seth has been discovered there.

Early photographs show the extent of sand encroachment on the monuments before they were cleaned by the Antiquities Service. Here, the façade of the Temple of Hathor at Denderah can be seen, with its impressive Hathor-headed columns. This temple was built and decorated in the Graeco-Roman Period.

In 1897, a short distance north of the village of Nagada, De Morgan discovered a large, much-damaged mudbrick mastaba tomb, with a palace-type façade. This contained ivory tablets, fragments of vases, and clay sealings, with the names of Hor-aha, a king of Dynasty 1, and Queen Neithetep who may have been his wife. One ivory label discovered here (each label was used to indicate the date and content of a vessel or receptacle to which it was tied) gives the name of Hor-aha and, in another group of hieroglyphs, there is a sign which reads as Menes, the first king of Dynasty I. From this evidence, several scholars chose to identify Menes with Hor-aha and to claim that this was Menes' tomb, but subsequent studies have shown that Menes was not Hor-aha and that this tomb was probably constructed not for a king but for an important local administrator of Dynasty 1.

Thebes
·········

The ancient Egyptian name for Thebes was Waset; for an unknown reason, it was given the name Thebai by the Greeks, and several ancient writers referred to the city's hundred gates as symbols of its size and power. Its geographical position, near the desert routes and Nubia and far from the earlier northern centres, ensured its importance, and it first became the country's capital in Dynasty 12. However, it reached its zenith in the New Kingdom as the capital of Egypt and its empire. The dry climate of the south has preserved its magnificent temples and tombs much better than those built in the northern centres.

The main part of the city was located on the east bank where the temple complexes of Karnak and Luxor can still be seen. Across the river, the palace of Amenophis III at Malkata and the royal necropolis workmen's village at Deir el-Medina have been discovered, but it is the Theban burial places and funerary temples that dominate the west bank.

The first tourists visited Thebes during the Persian Period, and graffiti show that many Greeks and Romans visited the most easily accessible tombs in the Valley of the Kings and also the Colossi of Memnon. The earliest known inscription left by a Greek tourist is cut into the wall of Ramesses VII's tomb and dates to 278 BC. Diodorus visited the Valley of the Kings between 65 and 60 BC; when Strabo was there between 24 and 20 BC, he found only scattered villages on the site of the ancient city, but he mentions 'around forty' royal tombs.

When Christianity spread, parts of some tombs and temples were turned into churches, but after the Arab conquest, Arab travellers and writers did not mention Thebes apart from a reference by the Armenian Abu Salih in the 13th century AD. Once European travellers began to reach Egypt, they started to extend their journey from Cairo, Giza and Alexandria, and the first description of the Temple of Karnak was given

Every temple had a Sacred Lake where the priests bathed several times daily and cleansed utensils used in the divine rituals. The Sacred Lake in the temple enclosure at Karnak is the most impressive. This early photograph shows the lake with temple pylons, columns and obelisks in the background.

by an Italian in 1589. In the 17th century, more people reached Thebes, and the first modern recorded visit to the Valley of the Kings was undertaken by two French monks and reported in Thévenot's account. However, it was Father Claude Sicard who first identified the monuments at Karnak and Luxor as the remnants of ancient Thebes.

In more recent times, several important contributions were made to the existing knowledge of Thebes. Richard Pococke, who visited the area twice in 1738, made the first accurate plan of the Valley of the Kings and mapped the tombs of Ramesses IV and VI, Sethos II and Tausert; another traveller, James Bruce, entered seven tombs and discovered the tomb of Ramesses III; and when Napoleon's savants made detailed studies of the Theban monuments, Denon sketched the ruins while others discovered new tombs. In the expedition's 1821 publication, Jomard and Costaz provided the most detailed record then available of the royal tombs,

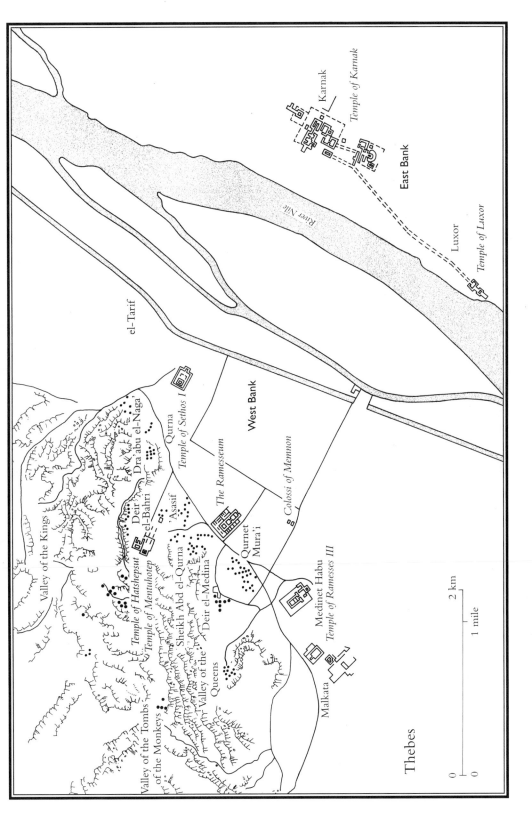

THE SITES

Temple of Karnak

Karnak

East Bank

River Nile

Luxor

Temple of Luxor

Temple of Luxor

el-Tarif

Temple of Sethos I

West Bank

Qurna

Dra abu el-Naga'

Deir el-Bahri

Asasif

The Ramesseum

Colossi of Memnon

Temple of Hatshepsut

Temple of Mentuhotep

Sheikh Abd el-Qurna

Valley of the Kings

Qurnet Mura'i

Deir el-Medina

Valley of the Tombs of the Monkeys

Valley of the Queens

Medinet Habu
Temple of Ramesses III

Malkata

Thebes

2 km

1 mile

0

0

81

although this concentrated on the architecture rather than the decoration of the tombs.

Wilkinson (after 1821), Hay (after 1824), Burton (after 1824) and Nestor l'Hôte (1838–39) also made copies of the tombs, and Champollion's expedition spent three months in 1829 in the Valley of the Kings. He was the first to realize that the texts on the tomb walls referred to the king's afterlife and not to his deeds in this world, and to become aware that some texts and scenes appeared to be repeated in almost every tomb. The Prussian expedition led by Lepsius spent the winter of 1844–5 surveying the entire valley, clearing some of the tombs and copying examples of the wall decoration.

The East Bank

The Temple of Karnak

In reality, Karnak (the name is taken from the nearby modern village but the Egyptians called it Ipet-isut, meaning 'The most select of places') is a complex of temples dedicated to the Theban triad of Amun, Mut and Khonsu, and several other deities. When Thebes became Egypt's capital in Dynasty 12, this cult-centre of Amun was established as a most important shrine, and the rulers of Dynasty 18 extended and enhanced it as the seat of their great deity Amen-Re. Most kings of the New Kingdom made additions to the complex, and it became the largest and most powerful religious centre in Egypt. There are three main areas – the precincts of Amun, Montu and Mut – and the complex was visited and recorded by many early travellers including Pococke, Burton, Hay, Wilkinson, Nestor l'Hôte, Champollion and Rosellini. Rifaud also mentions a visit in his *Voyage en Égypte, en Nubie* (1830).

The precinct of Amun includes the Great Temple of Amun, consisting of a series of pylons (gateways) interspersed with courts or halls which lead to the main sanctuary. There are also several smaller temples and chapels and the great Sacred Lake; to the east of the enclosure was the Temple of Aten, built in the early years of Akhenaten's reign and later dismantled during the counter-revolution.

Various major works were undertaken at Kar-nak, including Mariette's clearance of the site, and studies by Pillet, Legrain, Leclant, the University of Chicago Oriental Institute, Chevrier and Drioton, Barguet, and Firchow; Robichon with Christophe, Barguet and Leclant undertook important researches in the early 1950s for the Institut français du Caire. Lacau and Chevrier published the exquisite Shrine of Sesostris I which was discovered here and which has now been restored and set up in the Open-Air Museum at Karnak.

In the Temple of Amun, extensive excavations and restorations have been undertaken since 1895 by the Egyptian Department of Antiquities, particularly to strengthen the foundations and reinstate the massive columns of the Great Hypostyle Hall. Outside this temple, near Pylon 7, the Karnak Cachette was discovered in 1902–9; this included 779 stone and 17,000 bronze statues which represented the art of most periods. It was also discovered that the 'talatat' (blocks of stone) used as infill in Pylons 2, 9, and 10 had once belonged to the Aten Temple which stood at Karnak, and these have formed the basis of the work of the Akhenaten Temple Project, undertaken in the 1960s and 1970s by Winfield Smith and his colleagues.

This enclosure also accommodated the Temple of Khonsu (Amun's son) which was built and decorated under Pinudjem I, Herihor, and Ramesside and Ptolemaic rulers, and the Temple of Opet. Dedicated to the hippopotamus-goddess, this was built by Ptolemy VIII Euergetes II and decorated in the reigns of later kings including Augustus. Studies of the building and its inscriptions have been undertaken by Varille, De Wit and De Rochemonteix. Another major temple in this precinct, dedicated to Ptah, was built and decorated by Tuthmosis III, Shabaka, the Ptolemies and the Roman Emperor Trajan.

The northern precinct of Montu is the smallest; it includes the main temple dedicated to Montu, god of war, with an avenue of human-headed sphinxes, which was built by Amenophis III and later modified by Taharka and the Ptolemies. An earlier temple of Montu, founded by Tuthmosis I, was discovered outside the enclosure wall in 1970. The precinct has several other temples and a Sacred Lake, and the whole enclosure has been the subject of a number of detailed studies.

The southern enclosure of Mut, Amun's consort, was joined to his precinct by an avenue of ram-headed sphinxes. It contains Mut's temple, built by Amenophis III with later additions by Taharka, Nectanebo I, and the Ptolemies, and a crescent-shaped lake, as well as other temples. A major feature of Mut's temple were the hundreds of black granite statues of the lion-goddess Sekhmet placed there by Amenophis III. The temple was excavated and published by Benson and Gourlay.

The Temple of Luxor

This temple was the 'southern harem' of Amun where he took the form of the fertility god Min. Every year, during the inundation season, the great festival of Opet was held in which Amun's statue was brought to Luxor amidst great public rejoicing. The two temples were physically linked by an avenue of human-headed sphinxes built by Nectanebo I. The present temple, built on an earlier site, was mainly constructed in the reigns of Amenophis III and Ramesses II, although additions were also made by Tutankhamun, Horemheb and Alexander the Great. Later, in Diocletian's reign (c.300 AD), an innermost chamber was converted into a sanctuary for the observance of the imperial cult, and eventually part of the temple became a Christian church. In the 13th century AD the mosque of Abu el-Haggag, a local saint, was built in the temple court erected by Ramesses II; subsequent excavation of the temple left the entrance to the mosque well above ground level, and a new entrance has subsequently been made at the rear of the building.

Many travellers and scholars visited Luxor, including Norden, Denon, Wilkinson, Burton, Nestor de l'Hôte, Champollion, Minutoli and Lepsius. The temple has many points of interest, some of which were given special attention by

Known as the Southern Harem, the Temple of Luxor was the setting for the annual festival of Opet, when Amun's statue was brought there from Karnak. Here, columns are shown with their lotus-bud capitals. Like neighbouring Karnak, this temple was relatively accessible to early travellers.

the early writers: several colossal statues of Ramesses II which flanked the entrance were studied by Hay, Young, Pococke and Rifaud; Daressy in his *Notice explicatif des ruines du Temple of Louxour* (1893) investigated the Festival of Opet; and Lebas and others produced works on the obelisks (two red granite obelisks originally stood in front of the pylon, but the western one was removed to the Place de la Concorde, Paris, in 1835–6). On this same pylon are famous scenes and texts of Ramesses II's Battle of Kadesh, fought against the Hittites, which have been studied and translated by Rosellini and Champollion, Kuentz, and Breasted. A general account of the temple was published by Gayet in 1894.

The West Bank

Funerary Temples

Built on the plain between the river and the valleys where the royal burials were hidden, these temples were designed for the funerary cult of the kings. They continued the tradition of the temples attached to the pyramids, but now the burials in the valleys did not provide room for the temples to be built adjacent to the tombs. However, the function of these temples was the same: to ensure by means of rituals that the king attained immortality and continued as a god in the next world. Provision was also made in these buildings for worship of the gods, particularly Re-Harakhte and Amun.

The most important and best preserved temples are those of Ramesses II (The Ramesseum); Tuthmosis III and Ramesses III at Medinet Habu; Sethos I at Qurna; and Hatshepsut at Deir el-Bahri. The huge statues (the Colossi of Memnon) are all that remain of Amenophis III's funerary temple.

Deir el-Bahri

Two great temples were built here, one in Dynasty 11 as part of Nebhepetre Mentuhotep's unique royal burial complex, and the other for the queen regnant, Hatshepsut, in Dynasty 18.

Temple of Mentuhotep

The Theban king chose to be buried near his home in this unique building which incorpo-

rated a mastaba surrounded on all sides by a pillared ambulatory. It was originally excavated by Naville and Hall for the Egypt Exploration Fund in 1893–6 and 1903–6, when the discovery was made of six shrines which housed the funerary statues of royal princesses and of the four tombs which were associated with these shrines. Winlock later continued work here, clearing this site and the adjacent Hatshepsut temple for the Metropolitan Museum, New York (1911–31); he made many major discoveries at Mentuhotep's complex, including two intact burials belonging to the royal women and a mass burial of young soldiers. The anatomical evidence showed that they had suffered arrow and head wounds, and six of the bodies had been attacked by birds of prey. Their role in helping Mentuhotep achieve his military ambitions was obviously rewarded by transportation home and burial in the royal enclosure. Re-examination of the monument by Arnold for the German Archaeological Institute in Cairo (1966–71) led to the conclusion that originally a mastaba-type structure rather than a pyramid (as previously suggested) had stood at the centre of this monument.

Temple of Hatshepsut

This magnificent temple, partly cut into the Theban cliffside and partly built as a series of free-standing terraces, was originally surrounded by trees, flowers and statuary. Mariette made some preliminary excavations here, and in 1894–6 Naville uncovered the whole temple for the Egypt Exploration Fund. More recently, Winlock led an expedition for the Metropolitan Museum, New York, and cleared and excavated the temple; he discovered the smashed fragments of the queen's statues in pits on either side of the avenue leading to her temple and these were later restored and placed in the Metropolitan Museum, New York.

The temple has some particularly famous wall scenes, including the transportation of obelisks from Aswan to the Temple of Amun at Karnak; Hatshepsut's divine birth and coronation, underlining her legitimate claim to be pharaoh; and the trading expedition to Punt to acquire incense for the temples.

The mortuary temple of Ramesses II is known as the Ramesseum.
Belzoni removed part of a colossal granite statue of Ramesses from here;
it eventually entered the British Museum collection in 1817. The head
of a statue which once partnered it still remains at the Ramesseum.

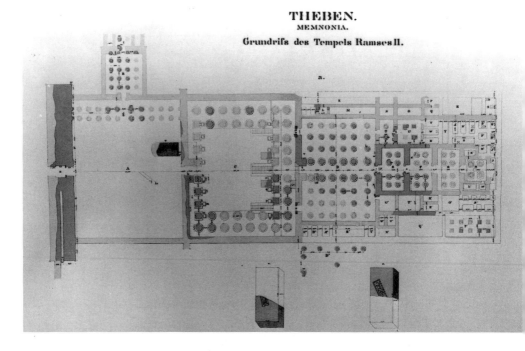

The information gathered by Lepsius on his expedition to Egypt (1842–5) filled seventeen volumes of the Denkmäler aus Aegypten und Aethiopien. *This plate shows a plan of the Ramesseum at Thebes.*

The construction of the temple appears to have been closely associated with Hatshepsut's most important courtier, Senenmut, who was Chief Steward of Amun. Winlock discovered the burial chamber he had prepared for himself under the front platform of the temple, but his power must have waned with Hatshepsut's own decline, and he was buried in another tomb situated, as befitted his status, amongst those of other nobles, in the hillside south of Deir el-Bahri.

By Ptolemaic and Roman times, Hatshepsut's temple had become a centre for the worship of two ancient sages, Imhotep (the vizier credited with the construction of the Step Pyramid at Sakkara and with the foundation of medical science in Egypt) and Amenhotep, son of Hapu (a wise man at the court of Amenophis III). Inscriptions on the walls of the upper terrace of the temple record the gratitude of the sick who were treated there, indicating that this became an important centre for medical treatment. Later, the temple was taken over by Coptic monks who, although they attempted to deface the wall inscriptions, retained the building as a monastery.

The Ramesseum

The Ramesseum was the mortuary temple of Ramesses II, although Diodorus described it as the Tomb of Osymandyas (this was a corruption of User-maat-re, one of the names of Ramesses II). In 1816, Belzoni achieved his first success for his employer Henry Salt when he removed part of a colossal granite statue of the king, which had once stood before the platform which lies in front of the hypostyle hall of the temple. It was originally one of a pair of statues, and the head of the other still remains in the Ramesseum, but Belzoni's prize was taken to London where it entered the British Museum in 1817. This statue, consisting of the upper part of the body across the waist, measures nearly 2.75 metres in height, nearly 2 metres across the shoulders, and weighs about 7 tonnes.

The remains of the temple that survive are substantial, and the building followed the traditional pattern, with two forecourts, a hypostyle hall, antechambers, sanctuary and subsidiary rooms. There are important wall reliefs on the First and Second Pylons which include scenes of the Battle of Kadesh. In addition to the temple, there are surrounding mudbrick magazines and other buildings which provide information about subsidiary structures found within a temple enclosure.

Near the Ramesseum, Petrie and Quibell undertook a number of excavations. In 1896, Petrie explored the remains of several other mortuary temples, and in 1896–7, he and Quibell investigated tombs of the Middle Kingdom and the Dynasty 22 tombs situated in brick buildings around the temple. The Berlin Museum expeditions, led by Anthes and Möller, excavated the area south of the Ramesseum (the Dynasty 22–25 cemeteries) in 1911 and 1913.

The Ramesseum, one of the major sites on the west bank, was recorded by many early visitors, including Sicard, Norden, Pococke, Burton, Champollion, Wilkinson and Lepsius. Eventually, a complete publication will be produced by the Centre of Documentation in Cairo.

Qurna

Temple of Sethos I

Sethos I built two mortuary temples which were both completed by his son, Ramesses II. The temple at Abydos is more elaborate and better preserved than his Theban temple at Qurna. This was dedicated to Amun and Sethos I's deified father, Ramesses I, as well as to the cult of Sethos I himself as a dead, deified king. It was visited by many early travellers, including Champollion, Hay, Wilkinson and Lepsius.

The Colossi of Memnon

These two great statues once flanked the entrance to the mortuary temple of Amenophis III which was later demolished and the material used to build Merneptah's mortuary temple. They represent Amenophis III, but in the Roman Period it was believed that they portrayed Memnon, the son of Eos and Tithonus, who killed Antilochus, Nestor's son, during the Trojan War. The northern statue was said to

'sing', a phenomenon first reported by Strabo who did not credit the story with much authenticity, but Pausanias and Juvenal accepted it as a fact. Caused by an internal vibration which had resulted from damage to the statue in an earthquake in 27 BC, the phenomenon ceased after the statue was repaired in AD 199, following a visit by the Emperor Septimius Severus. Earlier, in AD 130, the Emperor Hadrian, his wife Sabina, and a large retinue had spent several days here; according to the verses of the court poetess Balbilla (written in Greek on the legs of one of the statues), the statue sang for the emperor on three occasions, indicating how much he was respected by the gods. The Colossi were visited by many early travellers, including Sicard, Norden, Pococke, Roberts, Burton, Lepsius and Wilkinson.

Medinet Habu

The Medinet Habu enclosure contains two major temples and various subsidiary buildings.

Temple of Hatshepsut and Tuthmosis III

This temple, dedicated to Amun, was altered and enlarged several times in the reigns of Ramesses III, Shabaka, Taharka, Nectanebo I, Ptolemy VIII and Antoninus Pius. When Ramesses III built his own temple adjoining it, both buildings and the associated workshops, magazines, priests' houses and administrative offices were enclosed by a massive mudbrick wall. In the Ramesside period, Medinet Habu became the administrative centre of Thebes.

Temple of Ramesses III

Ramesses III's great mortuary temple was based on the design of the Ramesseum; in many aspects of his reign, this king attempted to emulate the achievements of his illustrious ancestor. Originally, the temple was linked with the Nile by means of a canal and landing quay. There are important historical wall reliefs in the temple, particularly on the exterior, where the king's campaigns against the Libyans, Asiatics and Sea Peoples are commemorated. Part of a brick-built palace located to the south of the temple's first court also survives. This was used by the king during religious ceremonies, and the Window of Appearances which linked the palace to the temple can still be seen.

In Christian times, a town was built inside the enclosure wall; the wall reliefs in the Temple of Ramesses III were plastered over and a church was put up in the second court. This church and town complex seems to have been abandoned by the 9th century AD, and in 1891 the temple court was cleared and the remains of the church were removed by the Antiquities Service.

The earlier temple was excavated by Daressy in 1894–5, as well as the tomb-chapels of the Saite princesses which were also found in this area. Medinet Habu was visited by many early travellers, including Burton, Champollion, Hay and Wilkinson, and from 1924 the Oriental Institute of the University of Chicago undertook an extensive epigraphic and architectural survey, under the direction of Nelson and Hölscher (an architectural historian from Hanover). This survey (with that carried out at Karnak) set new standards in copying and publishing temple reliefs; the epigraphers experimented with various techniques to provide near-exact copies of large wall surfaces which were covered with detailed scenes and texts, and used the skills and expertise of photographers, draughtsmen and Egyptologists. Studies of the important historical texts of Ramesses III have also been published by Edgerton and Wilson.

Domestic Buildings
Malkata

The Palace of Amenophis III

To the south-east of the Medinet Habu complex lay the royal town built by Amenophis III, which included a large palace known as the House of Joy. It was the custom for every king to build a new palace and, unlike the temples and tombs, these were mainly of mudbrick construction and included not only the private royal apartments but also major administrative quarters. This palace contained state apartments for Amenophis III, a residence for his chief wife, Queen Tiye, quarters for his harem and courtiers, a festival hall for the celebration of his

second jubilee festival, and various administrative buildings and workshops. His son, Amenophis IV-Akhenaten, spent the early years of his reign in residence here. The site, known today as Malkata, was excavated by Daressy; in 1901–2, Robb de Peyster Tytus joined Newberry to investigate the palace and a preliminary report was published in 1903. Later, further excavations were undertaken (1910–18) by Winlock and Lythgoe for the Metropolitan Museum, New York, and Hayes published the inscriptions from the palace.

Deir el-Medina

The village and cemetery of the royal necropolis workmen and their families lie on the Theban west bank, in a desolate location behind the hill of Qurnet Mura'i and some distance from the cultivated plain. The village, with its rows of some seventy terraced houses, was built by Tuthmosis I and, as the workforce expanded during the New Kingdom, more houses were built outside the village enclosure wall. The tombs of the workmen's families display some of the most interesting scenes of the Ramesside period; they have shafts leading to rock-cut burial chambers, and above there is a partly or completely free-standing tomb-chapel which incorporates a pylon, open court, portico, and vaulted chapel with a niche for the owner's statue. A small brick-built pyramid originally stood above the tomb. The wall scenes, usually painted but sometimes also carved, show many aspects of daily life and religious or funerary activities. There are also the chapels of the local gods near by, and the village rubbish heaps have provided a wealth of information regarding the social and legal arrangements of the inhabitants, as well as the working conditions of the Royal Gang. Amongst this material are the earliest references to the industrial action undertaken by the workmen in the Ramesside period. The community dwindled away at the end of Dynasty 20 when the royal cemetery was moved from Thebes to Tanis.

The Institut Français d'Archéologie Orientale has excavated here since 1922, and their series of volumes provides the most complete publication of a site in the Theban necropolis.

Bruyère, Nagel and ˘Cern´y undertook excavation and translation of texts from the village and tombs; Bruyère excavated two tombs of particular note belonging to Pachedu and Sennedjem, and also investigated the workmen's rest-houses where they stayed while working on the tombs in the Valley of the Kings, and the later tombs of Saite princesses. With Baraize, he excavated the votive chapels and the local Temple of Amenophis I (the community's patron); Baraize supplied Schiaparelli with objects for the Turin Museum and also excavated inside the local Ptolemaic temple enclosure in 1912. The Berlin Museum expedition, led by Möller, also undertook work at Deir el-Medina in 1911 and 1913.

Earlier travellers who had recorded the local Temple of Hathor, goddess of this area, included Rosellini, Burton, Prisse, Hay and Wilkinson.

Tombs

The cemeteries on the west bank at Thebes present the most confusing archaeological picture in Egypt. The area was used during Dynasties 11 and 17 and throughout the New Kingdom (Dynasties 18–20) for royal burials and the associated tombs of courtiers and officials. From the time of Napoleon's Egyptian adventure onwards, most archaeological expeditions were working at Thebes but, until government concessions began to be granted in the mid-19th century, they kept few records, and thus in many cases details regarding the locations of tombs and objects found in association with them have been lost.

Royal Tombs

el-Tarif

The cemetery of the earliest rulers of Dynasty 11 was situated in the northernmost part of the Theban necropolis. These large tombs, similar to non-royal provincial structures elsewhere, are now known as saff or row tombs. The three tombs of Inyotef I, II, and III were originally excavated by Winlock, and have been re-examined by Arnold for the German Institute of Archaeology in Cairo (1970–4).

Dra'abu el-Naga'

Situated in the northern part of the Theban necropolis, this area contained the burials of the rulers of Dynasty 17 and their families. Not a great deal of information survives about the architecture of these tombs which were not elaborate, although they may have incorporated small brick-built pyramids, but Papyrus Abbott, which records an inspection which was undertaken in antiquity, preserves details of their location and ownership.

Mariette discovered and excavated the tomb of Kamose (1857), and of Antef Nebkhepere in 1860; a year earlier, in the tomb of Queen Ah-hotep, his workmen had found a toilet box, weapons, and the jewellery which was to become the subject of conflict between Mariette and the governor of Qena. Other tombs were found by Passalacqua and the expedition financed by the Marquis of Northampton. Winlock also produced a study of this area, and agreed with Carter's identification of Amenophis I, the second ruler of Dynasty 18, as the owner of one specific tomb, although in fact its exact location still remains unknown.

The Valley of the Kings (Biban el-Moluk)

The Valley of the Kings accommodated the burials of most of the rulers and a few non-royal tombs of the New Kingdom (Dynasties 18–20). Chosen for its proximity to the capital city of Thebes, the area is dominated by the mountain formation which rises to a peak, the natural shape of which may have reminded the Egyptians of the pyramid form. The Valley has two main branches: an eastern valley contains most of the tombs but those of Amenophis III and Ay were found in the western valley. So far, sixty-two tombs have been uncovered but the only royal tomb which remained largely intact was that of Tutankhamun. The first king to build his burial place here was Tuthmosis I and the area was used until the reign of Ramesses XI at the end of Dynasty 20. Since there was no space to accommodate the royal mortuary temples adjacent to the tombs, these were now built on the edge of the cultivation.

Most tombs follow a general plan in which a rock-cut corridor inclines downwards to the burial chamber (before the end of Dynasty 18 this corridor turned either to the right or left, usually at a right-angle, but in later times, it was straight). The corridor is interrupted by one or more halls which sometimes have pillars which are all cut from the rock.

The wall and ceiling decoration of these tombs (unlike non-royal tombs which concentrate on aspects of daily life) is primarily concerned with the king's passage from this world to the next, and the scenes and inscriptions are taken from various funerary papyri, including the Books of the Dead, the Netherworld, Gates, Caverns and the Litany of Re. Naville published several of these texts, including the standard edition of the Book of the Dead, and in 1883, Lefebure made an inventory of all the information then available in the necropolis which was published in his *Hypogées royaux de Thèbes.* Maspero's studies, published in 1888–9 in the *Revue de l'histoire des religions,* pursued the subject further, and he was the first to identify the religious significance of many of the representations found in the sacred funerary books. Schiaparelli published his *Book of the Dead* (1882–90), and Piankoff, a Russian scholar who worked in Egypt from 1930 to 1966, overturned the earlier view that these tomb decorations were unworthy of further consideration and was able to demonstrate their true significance.

The first complete publication of a royal tomb, with an inventory, description, and translation of each part of the scene, was produced in 1954, as the result of the photographic survey of the tomb of Ramesses VI undertaken by the Bollingen Foundation for Piankoff in 1949–51. Hornung has continued Piankoff's important work in recording these tombs and subjecting them to scientific analysis, with the ultimate aim of studying all the royal tombs in the Valley.

In addition to the various expeditions and copyists who visited the Valley, Daressy produced an account, *Fouilles de la Vallée des Rois* (1898–9), which was one in the series of Cairo Museum Catalogues. Some of the most important discoveries and excavations of tombs include:

Tuthmosis I and II

Excavated by Loret in 1898–9, these were the earliest decorated tombs in the Valley and they provided new information for a study of the funerary texts.

Hatshepsut

This was excavated in 1903 by Carter for Theodore M. Davis, a wealthy businessman of Newport, Rhode Island. He gained the concession to have a monopoly to excavate in the Valley of the Kings, and engaged several archaeologists to undertake this work. Hatshepsut's tomb contained two sarcophagi, one for her own burial and one to receive the body of her father, Tuthmosis I, which she planned to transfer from his own tomb. She also had another tomb made in the cliff near Deir el-Bahri which had been prepared when she was principal queen, but once she seized the kingship she exercised her right to have a tomb in the Valley of the Kings, although it is unlikely that she was ever buried there.

Tuthmosis III

This tomb was discovered by Loret.

Amenophis II

In 1898, Loret discovered in this tomb the second cache of royal mummies, including those of Amenophis II, Tuthmosis IV, Amenophis III, Merneptah, Siptah and Sethos II.

Tuthmosis IV

Carter discovered this tomb in 1903 while he was excavating for Davis; it contained some funerary furniture, including a decorated chariot.

Amenophis III

Situated in the Western Valley, the tomb was discovered by Jollois and de Villiers of Napoleon's expedition, although they could not read the hieroglyphs and identify it correctly. It was later excavated by Davis, and by Carter and Carnarvon.

Tutankhamun

This tomb, complete with most of its treasure and the king's mummy, was discovered by

Carter on 4 November 1922 and opened shortly afterwards on 26 November.

The story of the tomb's excavation is one of the great romances of Egyptology; not only was this the greatest royal treasure ever found in Egypt but the discovery was followed by a spate of rumours about an ancient curse that would condemn to death all those connected with the excavation and disturbance of the boy-king's burial. Carter's patron, the 5th Earl of Carnarvon, died in April 1923 from pneumonia brought on by an infected mosquito bite, and this inspired the rumour of the curse. However, most members of the expedition lived a full span, and two of the ten staff were still alive forty years later.

Carnarvon, who had originally gone to Egypt in 1903 to restore his health, became fascinated with Egyptology and took on Howard Carter to excavate at Thebes on his behalf. Carter had worked as an artist many years earlier, recording tomb scenes for the Egypt Exploration Fund, and he later worked as an archaeologist, becoming Inspector of Monuments in Upper Egypt and Nubia in 1899.

Carter and Carnarvon worked on several projects at Thebes and when Theodore M. Davis relinquished his concession in the Valley of the Kings in 1914, they took it over. The war intervened, but in 1919 they resumed their search for Tutankhamun's tomb, and finally concentrated their efforts on a triangle of ground on the western side of the valley, marked by the tombs of Ramesses II, Merneptah and Ramesses VI. The pile of rubble, quarried when the latter tomb was built, remained at the site and effectively hid the entrance to Tutankhamun's tomb both from robbers in antiquity and also from the archaeologists.

However, Davis' earlier discovery of a small pit to the south-east of the place where Tutankhamun's tomb would be found guided Carter to his great discovery. The contents of this pit, which Winlock, visiting Davis' dig, correctly identified as materials used in Tutankhamun's mummification and the remains of his funerary meal, indicated that his tomb was in the vicinity.

It was to be Carter's final season of work in the Valley, as Carnarvon, disappointed with their lack of success, had decided to terminate his concession. Work started on 1 November and three days later the entrance to the tomb was revealed; a stone staircase led down to an intact sealed doorway, and ultimately to the burial and treasure beyond.

Carter, a patient and meticulous worker, took ten years to excavate and clear the four rooms of the tomb, and to make a detailed record of the treasures. They were cleaned, restored and photographed, and finally removed to the Cairo Museum. The staff who worked with Carter on this enormous task included Callender, Lucas (the Chief Chemist of the Egyptian Survey Department), the philologists Gardiner and Breasted, and, courtesy of the Metropolitan Museum in New York, the services of Mace, Burton (the photographer), Hall and Hauser (the draughtsmen).

However, bitterness and wrangling soon developed over the fate of the treasure and whether it should remain in Egypt or be divided between the Egyptian Government and the excavators. The concession had specified that, if an intact tomb should be found, the complete contents should remain in Egypt, but since the tomb had been plundered twice in antiquity, the situation was somewhat ambiguous. In the end, the treasure in its entirety remained in the Cairo Museum. However, the expedition's detailed notes and photographs are held at the Griffith Institute in Oxford. Although Carter and Mace published a general account of the discovery (*The Tomb of Tut-Ankh-Amen*, 1924), a definitive study of all the objects from the tomb remains to be completed.

Tomb 55

Discovered by Weigall for the Davis expedition in 1907, ownership of this tomb and its contents has been the subject of continuing controversy. The tomb contained a badly deteriorated mummy which was originally declared to belong to a woman; it was presumed to be the remains of Queen Tiye, wife of Amenophis III, and in 1910, the discovery was published under the title of *The Tomb of Queen Tïyi*. However, in a subsequent examination, Elliot Smith, Professor of Anatomy in Cairo, claimed that the body had belonged to a man aged around twenty-five at death; he also stated that the skull showed the characteristic distortion associated with hydrocephalus. It was speculated that this could be the body of the heretic king Akhenaten, brought back from Amarna to Thebes for a secret burial. Another examination by Derry, Elliot Smith's successor at Cairo, brought the age at death down to twenty-three and he could find no conclusive evidence of hydrocephalus. Also, since inscriptional evidence gives Akhenaten a reign of at least seventeen years, this body had to belong to someone else.

During the 1960s, further anatomical and serological studies carried out by Harrison and his colleagues indicated that this was the body of a man in his early twenties who was a close relative of Tutankhamun (probably a brother or half-brother) and of Amenophis III (perhaps his son). It has been suggested that it could belong to Smenkhkare who ruled briefly at Amarna.

Ay

This was one of the tombs in the Western Valley which was discovered by Belzoni in the early 19th century.

Horemheb

This tomb, built when Horemheb became king (earlier, when he was still a commoner, he had prepared a tomb at Sakkara), was discovered in 1908 by Ayrton for the Davis expedition. It contains fine reliefs and the earliest version of the Book of Gates, and, as it is partly unfinished, it demonstrates the sequence of tomb decoration.

Ramesses I

This was discovered by Belzoni in the early 19th century.

Sethos I

This tomb with its superb bas-relief wall decoration and painted ceilings is the finest in the Valley; the scenes represent the Books of the Netherworld, Gates, and the Celestial Cow, the Litany of Re and the Ceremony of Opening the Mouth. The deepest of the royal tombs, its discovery in October 1817 was the highlight of Belzoni's archaeological career. He and his

wife Sarah, with the artist Alessandro Ricci, recorded the wall scenes in a series of drawings and watercolours made in preparation for the model which was constructed and exhibited in London in 1821. Only a few of these paintings were used in Belzoni's publication but most of the originals are now in the Bristol City Museum; although they do not provide a perfect record, they are more reliable than many later copies, and preserve details which have subsequently been lost.

In April 1818, Belzoni returned to Thebes to remove the alabaster sarcophagus and other objects from the tomb. The sarcophagus, decorated with scenes from the Book of Gates, was put on display with the tomb model in London, and eventually, because of a dispute with the Trustees of the British Museum for whom it was intended, it entered Sir John Soane's collection. The mummy of Sethos I was found in one of the royal caches and is now in the Cairo Museum.

Ramesses III

Discovered by the early explorer James Bruce in 1769, this has sometimes been known as Bruce's Tomb or, on account of its wall decoration, as the Harper's Tomb.

Siptah

This tomb was discovered by the Davis expedition and part of the tomb equipment is now in the Metropolitan Museum in New York.

Ramesses VI

This was named La Tombe de la Métempsycose by Napoleon's expedition and the Tomb of Memnon by British scholars, since Ramesses VI had one of the same names as Amenophis III whom the Greeks had called Memnon.

It has been published in great detail by Piankoff.

Ramesses IX

This has been published by Guilmant, and by Maystre and Piankoff for the Mission archéologique française au Caire.

Yuya and Thuya

The parents of Tiye, Amenophis III's Great

Royal Wife, Yuya and Thuya were accorded the great honour of burial in the Valley although they were commoners. The tomb was discovered by Weigall for the Davis expedition in February 1905; the door seals had been broken and reinstated in antiquity, so the archaeologists knew that the tomb had been entered but when they gained access, they found the mummies, golden coffins and a considerable amount of treasure. This was the most complete burial discovered in the Valley until Tutankhamun's tomb was revealed seventeen years later. The treasure was removed within three weeks, and taken to the Cairo Museum.

Hatshepsut's Officials
The queen permitted several officials to be buried in the Valley in undecorated tombs, and some were even allowed to use the royal funerary texts. The vizier User was allowed to include scenes from the Book of the Netherworld and the Litany of Re, but this was a rare privilege for a non-royal person.

The Valley of the Tombs of the Monkeys
Here, Lortet, a French naturalist who made a special study of mummified animals, investigated tombs prepared for the burial of monkeys.

Carter (who explored this area in 1915–17) discovered the tomb of Neferure, daughter of Hatshepsut, and Winlock found the gold and silver treasure of three princesses belonging to the reign of Tuthmosis III, which is now in the Metropolitan Museum, New York.

The Valley of the Queens
The tombs here, dating mainly to Dynasties 19 and 20, belong to some of the queens and also to other members of the royal family, especially the princes of the Ramesside period.

Many were described by Champollion and Rosellini, and Lepsius, and over seventy have been discovered and excavated. Most of this work was undertaken in 1903–20 and 1926–7 by the Italian Archaeological Mission directed by Schiaparelli. Many of the tombs were unfinished and undecorated, but some superb wall scenes were also found here. The most famous tomb belonged

to Queen Nefertari, wife of Ramesses II, and although the painted reliefs have suffered considerable deterioration, a recent international project has undertaken extensive restoration of the tomb and will, it is hoped, arrest further decay.

Royal Caches
In the two great caches of royal mummies of Dynasties 17–20 which have so far been discovered, the human remains and coffins were gathered together and reburied in Dynasty 21. Although their original tombs had been plundered, the owners were thus given another chance to make use of their bodies to obtain sustenance on earth.

The first cache, discovered by a villager from Qurna in 1871 in Tomb 320 to the south of the Deir el-Bahri temples, came to official attention in 1881–2 when Maspero finally ordered the group to be moved to the Cairo Museum.

The second cache was discovered by Loret in 1898 in the tomb of Amenophis II in the Valley of the Kings, and transported to the Cairo Museum in 1901.

Non-Royal Tombs
The non-royal or private tombs belonging to courtiers and officials are scattered across several areas on the west bank, including Dra'Abu el-Naga', Deir el-Bahri, El-Khokha, 'Asasif, Sheikh Abd el-Qurna, Deir el-Medina and Qurnet Mura'i. Altogether, there are some five hundred numbered tombs which date from Dynasty 6 down to the Graeco-Roman Period, although most belong to the New Kingdom. Gardiner and Weigall listed 409 tombs supplied with the official numbers of the Antiquities Service in *A Topographical Catalogue of the Private Tombs of Thebes* (1913), and Bruyère, Davies and Fakhry have since added others.

There is considerable variation in the design of these tombs, although a general plan had developed during the New Kingdom. Many had an open rectangular forecourt behind which lay an inverted T-shaped chapel cut into the rock. At the rear of the chapel, or in a corner of the forecourt, a shaft descended to one or more subterranean burial chambers. Sometimes, the walls of the burial chamber were decorated with scenes,

A stone false door from a tomb at Sakkara (Old Kingdom, c.2500 BC). The spirit of the deceased was believed to enter through the false door into his tomb so that he could take possession of his mummy and gain sustenance from the food offerings.

but more usually these were restricted to the chapel. The transverse hall sometimes also had stelae set into the walls; a passage ran longitudinally from the centre of this hall back into the mountain, and at the far end, a small sanctuary contained a niche for statues of the tomb-owner and his wife, or sometimes a false door through which the owner's spirit could return to partake of the food offerings. The portico tombs belonging to the nobles of the Middle Kingdom provided the model for these Theban tomb-chapels which were introduced early in Dynasty 18, and this remained the standard form from which later designs were developed.

The scenes in non-royal tombs concentrated on the daily activities of the tomb-owner, his family, servants and subordinates, so that after death he could continue to retain his status and to experience the events he had enjoyed when he was alive. The Opening of the Mouth Ceremony, performed at the time of burial, was believed to bring to life by means of magic all the elements found in the scenes which, in addition to everyday events, also showed the owner's funeral and various other religious concepts.

Copyists who faithfully recorded many scenes in the Theban private tombs included Wilkinson, and Norman and Nina de Garis Davies. Wilkinson worked at Thebes in the 1820s, making detailed copies of inscriptions, reliefs and paintings, and preserving information about the tombs which sometimes have been subsequently damaged or destroyed, or have become inaccessible, or still await full publication.

The working partnership of Norman and Nina de Garis Davies provided some of the finest results ever achieved in copying tomb paintings. Norman de Garis Davies was commissioned by the Metropolitan Museum of Art, New York, to record principal tombs at Thebes, and his wife worked there for the Egypt Exploration Fund on *The Theban Tomb Series* (1915–33), edited by Gardiner. Three of the five volumes are entirely her work, and her husband co-operated with her on the other two volumes. Apart from brief periods at Amarna (1925–6) and Beni Hasan (1931–2), she worked entirely at Thebes (1908–39).

Nina de Garis Davies is acknowledged as one of the finest copyists of Egyptian paintings, in the tradition of Burton, Hay, Wilkinson and Carter. She set new standards in copying line and colour, and her brushwork most closely produced the original strokes of the ancient artists.

The main excavations and details of a small selection of some of the private tombs are mentioned here:

Dra'abu el-Naga'

There have been several excavations in this area, including those of Passalacqua (1822–5), Spiegelberg and Newberry for the 5th Marquis of Northampton (1898–99), Petrie (1908–9), Carnarvon and Carter (1908–13), and the University of Philadelphia (1921–3).

Important tombs include those of Panhesy (reign of Ramesses II) which has been published by the Mission archéologique française au Caire; Mentuhirkhopshef (reign of Tuthmosis III), published by Davies; Nebamun (Dynasty 18), published by Fakhry; and Antef (reigns of Hatshepsut and Tuthmosis III), published by Säve-Söderbergh; and Kenamun (Dynasty 18), published by Daressy (1895), and Davies and Faulkner (1947). In addition, the tomb of Neferhotep (probably reigns of Tuthmosis III to Amenophis II) was mentioned by Cailliaud, Hay, Wilkinson, and Rosellini, and was known as Mr Salt's tomb, but its exact location is now lost.

'Asasif

In this area, near the causeway of the temple of Hatshepsut at Deir el-Bahri, exploration was undertaken by Lepsius and Passalacqua who discovered some Middle Kingdom tombs; the concession was later assigned to Carnarvon and Carter who worked there for five years, and to the Metropolitan Museum, New York. The burials date from the Middle and New Kingdoms, and the Saite Period. Important tombs include those of Kheruef (reigns of Amenophis III and IV), published by Davies and by Fakhry; Pedamenopet (Saite), published by Duemichen; and Mentuemhet (Dynasty 25–26), published by Barguet, Goneim and Leclant.

Deir el-Bahri

Apart from the temples of Hatshepsut and Mentuhotep, a number of cemeteries were also excavated in this area.

In the Mentuhotep Temple area, burials associated with the temple were discovered when Naville and Hall found the pits containing the burials of the royal women, and Winlock uncovered the slain soldiers.

Near Hatshepsut's temple, the Metropolitan Museum excavations revealed the tomb of a queen of Amenophis II. Two great caches with group burials including coffins and other goods were also found. The first was uncovered by

Mariette in 1858 in the subterranean area of the temple, and it contained the burials of the priests of Montu, from Dynasties 22 to 26. The second group, belonging to the priests and priestesses of Amun (Dynasty 21) were discovered by Grébaut and Daressy in 1891, in a family tomb probably belonging to Thonefri which reused a Dynasty 11 pit. Most objects from these caches went to the Cairo Museum, but some found their way into other museums or private collections. Also, other tombs of priests and priestesses of the Third Intermediate Period were found in this area by Naville in 1894.

el-Khokha

The tomb of Userhet (reign of Amenophis III) was excavated in the 1860s by Rhind, who developed new scientific techniques of clearing and recording tombs.

Sheikh Abd el-Qurna

The tombs in this area include several excavated by Rhind (1855–7), the uninscribed tomb belonging to Senenmut's parents from which the objects went to the Metropolitan Museum, New York, and the Prince of Wales Tomb. The latter contained many coffins which dated to the reigns of Bocchoris and Tefnakht, but these had probably been brought together here so that they could be 'discovered' on the occasion of the Prince's visit to Egypt. Another group of coffins was found in 1823 by Lebolo in a pit dating to the Roman Period, and some of these went to Turin, Berlin and the British Museum. Fakhry also excavated here in the 1930s.

Several important tombs have been published, including those of User (reign of Tuthmosis I) by Davies; Dhout (reign of Amenophis II); and Amenemhet (reign of Tuthmosis III), both by Davies and Gardiner; Nakht (reign of Tuthmosis IV) by Maspero and by Davies; Ramose, sometimes called Stuart's tomb, by Stuart and by Davies; Haremhab (reign of Tuthmosis III) by Bouriant; Menkheper (reigns of Tuthmosis III and Amenophis II) by Virey; and Rekhmire (reigns of Tuthmosis III and Amenophis II), recorded by Champollion, Hay and Wilkinson, and by Virey, Newberry, and Davies.

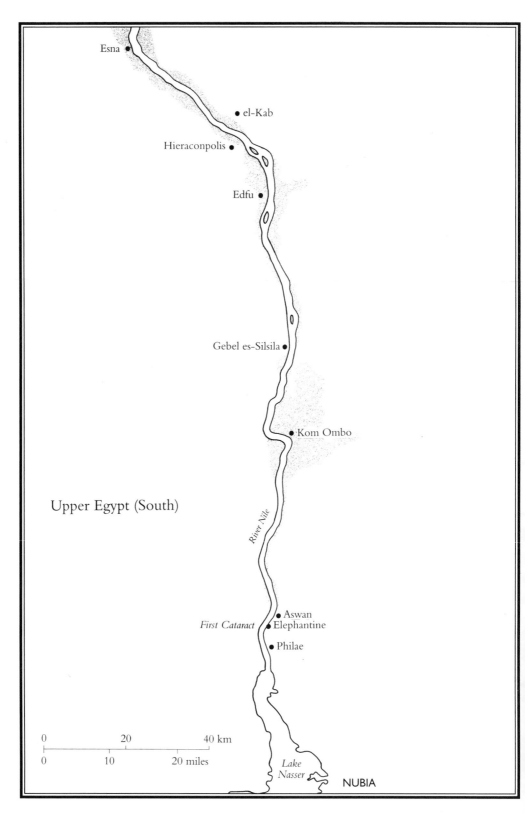

Esna

el-Kab

Hieraconpolis

Edfu

Gebel es-Silsila

Kom Ombo

Upper Egypt (South)

River Nile

Aswan
First Cataract Elephantine
Philae

0   20   40 km

0   10   20 miles

Lake
Nasser   NUBIA

Qurnet Mura'i

This area is in the vicinity of the Ramesseum. An important tomb belonging to Amenhotep called Huy, the Viceroy of Kush (reigns of Amenophis IV and Tutankhamun) was published by Davies and Gardiner.

Upper Egypt (South)

Esna

This ancient Egyptian town of Iunyt (Greek Latopolis) was the centre of veneration of the latos, a Nile fish.

. The necropolis contains burials dating from the Middle Kingdom to the Late Period, and there were apparently several temples in the area in antiquity. The main temple (only partly excavated) lies in the middle of the modern town; it was dedicated to Khnum and to several companion deities including Neith, Heka, Satet and Menheyet. Only the hypostyle hall is well preserved; the west wall (decorated with scenes of Ptolemy VI and VIII) was part of the inner area of the temple but the rest of the hall was completed in the Roman Period. Here, the reliefs dating from the first three centuries AD show the emperors as pharaohs, offering to the Egyptian gods. A series of texts on the columns provide a calendar of the festivals held during the sacred year at Esna. This temple is the latest of those built during the Graeco-Roman Period which has survived until today. It was visited by Napoleon's savants, Rosellini and Champollion, Pococke and Norden, and has been studied and published by Sauneron (1962). The tombs at Esna were excavated by De Morgan and Garstang.

el-Kab

The sites of the ancient town of Nekheb on the eastern bank of the river together with Nekhen (Kom el-Ahmar) on the west bank were very important settlements in the Predynastic and early Dynastic Periods. Nekheb was the cult-centre of Nekhbet, one of the royal patroness deities of predynastic Egypt who assisted in divine and royal births. In Graeco-Roman times she was identified with Eileithyia, the Greek goddess who assisted women in childbirth, and consequently the town was renamed Eileithyiaspolis. At one time, Nekheb was capital of the 3rd nome of Upper Egypt.

The ruins of Nekheb are surrounded by a massive brick enclosure wall which contains the main temple of Nekhbet (this building dates to the New Kingdom, with later additions), some smaller temples, a sacred lake, and earlier cemeteries of the Old Kingdom which Quibell excavated in 1897.

To the north-east of the enclosure, at the entrance to Wadi Hellal, there is a desert-temple built to the goddess Shesmetet during the Ptolemaic Period; to the south-east there is a chapel, probably used for the worship of Re-Harakhte, Hathor, Amun, Nekhbet and Ramesses II, which was constructed by Setau, Viceroy of Kush under Ramesses II (it was restored in Ptolemaic times); and another temple was built by Tuthmosis IV and Amenophis III for Hathor and Nekhbet.

The nearby hill contains over thirty tombs which date to the late Middle Kingdom, early Dynasty 18, or Ramesside Period. Particularly important tombs belonged to Paheri, the mayor of Nekheb (reign of Tuthmosis III), which has fine wall reliefs; Ahmose Pennekheb, who fought in the wars waged in the reigns from Amosis to Tuthmosis III and whose famous biographical text is in this tomb; and Ahmose, son of Ebana, whose tomb inscription records his life and military deeds in the war of liberation against the Hyksos.

el-Kab was visited by Burton, Champollion and Rosellini, Hay, Lane, Denon, Nestor l'Hôte, and Wilkinson. The town and cemeteries were excavated by Somers Clarke (1893) and Quibell (1897), and Somers Clarke also explored the desert temples.

Hieraconpolis (Kom el-Ahmar)

On the west bank of the river, opposite Nekheb (el-Kab), there are the extensive ruins of the ancient town of Nekhen (Greek Hieraconpolis). Nekhen and Nekheb had formed the capital of the Upper Egyptian kingdom in predynastic times, while the associated towns of Dep (Buto) and Pe in the Delta represented the capital of the Lower Egyptian Kingdom.

A detail of a capital in the Temple of Horus at Edfu. In these later temples composite capitals incorporating several plants replaced the simpler forms of Pharaonic times. The hieroglyphs shown here represent a late phase of the language which is known today as Ptolemaic Egyptian.

The chief god of Nekhen was the falcon Nekheny who was identified with Horus at an early date. In the temple at Nekhen, Quibell, Green and Somers Clarke (1897–9) found the cache (Main Deposit) of votive offerings which had been presented to the temple in earlier times and subsequently gathered together and placed in this deposit. This included carved maceheads, stone vessels, the statuettes of King Khasekhem, and slate palettes – in particular, the famous Narmer palette that commemorated the king's conquest of the north and the unification of Egypt. Narmer and Khasekhem had contributed most of the votive offerings in this temple (which is the earliest such building yet found) but there were additions from many later peri-

ods, the most important being two large copper statues of Pepy I and Merenre.

This town enclosure of Dynasty 1 (known as Kom el-Ahmar) had replaced an earlier settlement on the edge of the desert. The predynastic areas were extensive, and at the end of the 19th century a brick-built underground tomb was discovered in the eastern part of the settlement; it is known as the Decorated Tomb 100, but its location is now lost. However, the record of this tomb is of considerable importance because, on the west wall, there was a large painting of men, animals and boats which provides early evidence of the development of tomb decoration, although the 'typical' Egyptian tomb art, with its horizontal registers of scenes and formalized figures does not emerge before the Old Kingdom. The tomb probably belonged to a local predynastic ruler.

Hieraconpolis also had a series of decorated and inscribed rock-cut tombs, dating from Dynasty 6 to Dynasty 18. In addition to the work of Quibell, Green and Somers Clarke, excavations were carried out here by Petrie, Brunton, Garstang and Lansing, and Bouriant produced studies of the tomb inscriptions.

Edfu

This was the site of the ancient town of Dbot, which was known in Graeco-Roman times as Apollonopolis Magna, after the chief god Horus-Apollo. It was the capital of the 2nd nome of Upper Egypt.

The site has a long history: mastaba tombs have been excavated here (by Alliot for the Institut Français), and the ancient town lies partly under the modern dwellings, but the temple (built and decorated from 237 BC to 57 BC and based on buildings that go back to the Old Kingdom) remains the best-preserved example in Egypt. The Building Texts inscribed on the outer girdle-walls provide details of its construction, and also preserve information about the mythical interpretation of this and all other temples as the Island of Creation. There are also important scenes and inscriptions of the Sacred Drama which related the age-old conflict between Horus and Seth.

The temple was dedicated to Horus, Hathor of Denderah, and the young Horus. Each year, Hathor travelled south from her temple at Denderah to visit Horus at Edfu, and this event marking their sacred marriage was the occasion of a great festival and pilgrimage.

The temple was visited by Napoleon's savants, Rosellini and Champollion, Bonomi, Hay, and Norden. It was cleared by Mariette, and studied and published by De Rochemonteix and Chassinat.

Gebel es-Silsila

North of Aswan, the steep sandstone cliffs on both banks converge so that the river is substantially narrowed and provides a natural barrier. In very early times, this place was regarded as the source of the Nile, and later there were special festivals held here for Hapy, the river-god.

From the New Kingdom until Graeco-Roman times, the quarries on both banks were worked extensively, and many rock stelae and graffiti still remain; in the reign of Ramesses II, it is recorded that some 3,000 men were employed

here to cut stone to build the Ramesseum at Thebes.

The two banks have many rock-cut shrines or cenotaphs belonging to rulers and high officials. On the west bank there is the Great Speos (rock-cut chapel) of Horemheb, dedicated to the king and other deities. Other cenotaphs were placed at Gebel es-Silsila by Sethos I, Ramesses II and Merneptah. An interesting stela of Akhenaten (on the east bank) records that he ordered an obelisk to be quarried here for his Aten temple at Karnak.

Several early travellers visited this site, and studies of the stelae, shrines and graffiti have been made by Griffith and Legrain.

Kom Ombo

This ancient Egyptian town of Ombos was a strategically important site, but it only became a major centre in Ptolemaic times, when it became the capital of a separate Ombite nome. The temples were built by the Ptolemies and later additions were made in the Roman Period; early sanctuaries have left few traces, although Champollion reported a gateway of Dynasty 18 in the southern enclosure wall, when he visited the site.

The building is unique in that it is a 'double' temple, with the courts, halls, sanctuaries and rooms duplicated for two sets of gods: Sobek (the crocodile god) with Hathor and Khonsu in the southern half, and Haroeris (Horus the Elder), with Tasenetnofret (the Good Sister, a special form of Hathor) and Panebtawy (Lord of the Two Lands) in the northern part. The scene on the inner face of the rear wall of the temple is of particular interest, and probably represents a set of surgical instruments. In the courtyard there are several subsidiary features including a birth house and a well.

All the temple buildings in the southern part of the plateau were cleared and restored by De Morgan in 1893. The site was visited by Norden, Belzoni, Nestor l'Hôte, Champollion and Wilkinson, and studies have been made by Bouriant, Legrain, Jéquier and Barsanti.

Aswan and Elephantine

The district around modern Aswan, including the island of Elephantine, was the ancient Egypt-

The monuments on the island of Elephantine at Aswan demonstrate the importance of the place in antiquity as the gateway to Nubia. The buildings were described by many early travellers. This scene of one of the ruined temples is from Pococke's Travels in Egypt *(1814).*

ian town of Yebu (Greek Syene). It was the capital of the 1st Upper Egyptian nome, and was always of great importance to the Egyptians because it lay just north of the First Cataract which was the natural barrier between Egypt and Nubia. In addition to its role as a garrison town, it was near to the mineral deposits and the granite quarries, and was also a great trading centre from which expeditions set out to Nubia and the Sudan. It was almost continuously important from early dynastic times, and there are remains of monuments from many periods.

The Island of Elephantine

The main town and temple areas are at the south end of the island. Excavation has revealed material from an early dynastic votive deposit; there is a small temple erected by Trajan, reusing blocks from New Kingdom buildings, and the remains of a large temple built by Alexander II. Burials of rams, sacred to Khnum, have also been excavated, and these mummified animals were provided with gilded cartonnage headpieces and stone coffins. The buildings on the island were described by Napoleon's expedition, Prisse, Norden, Champollion, Minutoli,

Wilkinson, Firth, Hay, and Bonomi, and they record that part of a small temple of Amenophis III and a building of Tuthmosis III were almost complete in the early 19th century. The town and temple enclosure were excavated by Honroth and others (1906–8) and by Strazzulli and others in 1918, and the ram cemetery was explored by Clermont-Ganneau and Clédat.

The most famous monument on the island is the Nilometer. Strabo's account describes it thus:

The Nilometer is a well built of regular hewn stones, on the bank of the Nile, in which is recorded the rise of the stream, not only the maximum but also the minimum and average rise, for the water in the well rises and falls with the stream. On the side of the well are marks, measuring the height sufficient for the irrigation and other water levels. These are observed and published for general information… This is of importance to the peasants for the management of the water, the embankments, the canals and so forth, and to the officials on account of the taxes, for the higher the rise of water, the higher are the taxes.

The Nilometer has a staircase leading down into the river, beside which are cubit markings for measuring the height of the water. The records of the inundation levels which can be seen date to the Roman Period; the Nilometer was reinstated for use in 1870 AD. It was visited by Pococke, Bonomi, Young and Wilkinson, and studied by De Morgan, Borchadt and Jéquier.

An important discovery was made on the island in 1900–6. Wilbour had bought several papyrus rolls in 1893 from women on Elephantine; he showed them to Sayce who recognized that they were inscribed in Aramaic, and when others were subsequently discovered, they revealed the existence of a Jewish colony on Elephantine during the Persian Period. This community served as a garrison of frontier soldiers who lived here with their families, and they were allowed to build their own temple to Yahweh, although there were some conflicts with the local priests of Khnum.

Granite quarries

South of Elephantine, situated in the hills, are the famous granite quarries where the Egyptians acquired the hard stone for their building projects. Two colossal pieces were left *in situ* here: an almost complete figure of Osiris, and an unfinished obelisk which was abandoned because it developed severe faults during the quarrying process. The quarries are mentioned by Napoleon's expedition and De Morgan.

Rock-cut tombs

On the west bank to the north of the town at Qubhet el-Hawa are the tombs of local dignitaries of Elephantine – the men who led the Old Kingdom trading expeditions to the south, the Middle Kingdom nomarchs, and New Kingdom officials.

One group was discovered by Grenfell (1885–7), and there have been various studies by De Morgan, Bouriant, Legrain, Jéquier and Barsanti; others were excavated in 1902 by Lady William Cecil. The tombs of Dynasty 6 are decorated in the provincial style but include some interesting texts: most important are those of Mekhu, Sabni, Hekaib (who was later deified and had a local cult in the Middle Kingdom), and Harkhuf (who provides details of four expeditions to Nubia and includes the text of Pepy II's letter in which the boy-king anxiously enquires after the dwarf which Harkhuf is bringing back for him). The tomb of Sirenput, an official in the reign of Ammenemes II, has particularly impressive wall decoration and inscriptions and has been studied by Budge and Gardiner.

Nubia

South of the First Cataract lies the region the ancient Egyptians called Nubia (which covers the modern districts of southern Egypt and northern Sudan). As a major source of gold, minerals, stone and exotic goods from further south, Nubia was exploited and then colonized by the Egyptians. The trading expeditions of the Old Kingdom were replaced by a policy of direct military control in the Middle Kingdom, when fortresses were built as far south as the Second Cataract. In the New Kingdom, Egyptian control was extended beyond the Fourth Cataract, many impressive temples were built, and the area was effectively Egyptianized. In the Late Period the kings of Dynasty 25 came from Nubia and reversed the power balance, ruling the Nile Valley until the Assyrians drove them back to the south beyond the Fourth Cataract, where they continued a form of Egyptian civilization which is often referred to by modern scholars as the Meroitic culture.

When the Aswan Dam was built and subsequently raised in the early 1900s, many of the sites and monuments were threatened by the increased water level, and the Egyptian Survey Department inaugurated an Archaeological Survey of Nubia. This rescue project involved a general description of the entire area, detailing the sequence of cultures, and a rapid excavation of sites which were deemed to be of particular importance. Reisner developed the basic methods and principles which were used for this survey (1907–8) and his meticulous attention to detail and his ability to gain an overview of the culture enabled him to establish the foundations for later work in Nubia. Another important aspect of the survey – the excavation and examination of large numbers of skeletal remains – was undertaken by Elliot Smith and Wood Jones.

With the decision taken by the governments of Egypt and the Sudan in the late 1950s to build the new High Dam at Aswan, there was an urgent need for further action. This construction involved the creation of a great lake behind the dam which would flood an area of some 300 miles of Nubia and result in the loss of many archaeological sites, including over twenty temples. An appeal was made through UNESCO for international help to save as many monuments as possible before completion of the dam in 1965, and generous terms were offered to participating countries who were willing to provide architects, engineers, archaeologists and copyists. In return for their contribution, they would receive a major division of the objects found in the course of excavation and, in some cases, temples which would otherwise have been lost were presented to these countries, to be relocated abroad.

The project was extremely successful: two high profile rescue missions were undertaken at Abu Simbel and Philae to remove the temples and re-establish them in safe positions near to the original sites; several temples and monuments were removed from their original situations and rebuilt at New Kalabsha near Aswan in an open-air museum; and other temples were transported to Europe and America. The scope and scale of this international co-operation of the 1960s were unprecedented in the history of archaeology.

Major Unesco Salvage Operations

Philae

The original island of Pi-lak, situated at the First Cataract, was adorned with a number of monuments; because of its visual appeal and historical interest, it was visited and the buildings were recorded by many early travellers, including Rosellini, Hay, Bonomi, Norden and Lepsius.

The oldest buildings on the island date to Nectanebo I, but there are blocks which can be traced back to Dynasty 25. The temples were mainly built by the Ptolemies and the Roman Emperors. The last known hieroglyphic inscription (ad 394) survives here, and even when Egypt had become Christianized and two churches were established at Philae in the middle of the 4th century ad, the ancient cults continued to be practised until Justinian (ad 527–565) finally obliterated them, and some of the temple chambers were then converted for Christian services.

The island represented the primeval mound where creation had taken place, and the main cult was dedicated to Isis; Osiris (whose tomb – one of many – was situated on the neighbouring island of Biga), Nephthys, Hathor, Khnum and Satet were also worshipped here.

Lyons published a report on the island and its temples in 1896, and Bénédite also produced a study of the main temple.

With the heightening of the first Aswan Dam in the early 20th century the island became submerged for most of the year. When the High Dam was built, the temples were completely dismantled and rebuilt on the neighbouring island of Agilkia and this has ensured that they now remain above the water level throughout the year.

Abu Simbel

The two great rock-cut temples built by Ramesses II at Abu Simbel are amongst the most spectacular monuments in Egypt.

The Great Temple was dedicated to Ptah, Amen-Re, Re-Harakhte and Ramesses II, who was deified during his own lifetime, and contains important scenes of his military successes at the Battle of Kadesh and in the Syrian, Libyan and Nubian wars. On the south wall in the forecourt there is a stela which commemorates the king's marriage to a Hittite princess, marking the end of hostilities between the Egyptians and the Hittites.

Burckhardt was the first modern traveller to discover the temple, in 1813, and apparently as a result of his information, Belzoni went south to excavate it in 1817. It was cleared of sand-drifts by Lepsius and again by Mariette (1869), and in 1909 Barsanti undertook further work there, removing the rubbish which covered the northern colossal statue at the front of the temple. To the south of the temple is a small chapel which Amelia Edwards and her fellow travellers discovered in 1874.

The Smaller Temple, also built by Ramesses II, was dedicated to Hathor and his favourite wife, Queen Nefertari. The king and queen are represented by six large standing figures on the façade of the temple.

Both temples were moved between 1964 and 1968, in one of the most dramatic exercises of the UNESCO Salvage Campaign, to a new location slightly further away from the river and at a higher level, so that they would not be submerged by the rising waters of the lake which was created by the construction of the High

In early photographs (as here), monuments on Philae sometimes appear partly covered by the annual inundation. When the first dam was built at Aswan, the island was submerged for most of the year. After the construction of the High Dam the temples were dismantled and moved to a neighbouring island.

Dam. A cofferdam was built to hold back the waters of Lake Nasser while the temples were cut into large blocks and dismantled. The façades and interior walls were then rebuilt in their new positions; this also involved the construction of concrete dome-shaped buildings which would act as replacements for the original mountain into which the temples had been cut. The temples were reopened in 1968 and are an appropriate and impressive tribute to the international co-operation of the UNESCO operation to save the Nubian monuments.

Temples Rebuilt at New Kalabsha

These temples were transported from their original sites and re-erected on a promontory near Aswan; this work was undertaken by the German Archaeological Expedition.

Beit el-Wali

This rock-cut temple, originally located north of the Temple of Kalabsha, was built by Ramesses II and dedicated to Amen-Re and other gods. It has important historical scenes showing the king conquering the Nubians, and the Syrians and Libyans. Many early travellers visited the temple, and it has been published by Roeder.

Kalabsha

This important monument – the largest free-standing temple in Egyptian Nubia – was originally located near the ancient town of Talmis. Built on an earlier sanctuary of Amenophis II, the temple was constructed in Augustus' reign but was never finished; it was dedicated to the Nubian god Mandulis.

The temple was visited by Champollion, Bonomi, Belzoni and Wilkinson, but it had been submerged for most of the year since the first Aswan Dam was built early in this century. It was dismantled in 1963 and rebuilt at New Kalabsha; the gate was transported to the Ägyptisches Museum in Berlin. The temple has been published by Gauthier and by Gau.

Monuments Rebuilt Elsewhere In Egypt

Amada

This temple, built in Dynasty 18 and dedicated to Amen-Re and Re-Harakhte, had further additions made by Ramesside kings. Two important historical inscriptions describe Amenophis II's campaign in Asia and Merneptah's defeat of the Libyan invasion. Between 1964 and 1975 the temple was moved to a new location near the original site. It was described by several early travellers, and has been published by Gauthier.

el-Derr

This temple was built by Ramesses II for Re-Harakhte, in the style of his great temple at Abu Simbel, and it includes wall scenes showing the king's Nubian campaign. It was dismantled in 1964 and relocated near the Temple of Amada. Early travellers visited the original site, and it was studied and published by Blackman.

Aniba

This was the site of the ancient Mi'am, the capital of Wawat (situated in Lower Nubia between the First and Second Cataracts) in the New Kingdom. It probably developed from a Middle Kingdom fortress, and there are extensive Middle and New Kingdom cemeteries which were excavated by Steindorff for the von Sieglin expedition (1912–14). Other work was undertaken here by Woolley and Randall-MacIver, and by the University of Pennsylvania. The site was visited by several early travellers, and the rock-cut tomb of Penniut, the Viceroy of Wawat under Ramesses VI, has now been moved to a new site near Amada.

Below: The Temple of Amada appears in its original location in this early photograph; it was moved elsewhere between 1964 and 1975. Built in the New Kingdom, it preserves two important historical inscriptions which describe famous military campaigns.

Right: Colossal figures of the god Osiris are an impressive feature of the main hypostyle hall of the temple at Abu Simbel. Shown here in their original location, they were moved by the UNESCO project in the 1960s.

el-Sebu'a

This was the site of two temples; the earlier one was built by Amenophis III and restored by Ramesses II, who also built the large temple dedicated to his own cult and those of Amen-Re and Re-Harakhte. Visited by several early travellers, the site was published by Gauthier, and the monuments have been moved by UNESCO to a new location a short distance away.

el-Dakka

This temple at the site of the ancient Egyptian Pselqet (Greek Pselchis) was built by the Ptolemies, a Meroitic king, and Augustus and Tiberius on the site of an earlier monument. Early travellers came here, and the site has been studied by Firth (1909–10), and Roeder. It was

Details of a doorway and registers of scenes can be seen in this early photograph of a temple built by Augustus. Known in modern times as the Temple of Dendur (after a nearby village), it has been dismantled and re-erected in the Metropolitan Museum, New York.

dismantled between 1962 and 1968 and moved to a new location near el-Sebu'a.

The Fortress at Qasr Ibrim

This important site, lying south of the modern village of Ibrim on the east bank of the river, is situated on top of a hill. Known as Qasr Ibrim (the Castle of Ibrim), it was partly constructed in Roman times under the prefecture of Gaius Petronius, during Augustus' reign. However, it was probably originally a pharaonic site, and material from the New Kingdom and from later periods has been found here. In the west slope of the fortress hill there are a number of rock-cut memorial chapels dedicated by various Viceroys of Kush to New Kingdom rulers and various deities. The reliefs from these buildings were removed by UNESCO to a new location near el-Sebu'a, and a large New Kingdom rock stela which was once situated south of the fort was taken to New Kalabsha.

The site was visited by several early travellers and was excavated by Randall-MacIver and

Woolley for the Eckley B. Coxe Expedition for the University of Pennsylvania (1911); more recent work has been undertaken there by the Egypt Exploration Society.

Nubian Temples Transported Abroad

Dabod
Built by the Meroitic king Adikhalamani in the early 3rd century BC and enlarged by the Ptolemies, this temple (dedicated to Amun) was visited and studied by Burckhardt, Wilkinson, Belzoni, Champollion, Bonomi, and Rifaud. It is mentioned by Irby and Mangles, travellers who reached the Second Cataract and published their account in *Travels in Egypt, Nubia, Syria and Asia Minor in 1817 and 1818*, and it has been published more recently by Roeder. Dismantled in 1960–1, it was presented to Spain and re-erected (1970) in a park in Madrid.

Tafa
Two temples of the Roman Period originally stood here, and were visited by Burckhardt, Wilkinson, Bonomi and Norden, but the southern temple disappeared in the 19th century. The unfinished northern temple was dismantled in 1960 and presented to the Rijksmuseum van Oudheden in Leiden, Holland. It has been published by Roeder.

Dendur
This small temple originally stood opposite the modern village of Dendur; it was built by Augustus and dedicated to several gods including the deified sons of Quper, named Peteese and Pihor. The temple was visited by Champollion, Bonomi, Wilkinson, Irby and Mangles, and was studied and published by Blackman. Dismantled in 1963, it was presented to the USA and re-erected in 1978 in the Sackler Wing of the Metropolitan Museum in New York.

el-Lessiya
Several rock-cut grottoes on the east bank of the river included a chapel of the reign of Tuthmosis III with a niche which originally contained statues of the king and various deities (damaged in the Amarna Period), and decoration showing Tuthmosis III in the company of several gods. This was recorded by Hay, Lepsius and Weigall, and in 1966, the chapel was presented to Italy and is now in the Turin Museum.

Sites In Upper Nubia

To the south of Abu Simbel there are many important sites which span the southernmost area of Egypt and northern Sudan. They are not easily visited today but were of considerable importance in antiquity and so a brief account of them is given here. There are three main categories: the fortified towns established in the Middle and New Kingdoms to consolidate Egypt's power in the area; the towns and temples built by New Kingdom rulers to impress the local population with their might; and the towns, pyramid fields, and temples built by the kings of Dynasty 25 and their descendants (the rulers of the Napatan and Meroitic kingdoms).

Early travellers who made their way to the Sudan included Champollion, Rosellini, Bankes, Prudhoe, Lepsius, Wilkinson and Hoskins; a particularly interesting account is given by Cailliaud in his *Voyage à Méroé au Fleuve Blanc, 1819–22*. There have been several major archaeological expeditions, including those of Randall-MacIver and Woolley for the University Museum of Pennsylvania (the Eckley B. Coxe Jr. Expedition) in 1909–11; of Griffith (the Oxford University Expedition, 1910–12); Garstang's excavations at Meroë (1909–14); and the work undertaken at the Napatan and Meroitic sites by Reisner, Dows Dunham, and Chapman for the Boston-Harvard Expeditions from 1913 until the 1950s. The Egypt Exploration Society has worked at Buhen, and Griffith pioneered the study of the Meroitic inscriptions.

Fortresses
These were built in the region of the Second and Third Cataracts during the Middle and New Kingdoms, and were garrisoned by Egyptian soldiers. The best known are Serra East, Kor, Mirgissa, Uronarti, Kumma (Semna East), Semna, Semna South, and Sai.

Buhen, on the west bank of the Nile south of Wadi Halfa, was particularly significant in protecting the region of the Second Cataract. It was developed as a fort in the Middle Kingdom and had two major temples of New Kingdom date (both of these have now been removed to Khartoum). The North Temple, built by Amenophis II, was dedicated to Isis and Min, and the South Temple (cleared by General Sir Charles Smith in 1887) was constructed by Hatshepsut, Tuthmosis III and Taharka for the deity known as Horus of Buhen. To the west and north are the Middle and New Kingdom cemeteries excavated by Randall-MacIver and Woolley in 1909–10 (they also dug the Main Fort and the temples).

New Kingdom Sites

Important Egyptian temples and other monuments were built at several sites by rulers of Dynasties 18 and 19; these included Faras, Serra West, Dibeira East and West, Amara West, Sedeinga, Soleb, Sesebi, Nauri, and Tombos. The temples built by Amenophis III at Sedeinga and Soleb are of special interest, and the presence of an Aten temple at Sesebi indicates the geographical extent of Akhenaten's religious reforms; at Nauri and Tombos, various stelae with historical inscriptions provide important information.

Napatan / Meroitic Kingdom Sites

Much of the work at these sites, situated between the Third and Sixth Cataracts, was pioneered by Reisner, who moved to the Sudan prior to the First World War and excavated there for many years, at Napata (Gebel Barkal), el-Kurru, Nuri and Meroë, as well as further north at Semna and Kumma (Middle Kingdom fortresses) and Kerma (a Second Intermediate Period settlement and cemetery).

Some of the most important Napatan and Meroitic sites include: Kawa (temples of Amun); el-Kurru (where Reisner found the pyramids of the kings and queens of Dynasty 25 and twenty-four graves of horses with rich trappings, sacrificed at the time of the kings' deaths); and Napata. At this site, there is a high table-mountain (known today as Gebel Barkal) which was believed to be the dwelling of Amun, and tem-

ples and chapels were built to this god by the rulers of the New Kingdom, Dynasty 25, and the Napatan and Meroitic kingdoms. Napata, always a great trading centre between Egypt and the south, reached its zenith in Dynasty 25 as the capital of the local kings who now also controlled and ruled Egypt. It was enhanced with temples for Amun and other gods, and there is an extensive pyramid field near by. The site was explored by Cailliaud in 1822 and by Lepsius in 1844, and Reisner carried out excavations there in 1916 and 1919. Napata lost its prime importance when the royal residence was eventually moved south to Meroë, although it retained its religious significance as a centre of Amun's cult and its great cemetery continued to be used.

Another important site, Nuri, situated on the river-bank opposite el-Kurru, was also a major pyramid field; King Taharka of Dynasty 25 was buried here, and it was used for the rulers of the Napatan and Meroitic kingdoms after they withdrew from Egypt following the conflicts with the Assyrians. In addition, Nuri accommodated fifty-three smaller pyramids belonging to various queens and princesses.

The Napatan kingdom was finally overwhelmed by the Abyssinians and the capital was moved south to Meroë (c.300 BC–AD 350) which lies north of Khartoum. However, rival rulers continued to reside at Napata; both the kings at Meroë and the Napatan leaders still built pyramids and nearly fifty have survived at Meroë and eighteen at Napata. Reisner's excavations of the temples and pyramids at Meroë provide important information about this final stage, and indicate that the kings had revived the ancient custom of burying servants to attend them in the next life. Strabo recounts that it was the custom in Ethiopia for attendants to die at the same time as the ruler, but it remains uncertain whether they were buried alive or put to death before interment.

This capital city of Meroë had sanctuaries dedicated to various deities including the local lion-god Apedemak and Amun; there were also palaces and baths, and Garstang's excavations (1909–14), followed by those of Reisner, have revealed much of the city's original magnificence.

PART III

An Outline History of Egypt

Histories of ancient Egypt usually encompass the period from *c*.3100 BC, when the land was united into one kingdom, down to 332 BC when the Macedonian ruler, Alexander the Great, conquered Egypt and made it part of his world empire. However, the foundations for this civilization were laid down in the so-called Predynastic Period (*c*.5000–*c*.3100 BC); and many 'ancient Egyptian' beliefs and customs still survived during the Graeco-Roman Period (332 BC–AD 641), when Egypt was ruled first by the Ptolemies and then by the Romans.

Understanding ancient civilizations rests on interpretation of surviving literary and archaeological evidence, and in both areas the Egyptologist is well placed. Egypt's climate and the ancient burial customs have both ensured that the quality and quantity of surviving monuments and artifacts are probably unsurpassed, while the extensive literature that has survived, preserved on a variety of materials, provides insight into most areas of the Egyptians' lives.

The basis of our chronology of Egypt rests upon several sources. Probably the most important is provided by the Egyptian priest Manetho. He lived during the reigns of the first two Ptolemaic kings of Egypt (323–245 BC), and undoubtedly had access to source material which included ancient records and King Lists. Manetho prepared a chronicle of the Egyptian rulers, dividing the history into thirty-one dynasties, the first commencing with the unification of Egypt into one kingdom by King Menes in *c*.3100 BC. Modern research has revealed certain inaccuracies in Manetho's chronology, but it nevertheless remains the foundation of Egypt's pharaonic history.

Today, Manetho's dynasties are grouped into several major historical periods. The Archaic Period (Dynasties 1 and 2) follows immediately after the Unification in *c*.3100 BC, and ushers in the first great flowering of Egyptian civilization, known as the Old Kingdom (Dynasties 3–6). This highly structured society collapsed during the First Intermediate Period (Dynasties 7–11), but order and prosperity were restored by a strong line of rulers during the Middle Kingdom (Dynasty 12). Subsequently, in the Second Intermediate Period (Dynasties 13–17), centralized government was once again eroded, enabling foreign rulers to enter and take over the country. Driven out by a powerful family of local princes, the foreign rulers retreated, and Egypt entered the greatest period of strength and prosperity, the New Kingdom (Dynasties 18–20), when the kings established a great empire in Nubia, Asia Minor and Palestine, making Egypt the most powerful kingdom in the Near East. However, in the Third Intermediate Period (Dynasties 21–25), there was slow but inevitable decline in the country as well as a gradual dissolution of the empire, while in the Late Period (Dynasties 26–31), the Assyrian invasion of Egypt in Dynasty 25 was followed by Persian conquests, and ultimately by the arrival of Alexander the Great in 332 BC. The Graeco-Roman Period now commenced, when a line of Macedonian Greek rulers – the Ptolemies, descendants of Alexander's general, Ptolemy – controlled Egypt. The last of this line, Cleopatra, unsuccessfully attempted to prevent Rome's ambitions to take over Egypt in 30 BC , and the country was then ruled as another Roman province. The exact definition of the 'dynasties' into which Manetho divided the rulers is still unclear, and it is not always understood why one dynasty ended and another began. Generally, a dynasty included a line of rulers related to each other by family ties; if there were no successors or if another family seized power, then there was a change of dynasty, but sometimes families appear to span more than one dynasty, and the change from one to another was achieved under peaceful circumstances.

Another important source for understanding Egyptian chronology is provided by the King Lists. The Turin Canon of Kings (in the collection of the Turin Museum) is a Hieratic papyrus dating to around the reign of Ramesses II (1290–1224 BC). Although it was apparently in an almost perfect state when it was acquired by Drovetti, the French Consul-General in Egypt, it subsequently suffered damage, so that when Champollion later searched through the fragmentary papyri in the Turin Museum only fifty pieces of this document were found. The compiler, who apparently had reliable sources of information, recorded both the full years of each king's reign and any additional months and days. If this Canon were more completely preserved, it would be of considerable value, but only between eighty and ninety kings' names have survived. Nevertheless, results achieved by the German scholar Gustav Seyffarth in 1826, when he joined together the fragments and then translated the texts, were significant, and further work has provided more information. Certain details are in agreement with Manetho's account: both record that Menes was the first king of a united Egypt, following a line of gods and demi-gods.

The main fragment of another source, the Palermo Stone, is inscribed on diorite and housed at Palermo; when other pieces, probably from the same stone, were later recovered, they were placed in the Cairo Museum. When complete, this was probably an upright and free-standing oblong stone (stela), inscribed on both sides with horizontal registers, each divided vertically into compartments containing a hieroglyphic inscription. The complete stone would have given a continuous year-by-year record of the kings' reigns from Menes (the first king of Dynasty 1) down to (probably) Niuserre (the sixth king of Dynasty 5), with a special reference to some outstanding event in each year. These included victories over foreign tribes, expeditions to search for minerals, temple-building, festivals and so forth. However, the fragments of the stone do not provide a complete account and, in any case, it only recorded the events of the first five dynasties.

This stela was probably originally set up in a temple and, like other King Lists in temples, would have been placed there to play a part in the ritual performed in a royal mortuary temple on behalf of the dead king to whom the building was dedicated. They were in no way intended as historical lists and it was not necessary that they should be complete. The lists only include legitimate royal ancestors, whose acceptance was required before the king could rule on earth and ultimately join them as a god in heaven when he died. They usually only list the kings from King Menes down to the temple-owner's own reign and exclude those kings who were not deemed deserving of honour. Thus, the foreign Hyksos rulers were omitted, as were the heretic king Akhenaten and his three immediate successors, since they had worshipped the Aten and had not honoured the traditional gods. However, other omissions are less easily explained, and so far no lists have been discovered which are later than the reign of Ramesses II.

The most famous King List found in a temple is the Table of Abydos, inscribed in the Gallery of the Lists in the Temple of King Sethos I (1309–1291 BC) at Abydos. Occupying the whole wall, it shows Sethos I and his son Ramesses offering to seventy-six kingly ancestors, starting with King Menes; the kings are represented (and are therefore present in the temple) by their names written in hieroglyphs. Each name appears in a cartouche (the 'royal oval' in which the names of kings and queens were always depicted). In the ritual performed every day in these mortuary temples (known as the Ritual of the Royal Ancestors), the food and other offerings were brought from the god's altar in the sanctuary, where they had been presented to the divine statue, and were then offered up in front of the King List to the earlier kings, so that they could receive continuing sustenance after death, and would grant their approval to the temple-owner.

The Table of Karnak occurs in one area of the great Temple of Karnak at Thebes where the god Amen-Re was worshipped. This inscription dates to the reign of Tuthmosis III (1490–1436 BC), and, although it includes some kings not mentioned in other lists, it does not provide a correct sequence of the kings' names. When it was discovered in 1825, only forty-eight names were visible, although the list originally contained sixty-one.

The third list – the Table of Sakkara – originally included some fifty-seven earlier kings whom Ramesses II selected for worship, but only fifty remain legible because of damage to the wall (in the tomb of an Overseer of Works named Tjuneroy, at Sakkara). Together, the King Lists, Manetho's history and other written sources provide us with an incomplete chronological structure for Egypt's history.

The land which gave rise to the Pharaonic civilization, and indeed to the Neolithic cultures which preceded it, was physically very different in the Palaeolithic Period (before 5000 BC). Then, the two main areas – the Delta in the north and the Nile Valley in the south – were virtually uninhabitable; much of the Delta was covered with papyrus swamps, while the Nile Valley was either under the inundation waters of the river for three months of each year, or it was covered by lush and almost impenetrable vegetation which teemed with wild animals. During this time, people were forced to live on the desert spurs and to hunt the prolific game, but gradually the climate changed, the Nile Valley became drier and, once the annual inundation receded, they were able to move down into the Valley where they began to cultivate the land. During the Neolithic Period (between 5000 and 4000 BC), people began to gather together in settled communities and to replace their hunting activities with farming, growing grain and domesticating animals.

By now, the land would have displayed those distinctive natural features which would ultimately shape and mould Egypt's unique civilization. Dominated by the two great life-giving forces of the sun and the Nile, the Egyptians were constantly aware of the impact of the environment upon their beliefs and aspirations. Each day,

they observed the unremitting cycle of the birth, life and death of the sun, and annually they saw the parched land brought back to life by the flood-waters of the Nile. It took no great feat of imagination to presume that mankind's own existence had a similar pattern, in which birth, life and death were followed by individual resurrection, and the concept of continuing life after death soon became firmly established in Egyptian belief.

The contrast between life and death was always present in the very nature of Egypt's landscape. Although the total territory of the country is extensive, most of it is desert; the ancients feared this as a place of death and terror, the haunt of wild animals and nomads, and called it Deshret (the Red Land), after the predominant colour of the landscape (our own word desert is in fact derived from this). The main centres of population soon developed in the cultivated areas – the Delta and along the banks of the Nile. Despite a negligible rainfall, Egypt was made habitable by the phenomenon of the annual inundation of the river, thus giving rise to the frequently repeated quotation of the Classical writer Hecataeus that the country was the 'gift of the Nile'. This river – the longest in Africa – has always intrigued travellers and explorers. It rises far to the south of Egypt in the region of the Great Lakes (three degrees south of the Equator). It is known as the Mountain Nile in its upper course, but once it joins with the Bahr el-Ghazel it becomes the White Nile. Another river – the Blue Nile – rises in Lake Tana in the highlands of Ethiopia, and at Khartoum in the Sudan the Blue and White Niles join to become the great river that flows northwards through Egypt, ultimately to meet the Mediterranean. Between Khartoum and Aswan, the river is interrupted in its course by a series of six cataracts. These are not waterfalls, but simply scattered groups of rocks which stretch across the width of the river, obstructing the stream and, at the Fourth, Second and First Cataracts, impeding river navigation. The First Cataract, situated just south of Aswan (the location of the ancient town of Elephantine), marked the original southern boundary of Egypt; north of this, for some eleven hundred kilometres, the river flows uninterrupted to the Mediterranean coast. It was in the region of these northernmost

A view of men pulling a river craft by hand across the rapids at one of the cataracts on the Nile. It is taken from Cailliaud's Voyage à Méroé au Fleuve Blanc, *in which he describes his Nile journey (1819–22) to reach Meroë, the southernmost outpost of Egyptian civilization.*

cataracts that the early Egyptians fought and subdued the local population in order to gain ready access to the supplies of hard stone and gold that they required. They called this area Nubia or Gold Land.

Between the regions of Aswan and Cairo (a relatively modern city founded by the Arab conquerors), the Nile has forced a passage; along this valley, the scenery changes from dramatic rocky cliffs that sometimes descend to the river's edge to flat, lush, cultivated fields, which, in the distance, give way to the desert. This rich cultivation (which varied in width between ten and twenty kilometres) resulted from intensive irrigation of the land with the inundation water, and enabled fine crops to be produced every year.

Cairo, Egypt's modern capital city, stands at the apex of the Delta, not far distant from the sparse remains of the once-great ancient capital of Memphis. This area marks a change in the appearance of the river and the surrounding countryside; now passing over a low plain, the Nile fans out into a delta nearly 160 kilometres long and over three hundred kilometres wide at its northernmost perimeter. Although areas of the Delta can be cultivated, much of it is marshland; here, the land is crossed by the Nile's two main and other lesser branches. Finally, at Rosetta in the west and at Damietta in the east, it meets the Mediterranean.

The effect of the inundation on Egypt was, until recent times, dramatic and unpredictable. Modern construction of a series of dams along the river, culminating in the building of the High Dam at Aswan, now ensures that the volume of water can be held back and supplied as required for irrigation through a series of canals. However, in antiquity, the level of the inundation was uncontrollable and posed a constant threat to people's safety and prosperity. Every year, the rains falling on the highlands of Ethiopia increased the water in the river so that it became swollen, flooding out over its banks and bringing down with it the rich black silt which could be spread across the fields. It was

An alabaster offering-tray from a tomb at Medum, c.2700 BC. These were included in burials as part of the cult of presenting food to the tomb-owner to ensure eternal nourishment.

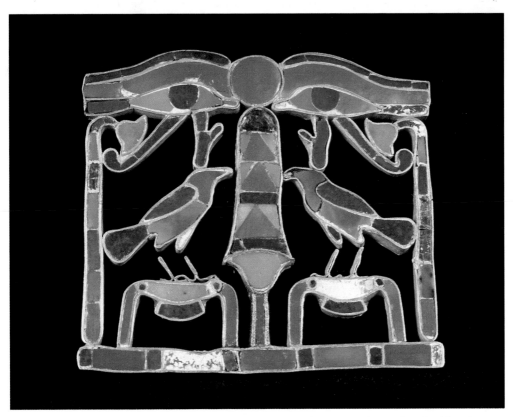

A pectoral (chest ornament) found on a mummy in a tomb at Riqqeh. Made of gold and semi-precious stones, it is a fine example of cloisonné work. The excavator found the body of an ancient tomb-robber lying across the mummy, killed when the roof partially collapsed.

The Royal Boat discovered in 1954 in a pit south of the Great Pyramid at Giza may have been used once at the king's funeral. Reassembled over forty years, it is now displayed in the Boat Museum.

The pyramids and Great Sphinx at Giza from a lithograph in David Roberts' *Egypt and Nubia* (1846).

One of the thrones from Tutankhamun's tomb, this is made of ebony and sheet gold inlaid with semi-precious stones, glass, faience and ivory. The king's names are given in the inscriptions.

A canopic jar from the Tomb of Two Brothers, Rifeh (c.1900 BC), with a human-headed lid; these jars were used to store the mummified viscera. Petrie discovered this tomb, complete with its contents, in 1905.

Part of the interior of the Temple of Sethos I at Abydos. The wall scenes are amongst the finest in Egypt. Many represent the rituals once regularly performed in the temple.

A wall scene from the Temple of Sethos I at Abydos showing a purification rite in which the gods pour sacred water over the king (centre). Sethos I had two mortuary temples, at Qurna and Abydos.

A carved stone relief from the Temple of Denderah showing the god Bes. He was a dwarf-god who was worshipped in people's homes to bring them good fortune in love and marriage.

The façade of the main temple at Denderah, dedicated to Hathor, goddess of love and beauty. It dates mainly to the Ptolemaic Period but probably occupies the site of a much older temple.

Part of the main pylon of the Temple of Amun at Karnak. Every temple was believed to be the residence of a god or group of gods, and also to recreate the island where creation had occurred.

A general view of the Karnak temples at Thebes, with the Nile, from the account of Lepsius' expedition, published in *Denkmäler aus Aegypten und Aethiopien* (1849–59).

The main pylon (gateway) of the Temple of Luxor, visited by many early travellers. There were originally two obelisks in front of this pylon but one was removed to Paris in 1835.

this silt which fertilized the soil and enabled the Egyptian farmers to produce abundant crops.

In Egypt, the inundation progressed from the region of the First Cataract in late June and reached the northern areas in late September, after which the waters gradually receded so that the river was at its lowest in the following April. Each year, the earth would become parched and cracked, and the people anxiously awaited the new inundation, always fearful that the Nile would not rise this time so that the land and its people would die. Although this never happened, they were well aware of the possibility of an extreme inundation, when an excessively high Nile could bring floods that would destroy the land and its crops, while a low Nile resulted in famine and disaster.

The contrast between the desert and the cultivation, between death and life, could not have been more marked, and whereas the desert was the Red Land, the Egyptians called their country Kemet (the Black Land). This referred to the colour of the rich silt and the soil it produced in the cultivated areas, which gave them their very existence. Here, in the cultivated strip along the Nile and in the Delta, the people had been aware since earliest times of a need to act communally to control and regulate the Nile waters, and to organize an irrigation system that would benefit all the Nile communities. A complex system divided the land into compartments of varying sizes by means of earth dykes; when the river rose, water was brought into these through canals and held there until the rich silt was deposited. Once the river level fell again, any remaining water in the compartments was drained off, and the land could be ploughed and crops sown. With effective organization, such a system brought together scattered communities, giving them a vital, common goal, and was undoubtedly instrumental in unifying Egypt as a state.

As well as the geographical division into desert and cultivation, the country fell naturally into two distinct northern and southern regions – the Delta and the Nile Valley – which were unified by the Nile as it flowed from south to north. The original isolated village communities gradually came together into larger units for their own mutual protection and because they needed to co-operate

over irrigation schemes. Each unit retained its independence, and had its own capital town and local chieftain; the people of the area worshipped their own god and cultivated the surrounding land to support the community. Gradually, common interest brought these units together into larger groups (which in later historical times became the 'nomes' or main geographical districts of Egypt); and in predynastic times these were organized into two kingdoms, each with its own ruler. The northern kingdom, centred in the Delta, may have extended southwards along the Nile Valley as far as Atfih; its capital city and the king's residence were at Pe which lay near to the town of Dep (later called Buto). Here, the cobra-goddess Edjo was worshipped; the kingdom was known as the Red Land and its ruler wore the distinctive Red Crown. The parallel southern kingdom stretched along the Nile Valley from the region of Atfih to Gebel es-Silsileh in the south. Known as the White Land, the capital city was situated at Nekhen (later known as Hieraconpolis) near Edfu; here, the king resided, and wore the White Crown. This was also the cult-centre of the kingdom's patron deity, the vulture-goddess Nekhbet. The Two Lands joined together when Egypt was unified in c.3100 BC, but the political duality of the country's origin was never forgotten; the king of a united land ultimately wore the two crowns, either separately or in a combined headdress known as the Double Crown. The two goddesses Edjo and Nekhbet were associated as the dual protectresses of the king of Egypt, and the symbols of the south (Upper Egypt) and the north (Lower Egypt) – the sedge, and the bee and the papyrus plant – continued to be used in art forms throughout Egypt's history. The north, facing the Mediterranean, became much more receptive to peoples, ideas and influences from Asia, Africa and Europe, and most of the major cities developed there. The south, hemmed in by the deserts, retained the Egyptian traditions more strongly.

Geographical factors clearly affected the distinctive nature and development of Egyptian civilization. A visit to any museum with an Egyptian collection will demonstrate that there was little superficial change in concepts or art-forms over a period of three thousand years.

It was only possible for such a unique culture to flourish and survive for so long because, compared with other ancient civilizations of the Near East, Egypt occupied a secluded position in Africa. Natural barriers afforded continuing protection against invaders, at least in the earlier periods when the foundations of art, architecture and religion were being established. Later, Egypt was able to absorb some foreign elements and incorporate them into the existing culture without altering basic concepts and ideas.

A glance at a map of the area will confirm that to the north of Egypt lies the Mediterranean, which was both a trading route between Egypt and her northern neighbours and also a deterrent to would-be invaders. To the south lay Nubia (straddling that area which today occupies southernmost Egypt and northern Sudan) and beyond this, the African hinterland. Nubia had important supplies of gold and hard stone – commodities which the Egyptians greatly desired – and so a policy of colonization of this area was assiduously pursued by the Egyptians. The Nubians became 'Egyptianized' and when ultimately a line of Nubian rulers established themselves as kings of Egypt in Dynasty 25, they had become more traditionally Egyptian than their subjects.

To the west lies the Libyan desert; here, scattered across this seemingly endless desolate area, there is an irregular chain of oases. The Egyptians always had close contact with the Libyan tribes and traded with them, but they did not threaten Egypt's security and political stability until later times. Further protection was afforded to Egypt by the Red Sea on the east, but above this, across the northern part of the Sinai Peninsula, there lay the one relatively easy route into the Delta and Nile Valley. A predictable climate and abundant crops made Egypt a country that attracted invaders, and this was probably the route of entry which the earliest infiltrators chose to follow. Nevertheless, the land was never subjected to the continuous waves of conquest which disposed of other early civilizations.

The Predynastic Period

The unification of Egypt and the commencement of Dynasty 1 with the reign of King Menes in c.3100 BC brought to an end the so-called Predynastic Period. Chronological sources such as Manetho describe a line of gods succeeded by several demi-gods (the Followers of Horus or exalted spirits) who immediately preceded King Menes and the historical period. These Followers of Horus were probably the kings of the northern and southern kingdoms centred respectively at Buto and Hieraconpolis, and reflect the existence of the Two Lands prior to the unification of Egypt, but it is evident that, for later generations, the origins of their history and culture were obscured in mythology.

Important excavations carried out at a number of sites at the beginning of this century first revealed the hitherto unsuspected development of the Predynastic Period. Near the modern village of Nagada, in 1895, William Flinders Petrie discovered and excavated cemeteries which belonged to the last two cultures of the predynastic era. At this time, the scattered communities throughout Egypt had certain features in common: they practised land cultivation, domesticated their animals, produced pottery, other domestic articles, and tools and weapons, and pursued religious beliefs and customs which showed great reverence for the dead and probably indicate a belief in continued individual existence after death. From the results of his excavations at several sites, Petrie was able to devise a method of relative dating for the excavated material, basing it on a comparison of the groups of pottery discovered in this series of graves. The system is still known as Sequence Dating. He went on to divide these cultures into three groups to which he gave the terms Amratian, Gerzean and Semainian (these are derived from the names of local modern villages which lay near to his excavations.) The Amratian and Gerzean periods of predynastic culture are continuous and some scholars still retain these terms, but it is now more acceptable to refer to the two stages as Nagada I and Nagada II, based on the evidence of Petrie's discovery of both these cultures in the cemeteries at Nagada. The term

Semainian is now only applied to the earliest dynasties, and the earliest known predynastic culture prior to Nagada I and II is named Badarian after the modern village of el-Badari, close to Assiut, where important excavations were carried out by Winifred Brunton and Gertrude Caton-Thompson. There is apparently a well-defined cultural break between the Nagada I and Nagada II periods, and Petrie sought to explain this in terms of the arrival in Egypt, c.3400 BC, of the so-called Dynastic Race. Today, not all scholars accept this theory, but prefer to regard these changes as the result of purely indigenous developments. Nevertheless, the possibility of the arrival of a new group or groups of people at this time cannot be entirely ignored. It is suggested that the newcomers brought advanced technology and new ideas, and that it was their fusion with the creativity and artistic genius of the indigenous population which ultimately resulted in the first flowering of Egyptian civilization in the earliest dynasties.

Certain specific developments can be noted in Egypt c.3400 BC which appear to have no direct precedents there. These include the first appearance of the earliest stages in the development of writing; the introduction of monumental brick architecture for the burials of the rulers; and the discovery of certain artifacts (stone maceheads and inscribed cylinder seals) together with the appearance on slate palettes of artistic motifs representing strange composite animals with entwined necks, quite alien to the Egyptian tradition.

There has been considerable conjecture concerning the possible homeland of the Dynastic Race; the newcomers presumably came from an area where these innovations were already established, and it has been suggested that they had contact with Mesopotamia. There, cuneiform writing predates any known Egyptian examples, although the materials used – mudbrick tablets in Mesopotamia or the less readily preserved papyrus in Egypt – may explain why Mesopotamia appears to be ahead in this field. Both cuneiform and Egyptian hieroglyphs are based on the use of pictographs, but the structure of the later languages that developed in the two areas and the appearance of the two writing systems were very different. If Egypt did adopt writing

from Mesopotamia, it was only the concept which was taken over. The second innovation – monumental brick architecture with recessed brick panelling as a façade decoration – may also have been introduced from Mesopotamia. However, in Egypt this was used for tombs whereas in Mesopotamia such building techniques and materials were only employed for temples. Thirdly, artifacts such as cylinder seals and maceheads which now appeared in Egypt were also found in Mesopotamia; and the artistic decoration on the slate palettes, particularly the composite animals, may also have been derived from Mesopotamian motifs.

Other homelands suggested for these people have included Syria, Iran, and even an as yet undiscovered area from which both Egypt and Mesopotamia could have been influenced. Contact between such peoples may have come about partly through trade, but there is also apparent evidence of some kind of armed conflict. This is shown in scenes carved on the ivory handle of the famous Gebel el-Arak knife, depicting a sea-battle between ships of Egyptian and Mesopotamian type. The scenes seem to represent an attempt at invasion, with the oppressors perhaps gaining entry to Egypt through the Red Sea before crossing the Eastern Desert into the upper part of the Nile Valley. Other land routes which may have been used could have included the one from Palestine to the Delta via the Sinai Peninsula.

There is, however, no evidence of a mass invasion; perhaps these newcomers entered in relatively small groups, some peacefully and some forcefully, through different routes. Yet, both tradition and archaeological evidence does support the theory that infiltration probably spread from the south to the north of Egypt. At sites in Upper Egypt – Nagada, el-Hammamiya, el-Mahasna and Armant – evidence of the Nagada II phase of development has been found. However, any such 'foreign' incursions appear to have stopped by the beginning of Dynasty 1, for by then the 'foreign' architectural and artistic innovations had either disappeared or been absorbed into Egyptian culture; also by now, the writing system had become distinctively Egyptian in structure and appearance.

From c.3400 BC (the Nagada II period), communities were organized into two kingdoms – the Red and White Lands – with their capitals at Pe and Nekhen. Then, c.3100 BC, Menes, the king of the White Land, conquered the north and unified Egypt. In 1897 J. E. Quibell was digging at el-Kab, a site on the east bank north of Edfu. This was the ancient city of Nekheb, the centre of the vulture-goddess Nekhbet, who protected the predynastic rulers of the Upper Egyptian kingdom. Quibell expected important results at the site, but he was disappointed there, although his pioneering excavations in 1898 at Kom el-Ahmar on the opposite bank (the ancient Nekhen or Hieraconpolis) brought to light in the temple a great cache of objects including the Narmer Palette. From his excavations, he was able to confirm that the two early kingdoms, centred at Nekhen and Buto, were historical realities, and also to show that they were unified by King Menes. Nekhbet became the protectress of Upper Egyptian kings, and always retained her role as assistant in the delivery of royal and divine births. In the north at Pe, the cobra-goddess Edjo became the patron of the Lower Egyptian kings and later continued to defend the King of Egypt against all his enemies.

Evidence to reconstruct the social and political history of these earliest periods is incomplete and there are no translatable written records to amplify the archaeological findings. However, from the Upper Egyptian evidence (where climatic and environmental conditions ensure better preservation of the artifacts than in the north), it can be construed that there were numbers of village settlements, each led by its own chieftain. People built their houses of perishable materials, and supported themselves by mixed farming. There is also evidence that trading contacts with the African hinterland provided ivory, while from the areas to the north they sought copper, and obtained turquoise from Sinai; shells were imported from the Red Sea and the Persian Gulf. By the Nagada II period, there were considerable advances in skills such as metal-working, pottery production and the manufacture of stone vessels, and they were able to import large quantities of silver objects. At Nagada, the cemeteries indicate the great importance of the ancient fortified town

they served, called Nubt (later known by its Greek name of Ombos). This name was probably derived from the Egyptian word 'nub' meaning 'gold', because the town apparently played an important role in early gold-working and trading. The gold mines in the eastern desert, accessible from the Wadi Hammamat, were not far distant, and this connection may have ensured the town's original rise to prominence. The local god, Seth (the Ombite), played an important role in early history.

Although excavation has revealed more of the physical culture of the Upper Egyptian sites from this early period, it is nevertheless most likely that the northern kingdom was also very significant. Early cities would have included Sais (a temple to Neith of Sais appears on a tablet of Hor-aha, a king of Dynasty 1), Pe and Dep, where the northern capital was situated, and Heliopolis, which later became the great religious centre during the Old Kingdom.

This predynastic era has posed many questions. Was there an overall culture or did communities in the north and south follow distinct patterns of development? Did the northern and southern communities develop from different racial origins? and which culture was earlier? However, interdependence between these communities, emphasized by the need to use the Nile water and irrigate the land, ensured that there was some degree of co-operation and it was this need to coexist that finally produced a common pattern of culture.

During the Badarian and Nagada I periods, our perception of these societies is limited by a lack of both written evidence and the dwellings of the living. Nevertheless, the graves and their goods provide some idea of their beliefs and customs, and it appears that in both the north and the south, the people had developed a belief in a continued existence after death. Their cemeteries show that the dead were provided with goods that could be utilized in the next life, and these included implements, personal adornments and food. Graves in the Badarian cemeteries, situated away from the dwellings of the living, were usually oval in shape, and contained single or double burials. A small pile of sand or stones marked the position of the grave. The body, in a contracted position on its side and enclosed in either coarse matting, a basket made of twigs, or an animal skin, was buried a few feet down in the sand. It was dressed in linen clothes and sometimes in a turban, and further adorned with jewellery and a beaded belt. The grave goods included jewellery, combs, ivory cosmetic vases, slate palettes, and cosmetics, the most important of which was probably the green malachite which was ground on a palette and mixed with oil or fat, and then applied to the skin. There were also flint tools, distinctive 'black-top' pottery, and female figurines, found in graves of both men and women, which may have represented a mother–goddess figure.

In these Badarian villages, evidence already existed of the importance of animal cults; the bodies of dogs or jackals, sheep and cows were wrapped in linen or matting and buried alongside the human graves. No grave goods were included for them but it is obvious that they were regarded as significant members of the community. Also, amulets (magic charms) in the shape of animals were placed in the human burials.

The burials of the Nagada I period are similar to those of the Badarian, and there was probably no marked cultural break between these two stages. The oval shape of the grave continued, but sometimes multiple burials (up to seven bodies) occurred in a single grave. The Badarian types of grave goods also continued, although there was an increased foreign influence: domestic pottery indicated contact with Asia, and imported items such as turquoise and lapis lazuli have also been found. Again, amulets found in Badarian graves, presumably offering magical powers to the deceased, continued in Nagada I; some of the slate palettes were now produced in the shape of animals, and there were also animal statuettes, suggesting an unbroken sequence of animal worship.

However, in the Nagada II period, possibly following the arrival in Egypt of the Dynastic Race, certain distinct changes occur. During this time, the isolated village communities came together in larger units, to afford mutual protection and to benefit from joint irrigation schemes. Although little is known of the political and social developments at this time, the irrigation of

the land was obviously a high priority, and towards the end of this period a king named Scorpion apparently initiated the digging of a canal (this is shown in a scene on a ceremonial macehead). It is possible that irrigation was already used throughout the land for the whole of this period but this scene may commemorate its introduction on a wider scale. Gradually, the communities drew together in increasingly large units, and ultimately formed the Two Lands – the northern and southern kingdoms.

There was also a dramatic change in the burial customs in the Nagada II period. Whereas previously the chieftain was regarded as an ordinary member of his community who acted on behalf of his people and who was buried in the same kind of grave as them, in this period and the succeeding dynasties the ruling classes had different burial arrangements from the masses. So marked is the difference that it has been suggested that such a change could only be explained in terms of the arrival in Egypt of a new racial group – the so-called Dynastic Race – bringing with them new beliefs and customs which their descendants perpetuated. Available evidence is inconclusive, although again it has been argued that the bodies in these and later tombs differ anatomically from those in the pit-graves. They are of larger build with wider skulls, and some claim that such differences could demonstrate the existence of two racial groups, the subjugated indigenous population buried in shallow desert graves, and the newcomers and their descendants (who became the new royal and noble classes of the first dynasties) with different, more elaborate tombs.

These tombs establish the pattern for royal and noble funerary architecture in the later dynasties, and today are often described as *mastaba* tombs. Rectangular in shape, each has a bench-shaped superstructure above ground (mastaba is the Arabic word for bench), where the grave goods were stored in several chambers; below ground, the substructure housed the burial. If racial differences were responsible for these early differences in burial customs, such a distinction was lost by the end of Dynasty 2 when presumably some degree of fusion between the two groups had occurred. Different burial customs still continued, but they now reflected individual social status rather than any variation in racial origin.

In the Nagada II period, the goods placed in the tombs perpetuated earlier customs, but a distinctive type of pottery was now introduced (this is known today as Decorated Ware). This is painted with scenes of a religious nature, often showing deities, festivals and river processions. The mother-goddess and her son-consort are also often depicted as symbols of fertility and rebirth after death, as well as gods (in animal forms) of the various districts.

Several gods known in later times were probably already important in the Predynastic Period. Generally, as the political units came together into two kingdoms, the local gods were also amalgamated, and gods of conquered or subordinated areas were assimilated into the victor's god who took on their powers and characteristics. Each nome (district) came to have its own chief deity who protected the chieftain. The amalgamation of the various cults produced a confusing pantheon, but individual worship probably continued to be directed towards one local god or group of gods.

The local or tribal gods often had animal or fetish forms in which the deity's spirit would reside. Animal worship continued throughout Egypt's history with some gods retaining animal forms, but throughout the early dynastic period, and even perhaps before, some animal forms were gradually replaced with a degree of humanization and deities were represented with bird or animal heads on human bodies. Later, some 'animal' gods acquired human forms, and other deities were always shown in totally human guise.

Any arrival of a Dynastic Race presumably would have had some effect upon the gods. However, older tribal deities certainly survived; the newcomers may have tolerated and adopted these, but now another group we call cosmic gods may also have been introduced. They appear to form a distinct group, associated with the celestial bodies and forces of Nature; always remote from mankind, some took over characteristics of the older gods, as well as their earthly cult-centres, but others never adopted such features.

The exact nature of divine worship in the towns and villages of predynastic Egypt remains unclear because the physical evidence is scanty, but from representations on ivory labels it seems that shrines were the earliest shelters for the gods' emblems. Built from wood, reeds and matting, these were very similar to surrounding domestic dwellings. Here, the community chieftain would have presented regular daily offerings and meals to the deity's symbol, in the same way that in later times the king or high-priest would approach the god's cult-statue in the great stone temple.

The evidence for this period is tantalizingly difficult to interpret. However, there is sufficient information available to us to attempt a reconstruction of the momentous events that occurred c.3100 BC, when the ruler of the southern kingdom, Narmer, took the northern land by force and created the unified state of Egypt. This unification is commemorated on a ceremonial slate palette discovered by the excavator Quibell in 1898, when he was digging the site at Kom el-Ahmar – the ancient city of Nekhen, later known by the Greek name of Hieraconpolis, where the falcon-god Horus was worshipped. The palette was one item in the great cache deposited there in the Temple of Horus, which included palettes, maceheads, stone vessels and carved ivory figurines.

Narmer and a later ruler, Kha'sekhem, had presented most of these votive objects which were later gathered together into the so-called Main Deposit of the temple. This magnificent and historically important palette may have been the king's ceremonial offering to his royal patron deity for his great victory. On the obverse, Narmer is shown wearing the Upper Egyptian crown, with his arm raised to smite a captive northern chieftain who cowers before him; in his upraised hand, Narmer holds a macehead to strike his enemy, above whose head a hieroglyphic group appears which should possibly be read as 'Horus brings (to the king) captives of Lower Egypt'. On the reverse, the action continues with Narmer, this time wearing the Lower Egyptian crown, inspecting the corpses of his northern enemies; this scene is possibly set on the battlefield, or perhaps at the temple of Hieraconpolis, where victims were perhaps sacrificed to celebrate the king's victory. On a macehead, there is a scene which may represent a marriage ceremony between Narmer and a northern princess; this would have consolidated his claim to the Red Land and united the inheritance of the Two Lands for his heirs.

Narmer's conquest of the north was obviously only the final stage in a series of campaigns waged by the south, but previous events remain obscure. An earlier southern ruler, King Scorpion, probably also played a major role in this conquest; scenes on a ceremonial limestone macehead discovered at Hieraconpolis show him engaged in fighting and also possibly inaugurating a widespread irrigation project. Narmer and his predecessors would have undertaken their conquests together with a coalition of local leaders. Ultimately, in *c.*3100 BC, Narmer was able to move his capital from the old southern city of This (near Abydos) to a new foundation in the north at the apex of the Delta, where he could more readily govern his newly united kingdom. We know this site by its later Greek name of Memphis, but it was originally called White Wall, probably referring to the gesso which covered the city's mudbrick buildings. The man named Narmer can almost certainly be identified with King Menes whom later tradition states was the founder of dynastic Egypt.

The obscure history of this predynastic period is further confused by the account given in one of Egypt's most famous myths, the Conflict between Seth and Horus. This myth relates the tale of conflict and jealousy between two brothers, Osiris and Seth. In the end, through the devotion of Osiris' wife Isis and the actions of their son Horus when he was engaged in combat with Seth, Osiris overcomes his enemy. Scholars have argued that the mythical Osiris may represent a human king who once lived in predynastic Egypt, whence he had led his followers from another homeland (perhaps in Syria, Libya, Africa or Asia Minor). It is claimed that Seth, who was worshiped by the people in the town of Nubt (Ombos), symbolized Egypt's indigenous population. Does the myth therefore describe the conflict between the Dynastic Race and the established communities in Egypt during the Predynastic Period, or does it reflect later events in Dynasty 2? If we accept the possibility of invasion in the Predynastic Period, Horus

may indeed have been the supreme god of another group of newcomers (perhaps loosely associated with the followers of Osiris) who were finally able to consolidate conquest of the indigenous people. It remains unclear whether the newcomers, if they did come, arrived first in the north or in the south of Egypt, and, generally, the events of this period remain obscure. Possibly the conflict between these groups continued into the early dynastic period. In Dynasty 2, further rivalry may have broken out between the followers of Seth and Horus, with a final resolution coming in the reign of King Khasekhemwy, who reasserted the unity of the country, married a northern princess, and finally ensured that Seth's supporters were vanquished.

The Archaic Period

In the same way that it revealed the Predynastic Period, archaeology has also thrown light on Egypt's first two dynasties. One of the greatest finds – the Narmer Palette – illustrates events during the southern ruler's conquest of the north and, in the tradition of such decorated palettes, it also demonstrates a cultural continuity between the end of the predynastic era and the beginning of the early dynastic period. A new capital was now established at Memphis, although This in the south remained the foremost religious centre. At the main royal residence in Memphis, a mudbrick palace housed both official and royal domestic quarters. The political structure had already begun to emerge and this became the foundation for the elaborate bureaucracy of the Old Kingdom. Centralized departments to deal with judicial and administrative matters as well as foreign trading contacts were already established at Memphis. The White House and the Red House (the treasuries of the Two Lands) were also situated there to receive and redistribute the national revenue. However, it was already recognized that a country such as Egypt, with some areas far distant from the capital, required some degree of local government and a network had probably been established to link Memphis with the provincial centres. Nevertheless, one striking feature of the

Archaic Period is the extent to which homogeneity now existed between the north and south and this is testified by the architecture and funerary goods found at both Memphis and Abydos.

During this period, the role of the king as an absolute ruler of a united land was established. The Narmer Palette clearly indicates the southern ruler's success in unifying the Two Lands, and an important macehead also shows him wearing the Red Crown of the north. However, modern controversy has surrounded Narmer's identification with Menes who, from evidence provided by the Palermo Stone, was the first ruler of Egypt. Herodotus, the Greek historian, mentions that the priests of the chief Memphite god, Ptah, informed him that Menes founded their temple and the city of Memphis; and a later Classical writer, Diodorus Siculus, also refers to Menes' foundation of Memphis. During the later historic period, the coronation rites performed at Memphis commemorated both this unification and the foundation of the city. In general, archaeological and literary evidence tends to suggest that the identification of Narmer and Menes as one person, the founder of a unified Egypt and first ruler of Dynasty 1, is correct.

Already there was a custom of identifying the king with the royal hawk-god Horus, and regarding him as the earthly embodiment of the deity. In life, the king held the title of Horus, and at death he conferred it upon his successor. Inscriptions found at Abydos by the Coptic scholar Amélineau were subsequently translated by scholars in Europe (most notably Griffith in England and Sethe in Germany). They showed that one set of royal names were actually the 'Horus-names' of kings already identified as the rulers of the first two dynasties in the chronology of Manetho and in the Ramesside King Lists. Amélineau had previously wrongly identified these royal names he found at Abydos as 'new' kings and had concluded that they were the predecessors of Menes listed in the Turin Canon of Kings – the so-called Followers of Horus. In early studies, the identification of a king's name found in one source with another name occurring elsewhere was often a problem, until it was fully realized that most kings possessed more than one name. Eventually, when inscriptions were discovered which included both

these names together, the proper identifications could be made.

By the Archaic Period, the definition of the roles of other members of the immediate royal family had also started. Queens were important figures; the king's mother is mentioned, probably indicating that a king's principal wife already played an important role in the succession. Later, every king was believed to be the offspring of a union between the previous king's principal consort – his Great Royal Wife – and the chief state god. Thus, every king inherited a nature that reflected both divine and human characteristics, and was able to exercise divine power on earth. His principal queen, as the future divine consort and mother of the next royal heir, gave her human husband the strongest claim to rule Egypt, and his marriage to her enabled him to defeat any rivals even if his own claim to rule was weak. The woman who became Great Royal Wife had usually been the Great Royal Daughter, that is the eldest daughter of the ruling king and queen. She was usually the full-sister or half-sister of the royal heir, although some claimants had only tenuous links to the throne and used marriage with the Great Royal Daughter to consolidate their right to rule.

The royal protective role of the gods was also already clearly established. Two goddesses who had supported the rulers of the Two Lands before Unification – Edjo and Nekhbet – now continued to act as divine patronesses of the king. Neith, responsible for hunting and warfare, with a centre at Sais in the Delta, was also important. Seshat, the goddess of writing, already existed, and Ptah, the creator of the world, had founded Memphis as the centre of his worship. He was one of the few deities who had a human rather than an animal form. Other gods shown on the early maceheads and palettes ruled the regions that had supported Scorpion and Narmer when they conquered the north; these included Thoth, the ibis-headed moon-god and patron of writing; Anubis, jackal-god of cemeteries; Wepwawet, the wolf-god of Assiut who was a god of warfare and the dead; and Min, the fertility god with centres at Koptos and Akhmim.

During the Archaic Period, the sun-god Re had already begun his ascendancy as the great royal god. He took over Iwnw (the Greek Heliopolis) as his cult-centre from the older resident deity, Atum. By Dynasty 2, the king, still protected by Horus, adopted the title 'Son of Re', indicating his growing allegiance to the sun-god. It is unclear if the later belief, that the deceased king joined the gods in a solar barque to encircle the heavens throughout eternity, was already present, but boat burials (similar to those found later in association with some pyramids of the Old Kingdom) have been discovered near large tombs at Helwan, Abu Roash and Sakkara.

However, Horus remained the supreme royal god in this earliest period, symbolizing the king's divine power; indeed, each king was regarded as Horus incarnate, exercising the deity's rulership on earth. The later myth of the conflict between Horus and Seth may have reflected the infiltration and conquest of the indigenous population (followers of Seth) by the newcomers (the followers of a falcon-god, Horus). As the so-called Dynastic Race, they perhaps brought their god from an unidentified homeland. However, it is possible that the myth reflects events at a later time, either immediately prior to Unification, or during Dynasty 2, when evidence from the royal names shows that some early kings continued to support Seth in preference to Horus. There appears to have been continuing rivalry between these two gods and their supporters, and the political and religious confrontation was only resolved when, in Dynasty 2, King Khasekhemwy established the supremacy of Horus and again united the country. Henceforth, the kings would give their allegiance to Horus, and Seth would be cast as the arch-enemy of divine order and the legitimate gods.

Divine worship remained a central feature of religion in the Archaic Period, and presumably offerings of food and drink continued to be presented to divine symbols or cult-statues in shrines or temples by the king (in the role once performed by each local chieftain) and his delegates. Little is known of the structure of such shrines; traces of them have been found at Abydos, Hieraconpolis and Sakkara, but the materials from which they were made have largely perished. However, representations in later hieroglyphic texts show them as stylized ideograms. They are also depicted on early dynastic cylinder seals and ivory and ebony tablets; one, dating to the reign of King Hor-aha of Dynasty 1, shows the main features of the shrine of the goddess Neith. Built of wood or wickerwork with a hooped roof, each shrine stood at the rear of an open courtyard enclosed by a fence. This design had existed since the Predynastic Period. The entrance to the courtyard was flanked by two poles with banners; the deity's symbol or emblem, mounted on another pole, stood in the open enclosure immediately in front of the shrine where the divinity's statue was housed. The primitive features of the hut shrines (which were merely larger versions of the village dwellings) would ultimately be translated into major architectural elements in the later stone temples, called Mansions of the Gods. Even as early as the Archaic Period, the shrines were probably gradually becoming more permanent 'temples', with the additional use of brickwork, solid wooden doors, and roofs constructed of wooden beams. Important religious festivals already occurred and references to these are found in the events of kings' reigns recorded on the Palermo Stone.

Unlike the scanty evidence for political and religious organization amongst the living, the Egyptians' funerary practices in the Archaic Period are well testified by the archaeological evidence. There continued to be two main types of burial, which may reflect the original customs of the indigenous population and the Dynastic Race. The traditional predynastic pit-graves remained in use for the lower classes, but the rulers continued to develop the mastaba tomb which had first appeared c.3400 BC. Altogether, Emery identified six main stages of development in the funerary architecture of the Archaic Period; each category is then subdivided further to reflect the status of the owner, from the king through to the nobles, aristocracy, officials, artisans and peasants. The mastaba tomb still had a substructure cut into the rock; this was divided internally by brick cross-walls into a number of cells or chambers where the body and some of the funerary possessions were housed. Above ground, the brick-built superstructure extended beyond the limits of the substructure; recessed brick panelling decorated the outer walls and recreated the contemporary design of the royal palaces, emphasizing the role of such tombs as 'dwellings for the deceased'. In the lower part of this superstructure, a further series of cell-chambers accommodated more funerary equipment. Outside the tomb, the area was encompassed by an enclosure wall.

Various changes and modifications were introduced in tomb design during Dynasties 1 and 2, but generally the aim was to provide greater protection for the funerary goods by deterring tomb-robbers. To do this, they first deepened and enlarged the substructure, and then they discontinued the store chambers in the superstructure, placing the goods instead in the less accessible burial chamber. The quantity of tomb goods was also gradually reduced in all non-royal tombs, and more attention was given to building an elaborate tomb structure. By the end of the Archaic Period, a standardized tomb had come into use for the royalty and nobility, although these still reflected differences in wealth. The substructure now included, in addition to the burial chamber, a reception hall, guest rooms, living room and harem, a bathroom and lavatory, and storerooms, reflecting contemporary domestic architecture and serving as a 'house' for the deceased.

Innovations introduced for the upper classes gradually worked their way down the social scale, and greater emphasis was placed on the construction of the burial place rather than elaborate funerary goods; even in the pit-graves, wooden coffins and brick lining of the burial pit became more common but, in some, only two pottery vessels for food and drink now replaced the collection of jars, tools, and toilet equipment formerly found there.

An important result of interring the body in the brick-lined mastaba tomb or the wood or brick-lined pit-grave was the deterioration of the body, because it was no longer directly surrounded by the heat and dryness of the sand. In earlier times, the sand had absorbed the bodily fluids and desiccated the tissues before the corpse had a chance to decompose and, as a result, bodies had been preserved through natural mummification, with skin tissue and hair often still left

intact. The Egyptians believed that the spirit or vital force of the dead continued to be tied to this world in some way and, although it still existed elsewhere in eternity, the spirit needed to return to the tomb from time to time to gain spiritual sustenance from the supplies of food and drink placed there. However, to allow this to happen, a person needed to have a preserved and recognizable body which could be used to take sustenance from the food.

With the new burial methods and the consequent decomposition of the bodies, it became imperative to find alternative methods of preserving the lifelike appearance of the body, and ultimately artificial mummification, using chemical agents, was developed. However, the Archaic Period witnessed a number of preliminary experiments in this area. There is no existing evidence of any attempt to remove the viscera to deter decomposition (a feature of later mummification), but one example indicates that natron (the main dehydrating agent used later) may have been applied to the skin surface underneath the bandages. Generally, the embalmers of the Archaic Period tried different methods to create a lifelike appearance. They moulded the shape and contours of the deceased on to his body, using layers of linen pads and bandages soaked in a resinous substance to recreate the plumpness of the face, torso and limbs. Inside, the decomposing body rapidly became skeletal, but the stiffened bandages continued to retain the outward appearance, and this was further enhanced by painting the details of the face, genitalia and breasts on to the bandages. This time-consuming procedure was only attempted for members of the royal family and the great nobles. They were still not entirely reassured by these procedures and some also provided themselves with almost lifesize wooden figurines in the tomb. These were perhaps intended to act as a substitute for the body if it should perish or be totally destroyed.

The royal tombs of the Archaic Period have been the subject of much controversy. In 1895, the French scholar Amélineau, who had no previous experience of excavating but managed to obtain funds from private sources, began to investigate the area known as Umm el-Ga'ab

(Mother of Pots) at Abydos. Here he uncovered the brick pit-tombs of a number of kings whom he erroneously identified as the rulers who had reigned immediately prior to the Unification. Subsequently, this error was corrected by a study of the inscriptions, and the kings were identified as the rulers of Dynasties 1 and 2. His excavation methods were also criticized by later archaeologists, particularly his successor at the site, William Flinders Petrie, who obtained permission to dig there in 1899. With his meticulous methodology and attention to detail, Petrie was able to produce highly successful results which he published quickly. He produced plans of the tombs, and uncovered many significant objects including stelae, inscribed stone vessels, jar-sealings, and ebony and ivory tablets.

Inscribed objects provided the names of one queen and all the kings of Dynasty 1 and two kings of Dynasty 2. Philological study helped to identify these with the early dynastic rulers listed by Manetho whom he associated with This at Abydos. Although no human remains were discovered in these tombs, this was explained as the result of plunder or marauding animals, and it was assumed that these were the tombs of early rulers built near to their great religious capital of This.

However, from 1938 onwards Emery made significant discoveries at Sakkara, the necropolis of Memphis. Here, in the Early Dynastic cemetery at the north-east corner of the necropolis, a large brick mastaba tomb was discovered which contained sealings with the name of King Hor-aha. A long row of twelve brick mastabas and their subsidiary burials were uncovered, and the plans of their structures showed that they were much larger and more complex than those uncovered at Abydos. The architectural evidence and the inscribed objects found inside these tombs indicated that they all dated to Dynasty 1, starting with the reign of Hor-aha. They were better preserved and had obviously been burial places, since Emery found human remains here. However, ownership of the Sakkara tombs remains uncertain since the inscribed material associated with them only identifies each tomb with one reign but does not state the specific owner of the tomb. Also, unlike

the Abydos tombs, there are no stelae (inscribed stones) to show individual ownership, and it has therefore been argued that the Sakkara tombs could belong to courtiers of the period.

The earliest dynasties therefore have two sets of funerary structures, but their exact use is uncertain. The royal ownership of the Abydos 'tombs' cannot be disputed, since this is attested by the mud-sealings and other inscribed objects and stelae with royal names found associated with each building; however, since no human remains have been found, kings and queens may never have been actually buried here. The Sakkara tombs, on the other hand, were used for burials, but their identification with specific rulers is uncertain. However, if the kings were buried at Abydos and their courtiers at Sakkara (where the tombs are larger), this would present some puzzling difficulties. It is most likely that both were royal sites, with the burials actually placed at Sakkara, while the empty set at Abydos acted as cenotaphs. This perhaps reflected the king's role as ruler of both north and south; it also continued the royal tradition of close association with the prime religious centre at Abydos. However, it would have been more convenient for the actual burials to be carried out at Sakkara, near the royal residence at Memphis.

A feature of many of the great 'tombs' at both Abydos and Sakkara are the extensive subsidiary burials. Long lines of small burial chambers adjoining each other surround the main tomb. At Abydos, more than 1300 subsidiary burials were found; these included the remains of royal servants, high-ranking members of the royal harem, and domestic animals, obviously intended to serve the tomb-owner in the next life. Such burials also occurred at Sakkara but they were less numerous and had been heavily plundered. It is apparent that the subordinates were buried at the time of the owner's death, since the evidence from Abydos indicates that the tomb superstructure was erected over both the main building and the subsidiary graves, built in rows parallel to the sides of the tomb.

Some of these individuals, according to accompanying inscriptional evidence, were persons of some importance, but most were menials, each buried in an oblong pit roofed with timber and covered with a low rectangular superstructure. The body, wrapped in linen, lay contracted inside a small wooden coffin, and food and toilet equipment were also provided. At Abydos, inscriptions on stelae give the names, and sometimes the person's sex and other details, so we know that these burials included many women, some war captives, dwarfs and even dogs. At Sakkara, the discovery of tools in the subsidiary graves may indicate that skilled craftsmen were buried with the tomb-owner so that they could continue to serve his needs and repair the tomb in the afterlife.

The skeletal remains suggest that these people were already dead when they were buried, perhaps as a result of taking poison. There is no evidence that they were buried alive, and some tomb complexes have subsidiary burials which are separate from the main superstructure, perhaps suggesting that these servants met natural deaths and were buried near their ruler at different times. The extent of human sacrifice in the Archaic Period remains uncertain, perhaps reaching its peak in the reign of King Zer whose tomb complex at Abydos incorporated over five hundred subsidiary burials. The practice seems to have survived longer in the south than in the north. However, it was considerably reduced in Dynasty 2, and by the end of the Archaic Period such barbaric customs had been discontinued. In later dynasties, tomb models of servants replaced these human sacrifices.

The Old Kingdom
························

During the Old Kingdom, Egypt reached its first peak of civilization when it developed from the loose and essentially tribal society of earlier years into a highly organized and centralized theocracy. The country now achieved great technological advances, and the absolute power of the king enabled him to use the natural resources and manpower to construct the greatest of royal monuments – the pyramids. Major developments in architecture, art and other fields, undertaken first to enhance the king's burial,

later filtered through to improve other aspects of society. Indeed some would claim that the achievements of the Old Kingdom were never surpassed, and they certainly became models which later generations attempted to emulate.

The king's role was the most important aspect of this hierarchical society. Regarded as half-human and half-divine, his unique status enabled him to act on behalf of mankind in approaching the gods, and gave him at least theoretical ownership of the land, its people and its resources. His absolute power, however, was tempered by the need to act according to precedent and to obey the dictates of Ma'at, goddess of order, truth and justice. In reality, many of his duties in the administrative, legal, political and military spheres were delegated to officials who, at least in the early Old Kingdom, were almost always members of the royal family.

After the king, the most important executive was the vizier, whose range of powers and duties was extensive. Local governors were appointed, at first on a non-hereditary basis, to administer the various districts (nomes). At the capital, Memphis, there was a bureaucracy staffed with officials who dealt with the efficient organization of revenue and expenditure, the armoury, granaries and department of public works. From Memphis, the priesthoods of the great temples were probably administered, as well as the king's pyramid complex with its attached residence city which housed the workers and officials who tended it. In addition to this centralized bureaucracy, local administration also existed in the various districts.

The next level was made up of craftsmen and artisans who lived at Memphis; they built the royal and non-royal tombs and produced the wealth of objects – furniture, jewellery, toilet equipment, pottery and so forth – which was placed with the burial. They achieved a high standard of excellence in many fields, and in sculpture and painting their definitive style is sometimes referred to as the Memphite School. Although their work was primarily directed towards funerary goods, they also produced items for the living, and many beautiful objects undoubtedly enhanced daily existence in the Old Kingdom.

At the base of this social pyramid, and perhaps comprising 80 per cent of the population, were the peasants. They worked the land, irrigating the soil, cultivating the crops and tending the animals, in order to feed themselves and provide food, through taxation, both for their superiors and for the eternal offerings placed at the pyramids and tombs. It has been suggested that for the three months of each year when the land lay under water because of the Nile inundation, these men were redirected towards labouring on the pyramid site. This would have averted starvation for themselves and their families and also removed the threat of a potentially rebellious population. However, this theory is not universally accepted, and most pyramid labour may have been raised locally by corvée-duty.

The peasants were also forced to undertake military duties since Egypt had no standing army at this time. Relations with Nubia (to the south of Egypt) were fairly amicable; Egypt needed the hard stone and gold found in Nubia, but the Nubians looked to Egypt for corn and such commodities as oil, honey, clothing and faience, and trading expeditions probably continued throughout the Old Kingdom. Later, the Egyptians colonized Nubia itself, but the First Cataract at Elephantine was the accepted border at this time. Inscriptions in tombs of local princes there, dating to Dynasty 6, reveal some information about Egypt's foreign relations: Prince Harkhuf's inscription, based on a letter written to him by the child-king Pepy II, relates how Harkhuf journeyed far south, perhaps beyond the Second Cataract, to bring back various commodities, as well as a pygmy for the king. The king was most concerned for the well-being of the pygmy and his letter urges Harkhuf to hurry to the palace, as he is more anxious to see the pygmy than all the other goods.

It is evident that there were conflicts with the Nubians, but generally the Egyptians were able to recruit them for their campaigns against the 'Asiatics'. Expeditions also went to Punt (somewhere on the Red Sea), the source of incense and various spices for the Egyptians. On the north-eastern border, constant harassment by the 'Sand-dwellers' had to be dealt with, and although some of these skirmishes involved the nomadic tribes of the Sinai Peninsula, other and more extensive dangers were probably presented by the inhabitants of southern Palestine. These Asiatics finally helped to overthrow Egypt at the end of the Old Kingdom. Ships also went to Lebanon to obtain the fine wood that Egypt lacked, and Egyptian influence was well established there in the coastal town of Byblos. Generally, the emphasis of Egypt's foreign relations was on procuring materials and luxury items for the king rather than on warlike campaigns.

During the Old Kingdom, it was believed that the king alone could expect an individual eternity; everyone else could only hope to participate in this vicariously, through their contribution to the king's well-being in life and their endeavour in preparing and maintaining his burial place. The construction of the royal pyramid complex became the focus of society, of paramount importance not only to the king but also to all his subjects, whose existence in life and after death depended on his survival.

By this period, there was a determined attempt to impose order on the multitude of gods and religious beliefs that had existed since predynastic times. The priesthoods of various powerful deities now sought to centralize and rationalize the cults of the many gods who made up this confusing pantheon and, although they were never entirely successful, some religious structure did now emerge. Certain cities became great religious centres associated with particular gods where the deities were arranged either in families, or groups of eight (ogdoad) or nine (ennead) gods. The priests of the most important centres – Heliopolis, Memphis and Hermopolis – promoted their own theologies in which they each claimed the primary role of their god in creating the universe, the other gods and mankind. These Creation Myths (cosmogonies) each claimed that their own city was the place of creation, and all described a mythical scene in which an island, emerging from the primordial waters, became the sanctuary of the first god, providing an ideal set of circumstances for the emergence and development of all the key elements of society.

The most famous creation myth came from Heliopolis, the city where the sun-god Re had assimilated the characteristics of an earlier god, Atum. Much information about Re's mythology is derived from the Pyramid Texts (spells placed inside certain pyramids to ensure the king's passage to the next world). Re's descendants (cosmic gods of air, moisture, earth and sky) and their offspring (Osiris, Isis, Seth and Nephthys) formed the Great Ennead, while Horus, son of Isis and Osiris, led the Little Ennead. The myth says that, at creation, Re-Atum (in the form of the mythical Bennu bird) had alighted on the Benben (a pillar which was the cult-symbol of the sun-god). This conical pillar probably formed the focus of worship at the Old Kingdom temple at Heliopolis.

Although Re had been an important deity since at least early dynastic times, in the Old Kingdom his power and influence reached their zenith. He became the supreme royal god, with the king taking the title of Son of Re, and eventually, in Dynasty 5, the kingship became subordinate to the god's cult. Whereas the king had originally been regarded as an equal with the gods, joining them in the heavens after death, he increasingly acted as the sun-god's offspring and delegate on earth and he now needed Re's acceptance to become eternal.

Throughout the Old Kingdom, it was envisaged that, after death, the king would gain access to the heavens which were imagined as a great semi-circular ocean curved above the flat surface of the earth. Here, welcomed and received by the gods, he would spend eternity travelling with the gods in their celestial barque. However, in order to obtain eternal sustenance, it was also essential that the king could return to earth at will; here, through his preserved body, his spirit could imbibe the essence of food and drink offerings which were continually brought to his burial complex.

It was to fulfil such basic requirements that the traditional pyramid complex of the Old Kingdom was developed. There is much support for the theory that the pyramid form was intimately associated with the cult of Re and that later kings who chose not to build pyramids, but reverted to mastaba-type tombs, were attempting to release themselves from the stranglehold of Re's cult and priesthood. Various explanations have been offered to explain the choice of a smooth-sided pyramid (the 'true' pyramid) as a place of royal burial. In architectural terms, it may have been designed to conceal the entrance from the tomb-robbers, who nevertheless plundered all these monuments. It may have represented the Island of Creation, as a place of great spiritual potency where the king's rebirth after death could be assured, or, as a major feature of the sun-cult, it perhaps symbolized a sun-ray. This would give the king, buried deep inside the pyramid, the means of ascent to heaven and the possibility to return down this 'ramp' from the sky to use the offerings placed in the mortuary temple adjoining the pyramid. Pyramid, derived from the Greek word *pyramis* meaning 'wheaten cake', was the term applied to these monuments by the Greeks when they first encountered them. However, the ancient Egyptian word for this building was *mer* which is translated as 'Place of Ascension', supporting the interpretation of the pyramid as a link between earth and heaven.

The true pyramid is a development of an earlier form. At the beginning of Dynasty 3, King Zoser's vizier, Imhotep, was responsible for the construction of a stepped pyramid as the king's burial place. This structure, which dominates the necropolis at Sakkara, was originally designed as a mastaba tomb, but later alterations and additions created a stepped building in which a series of six 'mastaba superstructures' of decreasing size were placed one on top of the other. As in earlier mastaba tombs, the burial chamber is placed in an underground substructure, although in later pyramids this was moved up into the body of the pyramid itself. The Step Pyramid – the world's earliest known sizeable stone building – is a magnificent achievement, but it is only the major feature in a complex of monuments designed to imitate the main elements of the king's Royal Court in life. An enclosure wall of white limestone (perhaps imitating the wall surrounding his palace at Memphis) encircled the entire complex; inside were many religious buildings – a mortuary temple, shrines, storehouses, altars, courts and subsidiary tombs. The complex was probably designed as a residence for the king after death, and some ritual buildings occur in pairs, perhaps to reflect the king's role

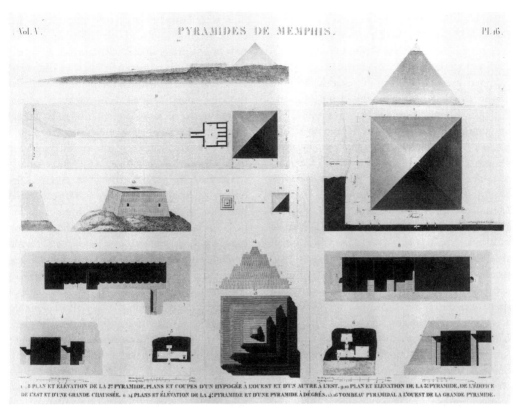

From Description de l'Égypte, *this shows plans and elevations of pyramids at Giza and Sakkara, cemeteries which served the ancient capital Memphis. The Step Pyramid at Sakkara probably developed its form from the mastaba tomb; the later change to a true pyramid may reflect a major religious change.*

as ruler of both Upper and Lower Egypt. A southern mastaba tomb, too small to accommodate a burial, may have been intended as a royal cenotaph to provide Zoser, together with the pyramid, with two 'tombs'. An interesting feature of this complex (which is unique: it has no known precedent and was never repeated) is the evidence of experimentation with building techniques. Inexperienced in large-scale stone masonry, the craftsmen here tried to express older forms in the new material: the stone fluted and ribbed columns are patterned on the earlier pillars made of reeds or wood but, uncertain yet of using free-standing columns to support the roof, the architects opted for engaged columns. Similarly, small stone blocks, imitating the dimensions of the mudbricks used in earlier buildings, are used here in place of the massive stone blocks found in later pyramid buildings.

Subsequently, several stepped or layered pyramids were built, but at Medum, at the beginning of Dynasty 4, the next stage in pyramid development can be clearly observed. Here, the original small step pyramid was extended to incorporate seven or eight superimposed layers; it was then transformed into a true pyramid by infilling the steps with local stone and facing the sides with white limestone. Unfortunately, this became the site of one of the world's first great architectural disasters. The angle of incline on all sides, combined with the increasingly heavy mantle as the pyramid changed form, produced such stresses that a great rockslide apparently occurred, causing the builders to abandon the pyramid and the site for future royal burials. Some twenty-eight miles to the north, at Dahshur, two other pyramids were also constructed at the beginning of Dynasty 4. The southern pyramid was always planned as a true pyramid, but when work had reached a point just beyond halfway up the

127

pyramid's height, the angle of incline (the same as that used at the contemporary Medum pyramid) was sharply decreased, producing a blunted structure, so that this is now known as the 'Bent' or 'Blunted' pyramid. It is possible that the Medum disaster may have prompted this change of plan.

The northern pyramid at Dahshur is the earliest example of a traditional true pyramid, planned and completed as such, but the most famous pyramids are found at Giza. Sneferu's son, Cheops, selected this magnificent and previously unused plateau because it was near to Memphis and to the excellent supply of limestone at Tura. His pyramid remained unrivalled in size, and he was also able to use the adjacent area for extensive subsidiary buildings. Here, members of his court were buried in two great cemeteries, in rows of mastaba tombs. In death they were forever overshadowed by this absolute ruler whom Herodotus later characterized as a hated despot. Perhaps this was an unfair assessment of the king, but undoubtedly he must have enjoyed supreme control over his country's resources and its people to enable him to envisage and complete such a monument. Archaeological evidence does, however, indicate that he was a pious and caring son. In the 20th century, the tomb of his mother, Queen Hetepheres, was found in the vicinity of his own pyramid, indicating that the queen's original burial place had been ransacked and her surviving relics, accompanied by a fine set of funerary furniture, given a new resting place near to Cheops' pyramid. The discovery later this century of a spectacular wooden boat in a pit near Cheops' pyramid also demonstrates that Giza can still provide a wealth of new information.

Cheops' son Radjedef started a pyramid north of Giza at Abu Roash, but another son, Chephren, returned to Giza and built alongside Cheops' monument. His pyramid is smaller than that of Cheops but, built on slightly higher ground, it appears to equal it in size. This is the only pyramid which has retained some of the original limestone casing, but even this appears only at the summit since the rest has been removed and taken elsewhere for use in more recent building projects. Instead of an adjacent family cemetery, Chephren's queens and chil-

dren were buried in rock-cut tombs to the east of his pyramid, but his pyramid complex is the only one to preserve the fully developed features found in standard pyramids of later dynasties. Such complexes included the pyramid itself (for the king's burial); an adjacent mortuary temple for the burial rites and presentation of perpetual food offerings to nourish and sustain the king's spirit; a covered causeway joining the mortuary temple on the desert's edge to the valley temple situated on the edge of the river; and a valley temple where the king's body was first received into the complex and where mummification may also have been carried out. Each part of the complex had important religious and ritual functions but, in practical terms, the layout was designed to join the pyramid on the desert's edge to the landing stage on the river. It also provided access for the movement of building materials in the early stages of construction and, later, for the funeral procession and subsequent supply of offerings to the mortuary temple.

Chephren's complex also incorporated a unique feature – the Great Sphinx. Already, however, the construction and maintenance of these extensive complexes had become a burden, since each king was responsible not only for his own monument but also for the upkeep and provisioning of his predecessors' pyramids. The third pyramid at Giza, built for Chephren's son Mycerinus, is modest in size and may reflect these economic pressures. His successor, Shepseskaf, completed this pyramid but chose to break with tradition by returning to an earlier style for his own tomb. Known as the Mastabat Fara'un, this is a type of mastaba tomb which may represent one ruler's attempt to break the influence of Re's priesthood. However, subsequently the kings of Dynasty 5 chose to promote the sun-god's cult to an unprecedented level. They revived pyramidbuilding and were buried first at Sakkara, and then established a new royal cemetery at Abusir, but their pyramids are built of very inferior materials. The solid stone internal construction of earlier pyramids is replaced with a core of small stones bonded together with a mortar of Nile mud. In all pyramids, the outer casing of limestone was subsequently removed for other building projects, thus exposing the

This drawing by Boudier is based on a photograph of 1881; it shows the archaeologist Maspero inside the burial chamber of the pyramid belonging to King Unas at Sakkara. The earliest known examples of the Pyramid Texts were found inscribed on the walls when it was opened in 1881.

interior, so here only the poorly preserved rubble core is now visible. The pyramids probably reflect a general political and economic decline, but other evidence indicates that both the nobles and the priests had gained power at the king's expense. The tombs of royal relatives and courtiers were no longer constructed near the king's pyramid but were scattered more independently across the necropolis, and the high quality of the wall-decoration in these tombs indicates their owners' increased importance.

Similarly, the priesthood of Re enjoyed an unparalleled status during Dynasty 5. Whereas the construction of the pyramids now declined, it is evident that the country's resources were directed towards building magnificent sun-temples at

Abu Ghurab. Indeed, archaeological and literary evidence suggests that this line of kings owed their rulership to the support of Re's priesthood. The Westcar Papyrus, a propagandist story designed for popular consumption, sets out to emphasize these kings' legitimacy and piety, and their claim, as the physical sons of Re, to rule Egypt.

In Dynasty 6 the general decline continued, and the pyramids reflect this trend. The last king of Dynasty 5, Unas, and various kings and queens of Dynasty 6 tried to reassert their power and ability to overcome death by resorting to magical means. In their pyramids, the walls were carved with hieroglyphic inscriptions – the Pyramid Texts. These consist of hundreds of spells, designed to ensure the king's victory over death and his acceptance as an equal by the gods whom he joined in heaven. As the world's earliest body of religious literature, they provide us with an unequalled insight into some of the earliest Egyptian beliefs.

Examples of another genre of literature which developed at this time, the Instructions in Wisdom, have often only survived in later copies. New pieces were added in later periods, but it was the hierarchical society of the Old Kingdom which gave birth to this literary form. Couched in terms of practical wisdom handed down from a sage (king, vizier or, later, a father) to his young charges or relatives, these texts provided the basic teaching for generations of boys who would become the country's officials. They illustrate the morals and ethics of Old Kingdom society, and are notable for the emphasis they place on clemency being shown to the poor.

Pyramids had been introduced for most kings and some queens, but the mastaba tomb continued and was developed as the typical non-royal burial place for the nobility. By Dynasties 5 and 6, these tombs were lavishly decorated with carved and painted scenes arranged in horizontal registers on the internal walls of the superstructure. The offering chapel for the continued presentation of food to the deceased was now situated in the superstructure and the burial itself was placed in a subterranean chamber. Unlike the king's celestial afterlife, it was envisaged that well-to-do but non-royal persons would continue to enjoy a limited existence after death within the confines of the tomb, obtaining sustenance from the food offerings and the scenes of food production carved on the walls. The rigid principles of Egyptian art had already been established; these conformed to certain rules to ensure that the dead person, by means of sympathetic magic, could possess and enjoy the objects and activities depicted in the wall scenes. These were 'brought to life' for the owner's eternal use by a ceremony known as 'Opening the Mouth' which was performed at the burial, when a priest touched the face, hands, and feet of the figures, as well as the owner's mummy, with an adze. Food offerings, scenes of food, and even a menu inscribed on the tomb wall ensured that the owner would not starve in the afterlife; it also became customary to include a statue of the deceased in the tomb. The funerary goods provided to enhance the tomb-owner's enjoyment give some idea of the luxurious lifestyle of the period.

However, the structured world of the Old Kingdom was not sufficiently secure to survive, and with the death of the elderly King Pepy II at the end of Dynasty 6, the society collapsed, ushering in a time of decentralization, disorder and disillusionment, now known as the First Intermediate Period. The main causes of this disintegration were political, economic, social and religious, and they had been present in the system from the beginning of the Old Kingdom. However, gradual deterioration and some additional factors now precipitated the final collapse.

At first, every effort had been made to emphasize the great difference between the king (supposedly divine) and his subjects. Buried in his pyramid, his individual afterlife in the heavens assured, the king alone could offer his people a chance of eternity, and he was responsible for giving the nobles not only their tombs but also land from the royal estates to provide their funerary offerings. Also, marriage to the Great Royal Daughter preserved the divinity of the royal line.

However, from Dynasty 4 onwards, there was a gradual equalization of wealth. The king's gifts of royal lands to the nobles became a continuous drain on royal resources, and this land was also usually exempt from taxation, thus compounding the problem. Additionally, each king was required to build and maintain a pyramid complex, and endow and support a staff of priests to perform the perpetual mortuary rituals. He was also expected to repair and provision his predecessors' complexes, and to provide tombs for his family and the Royal Court. Additional royal decrees – exempting the personnel and possessions of the pyramid mortuary temples and the associated residence cities from taxation and enforced labour drafts – further depleted royal resources. These 'benefits' were also extended to the nobles' tombs and to the priests who provisioned them with offerings.

The king's economic and political power declined, while the nobles' status was enhanced. There is clear evidence for this in the deterioration in pyramid construction and the more elaborate tombs of the nobility. Also, instead of arranging burial near the king, the local governors began to locate their tombs in their own districts, and gradually, the king's unique divine status lost credibility. Moves taken to arrest the royal economic decline now worsened the king's position. Increasingly, he began to marry into the wealthy but non-royal nobility, destroying the fictional divinity of the royal line. The kings of Dynasty 5 in particular needed the support of the priests of Re to rule, and the endowments and privileges of tax exemption enjoyed by the nobility were extended to the god's temples so that royal power and prestige were now also undermined by the state religion.

In Dynasty 5, the highest administrative posts were no longer given exclusively to the king's relatives, and lifetime or temporary appointments, subject to the king's approval and renewal, were replaced with hereditary governorships so that gradually these men felt free to pursue their own independence as local rulers far from Memphis. By the end of the Old Kingdom, centralized political power vested in the king had been replaced by conditions similar to predynastic times, when local leaders had held sway, forming alliances and fighting each other.

The final collapse was inevitable, and by the end of Dynasty 6 the internal stresses were exacerbated by waves of Asiatics on Egypt's north-eastern border who infiltrated and raided the country. The king, Pepy II, had sat on the throne for over ninety years, and he was unable to provide strong, effective leadership against the dangers that assailed his kingdom from all directions. This finely balanced, well-ordered, affluent society, once secure in its own beliefs and traditions, was overthrown and replaced by the chaotic conditions of the First Intermediate Period.

The First Intermediate Period

The First Intermediate Period is usually taken to include Dynasties 7 to 11. During this time, the centralized government at Memphis was overthrown, resulting in anarchy and fighting between the provincial rulers; this helped the Asiatics to infiltrate into the Delta. However, in Dynasties 9 and 10, a new line of Pharaohs emerged at Heracleopolis under a ruler named Akhtoy, but they soon came into conflict with a vigorous family of princes at Thebes (the first four were named Inyotef and the last three were called Mentuhotep). The resulting civil war was only resolved when Mentuhotep Nebhepetre succeeded in defeating the Heracleopolitans; he reunited Egypt under one king and established Dynasty 11, when the country began to flourish again. However, a new line (Dynasty 12) founded by Ammenemes I soon emerged to create the second great period of prosperity, known as the Middle Kingdom.

The historical and archaeological evidence for this troubled period is scanty, but literary sources probably cast some light on the turmoil and disaster which followed the end of Dynasty 6. A papyrus in the Leiden Museum, often referred to as the 'Admonitions of a Prophet', describes the conditions of revolution which prevailed at that time. It paints a picture of a society collapsing from within: chaos prevails over law and order; the roles of the rich and the poor are reversed; the neglected irrigation system results in famine and economic deprivation; the dead remain unburied, disease stalks the land, and thieves and murderers roam the countryside. Central administration, threatened by the people, collapses and, because nomads and foreign mercenaries now endanger Egypt's borders, the once flourishing trade with foreign lands falls away. In the midst of this chaos, the elderly king (almost certainly Pepy II) is in his palace, unaware of the dangers. A wise man called Ipuwer arrives and describes the conditions, urging action before it is too late. However, the warning goes unheeded and the old order collapses; apparently even the kingship is overturned: 'Behold, a thing has occurred that has never happened before; it has come to this that the king has been taken away by poor men.' As centralized order was overthrown, local rulers fought each other, and the certainties of the Old Kingdom disappeared. Men wished that they had never been born, but even death offered no solace because the materials for burial were often unobtainable and tombs were plundered on an unprecedented scale.

The pessimism of this text is reflected in other literature which probably also relates to this period. The most famous piece, sometimes known as the 'Dispute with his Soul of One who is tired of Life', expresses a dialogue between a man and his soul. The man is weary of life and seeks to end it by committing suicide, but his soul (described here as a separate entity) is anxious to persuade the man to live his normal span so that eventually they can both enjoy the benefits of a prepared tomb and funerary goods. They both present their viewpoints, but ultimately the soul wins the argument.

The profound political and economic changes of this period had a dramatic effect on religious beliefs and customs and on the associated art forms. Since the kingship was totally discredited, individuals now demanded their own eternity. Tombs were equipped in provincial districts for the local rulers, but gradually, democratization of beliefs came to affect all levels of society, and even the poorest classes hoped to achieve individual immortality. Closely associated with this transformation was the rise to universal prominence of the god Osiris who, as a resurrected mythical king, could offer his followers the chance of eternal life. Memphis had ceased to be the capital and main centre of arts and crafts and gradually the northern style was replaced by crude but vigorous provincial art. Generally, although sculpture and painting declined in excellence in this period, there was a considerable development in the literary forms; these provided new insight and expression which had grown out of the Egyptians' personal and national suffering.

Few facts survive about the rulers of Heracleopolis in Middle Egypt, although they are mentioned by Manetho and in the Turin Canon. However, their alliances with other local rulers must have provided some peaceful conditions, since these provincial rulers were able to prepare fine tombs for themselves near their courts, at such places as Beni Hasan, Akhmim and el-Bersha. At Assiut, in tombs prepared for princes who supported the Heracleopolitan kings, texts inscribed on the walls provide valuable information about the military conflict they had with the Theban rulers, but they also describe activities such as irrigation, farming and even swimming with the royal children. This suggests that some degree of peace and order prevailed in the district.

Meanwhile, at Thebes local princes were gradually expanding their influence. This line traced its ancestry to a noble named Inyotef the Great, and these rulers were the first to establish Thebes as one of Egypt's greatest cities. Later, in Dynasty 18, it would become the capital not only of Egypt but also of the Empire. Mentuhotep Nebhepetre founded Dynasty 11, after the Heracleopolitan rulers had been successfully vanquished, and he began to re-establish the unity and prosperity of the country. Little is known of his methods of administering Egypt, but he does not appear to have attempted to abolish the provincial rulers; their tombs continued to flourish, and he obviously reached some mutual agreement with them.

The royal residence was now established at Thebes. Restoration of temples was undertaken and peace and prosperity allowed a revival of the arts and architecture. The new capital became the centre of a distinctive but crude art style which was more angular than the forms of the old Memphite School. In the northernmost part of the Theban necropolis, three of the earlier princes of this line were buried in large rock-cut tombs, each with a large court at the back of which runs a series of door-like openings, giving the appearance of a pillared façade. Archaeologists use the term saff or row tombs for these monuments, and each has a modest burial chamber and other rooms cut into the rock behind the façade, as well as an associated brick valley temple.

However, Mentuhotep Nebhepetre chose a different burial for himself. In the cliffs at Deir el-Bahri on the west bank opposite Thebes, a unique and impressive burial place was designed for him. It incorporated elements of the Old Kingdom pyramid complex with several new features, again uniting burial place and mortuary temple in one location. There were also six shrines belonging to the royal ladies, queens and concubines, each with a shaft leading to a chamber which contained a finely carved sarcophagus. Much of the original impact of this monument is now lost, however, because it was later cannibalized by Queen Hatshepsut's builders to construct the even more magnificent adjacent temple.

The surrounding cliffs contained the tombs of the courtiers and officials of this period; excavated by Winlock for the Metropolitan Museum in New York, these provided further information, including a spectacular set of tomb models which illustrated many contemporary daily activities. Such models – 'brought to life' by magic to provide food and other services for the deceased throughout eternity – provide a real insight into the lifestyle and technology of that period.

Later generations regarded Mentuhotep Nebhepetre as the founder of the Middle Kingdom, and some historians place Dynasty 11 in the Middle Kingdom rather than in the First Intermediate Period. He was able to hand on a peaceful and prosperous kingdom to his successors, S'ankhkare Mentuhotep II and Nebtowere Mentuhotep III, but violent events marked the end of the latter king's reign when his vizier, Amenemhe, seems to have conspired to kill the king. Seizing the throne for himself, he became Ammenemes I, the founder of Dynasty 12.

The Middle Kingdom

When Ammenemes I usurped the throne he inaugurated a new and dynamic period of Egypt's history. A papyrus in the Museum of Leningrad entitled the 'Prophecy of Neferti'

attempts to glorify the king's reign in order to justify this line of rulers. It is set in the reign of the Old Kingdom ruler Sneferu when a lector-priest named Neferti gives a prophecy to the king. He describes a time of great disaster (reflecting the events already mentioned in the 'Admonitions of a Prophet') and the actions that will be taken by a new ruler, Ammenemes I, to save the country and reunite the people. The text refers to the non-royal birth of Ammenemes (his father was a commoner named Sesostris) and mentions that his mother was from Elephantine in Upper Egypt (it has been suggested that his features in surviving statuary show traces of a Nubian ancestry).

Ammenemes made several immediate changes. The rulers of Dynasty 11 had honoured Montu, god of war, as their patron deity but the new dynasty adopted Amun as royal god. He was identified with Min, the fertility god of Koptos, and his cult was honoured at Thebes. However, the political capital was now moved from Thebes to It-towy, just south of the Delta, so that the rulers would have greater control over the country, and on the west bank a new royal cemetery was started near the modern village of Lisht where the kings revived the idea of the pyramid for royal burials.

However, despite the king's undoubted strength and ability, the origins of Dynasty 12 were only questionably legitimate, and Ammenemes I and his successors employed a number of measures to ensure the continuation of the line. To prevent any rival claimant seizing the throne, Ammenemes I instituted the system of co-regency, placing his son and heir on the throne with him during his reign. Sesostris I probably took on an increasing number of royal duties, and at his father's death the succession was ensured and the throne passed to him. Co-regency became the custom throughout the rest of this dynasty and rulers in later times adopted it as a measure to secure the family line.

One of the greatest threats to the king's power towards the end of the Old Kingdom had been the strength and independence of the provincial nobility. Ammenemes I as a usurper needed their allegiance, and he restored some of the privileges which his predecessor Mentuhotep had removed. During his reign, they built fine tombs, reopened their local courts, raised their own troops locally and established the level of taxation on their subjects. However, their powers were kept in check and the king pursued a policy of demanding troops and ships from them when required, but it remained an uneasy alliance, and a later ruler of Dynasty 12, Sesostris III, finally resolved the situation. He again faced problems from the provincial rulers, but took a number of actions (which remain obscure) to deprive them of their privileges and close their courts. Their great tombs ceased to be built, and the old nobility never became a problem again; the king now advanced a new middle class, consisting mainly of small farmers, craftsmen and tradesmen who owed their allegiance to him. The administration was now organized so that the officials were directly responsible to the king and his delegate, the vizier.

During the Middle Kingdom, the kings again established relationships with Egypt's neighbours. Evidence suggests that incursions of 'Aamu (Asiatics) into the Delta now occurred and there are literary references to the Walls of the Ruler built by Ammenemes I to repel the danger, although their exact location remains uncertain. Small communities under the control of local princes probably occupied most of Palestine, and the kings of Dynasty 12 not only had contact with these but also penetrated further north. Egyptian influence was well established again at Byblos on the Syrian coast where trading contacts were renewed and two of the rulers received valuable gifts from kings Ammenemes III and IV. In Egypt, discovery of a treasure at Tod revealed objects of gold, silver and lapis lazuli, inscribed with the name of Ammenemes II but also displaying Aegean or Mesopotamian workmanship. Other objects of Egyptian style and manufacture which can be dated to this dynasty have been found at various sites almost as far north as the mouth of the River Orontes. More Asiatics were also employed in Egypt, working in households, at the pyramid building sites, or even in temples. They may have been brought to Egypt after military campaigns or they perhaps came as traders and craftsmen with specialized skills, but during this period there was

undoubtedly much greater contact between Egypt and her north-eastern neighbours.

Inscriptions and archaeological evidence also show an active policy towards Nubia in the south. A more aggressive people – known today as the C-group – had entered northern Nubia during the conflicts in Egypt in the First Intermediate Period, and they now prevented the Egyptians from gaining ready access to the essential gold and hard stone of the area. Ammenemes I therefore proceeded to subjugate Lower Nubia, and later kings continued this policy to ensure safe access to the area. A string of large brick fortresses was built along the river between the cataracts to subdue the local population, and Sesostris III, who most actively pursued this policy, established Egypt's southern boundary at the southern end of the Second Cataract. The fortresses became permanent stations, staffed with large garrisons and long-serving Egyptian officials and scribes.

Information about Egypt's relations with the south at this time comes not only from Nubia but also from inscriptions such as the narrative placed on the doorway of the tomb of Ameny, governor of the Oyrx Nome, at Beni Hasan. In this, he describes how he acted for two kings on missions to the south to obtain gold and other valuable commodities.

Middle Kingdom rulers also restored contacts with other areas: expeditions were sent to Punt to obtain incense, the turquoise mines in Sinai were reopened, and there was trade with Crete. There were also substantial developments at home. Ammenemes I completely reorganized his country, and in the 'Prophecy of Neferti' (which was probably composed to justify his reign), the king is described as the saviour of Egypt who banished chaos. However, another text, the 'Instruction of Ammenemes I', describes how the king met his death at the hands of conspirators. In this text, he revealed himself to his son in a dream in order to give Sesostris good advice, and warned him against friendship with his subjects who, like the murderous conspirators, would turn against him. Although the founder of this dynasty met a harsh fate, his line was strong enough to continue and to undertake great projects. Not only was the country's irrigation system restored, but Sesostris II and Ammenemes III also undertook a great land reclamation scheme in the Fayoum basin, around Lake Moeris. Classical legend actually credits Ammenemes III with construction of the lake although it was almost certainly a natural feature that he extended. He built a temple in the Fayoum to Sobek, the crocodile-god, and was probably also responsible for the Labyrinth, a construction famed in Classical writings and discovered by Petrie in 1889, near to the king's pyramid at Hawara.

Even in the Graeco-Roman Period, legend still perpetuated the memory of a 'King Sesostris' who performed great deeds; this legendary ruler was probably largely based on the character of Sesostris II who was regarded as one of Egypt's greatest rulers and received the rare honour of worship as a god in his own lifetime. In general, the kings of this dynasty supported the cults of many gods: the temples of Ptah at Memphis, Hathor at Denderah, Min at Koptos, Re-Atum at Heliopolis and Osiris at Abydos were all enhanced, and while Osiris became the most important and popular deity throughout Egypt, the rulers of Dynasty 12 promoted the cult of Amun as their own royal god. His temple at Karnak in Thebes was established and developed as a great religious centre, and one of the finest features to survive from the reign of Sesostris I was found there. It is an exquisite limestone shrine, now reconstructed in the Karnak temple precinct. Its blocks were later used in the construction of the Third Pylon (gateway) of the temple, but this kiosk was originally built to commemorate the king's first jubilee festival, and acted as a resting station for Amun's barque (sacred boat) which the priests carried around during the great festivals.

Thebes was now firmly established as a great religious centre, but the kings moved the political capital north to It-towy and their burial complexes were built in the same area. Ammenemes I and his son Sesostris I chose nearby Lisht for their sites, reinstating the classical pyramid complex of the Old Kingdom although some new Theban features were introduced. Around Ammenemes I's complex were the tombs of his family and some of his courtiers, but there was no return to the centralization of Cheops' pyramid and funerary city at Giza, and some officials of this reign chose to be buried at Thebes or in their own

provinces rather than at Lisht.

Other kings of Dynasty 12 chose different locations for their pyramids. Ammenemes II's monument at Dahshur was investigated by De Morgan in 1894, and although the king's tomb produced no treasure, the archaeologist found exquisite jewellery belonging to the royal princesses. Sesostris II, Ammenemes II's successor, moved away to Lahun for his burial but Sesostris III returned to Dahshur. De Morgan searched this pyramid but the burial had been robbed; however, within the enclosure, on the north side of the pyramid, he discovered another set of fine jewellery belonging to the royal women. The next king, Ammenemes III, built two pyramids – one at Dahshur and one at Hawara. The Dahshur monument was probably the king's cenotaph, and it is likely that he was actually buried at Hawara. This pyramid included various elaborate building devices (all in vain) to defeat the tomb-robbers, but its most interesting feature was the associated building known as the Labyrinth which was mentioned by Herodotus, Diodorus Siculus and Strabo. Petrie examined the Labyrinth in 1886 and made a more detailed study in 1911, although little survived of this famous construction. It apparently incorporated the funerary temple of the pyramid, administrative quarters, and possibly a royal residence.

The pyramid of Sesostris II at Lahun showed a number of innovations designed (again unsuccessfully) to thwart the tomb-robbers. These included a change in the positioning of the entrance; here it was located in a shaft outside the pyramid instead of in the northern face of the superstructure. Petrie, who examined the monument for several months in 1889, found only the superb granite sarcophagus inside. However, in 1914, with his co-worker Brunton, he had the good fortune to discover the jewellery of the king's daughter Princess Sit-Hathor-Iunut in her shaft tomb which, together with three similar tombs for members of the royal family, had been built south of the pyramid.

The eight groups of jewellery belonging to the queens and princesses of this dynasty are superb examples of the goldsmiths' and jewellers' crafts, demonstrating standards perhaps never surpassed in Egypt. They include crowns, pec-

Excavation at Kahun revealed builders' tools, the first ever found at a site in Egypt, although tools and building techniques are shown in tomb wall-paintings. This group contains a wooden mudbrick mould (centre), plasterer's float (right), and butterfly clamps used in masonry.

torals, armlets and collars, and feature a variety of semi-precious stones such as amethyst, carnelian, felspar and lapis lazuli, all set in gold and silver. Today, the jewels form part of the collections to be seen in the Cairo Museum and the Metropolitan Museum of Art in New York.

Near the pyramid of Lahun, Petrie made one of his most interesting discoveries. The town he called Kahun (its ancient name was Hetep-Sesostris meaning 'Sesostris-is-content') had housed the workforce engaged on the construction and maintenance of the pyramid, together with their families. All the ancillary services required to sustain a thriving community also grew up there. In the late 1890s, Petrie excavated two-thirds of the site, exposing the rows of purpose-built terraced houses for the workers, the larger villas for the officials, and the king's palace where he stayed when inspecting progress on his pyramid. For some reason, the town was apparently suddenly deserted about a hundred years later, long after the pyramid was completed. Most of the goods and chattels were left behind in the houses including the craftsmen's tools, spinning, weaving and agricultural equipment, women's toilet equipment and jewellery, children's games and toys, furniture and household possessions. These all provide a unique insight into the life of such a community because, unlike most Egyptian

material, they do not come from the tombs but are the articles used every day by ordinary people. Papyri were also discovered at the site: accounts and correspondence from the temple (situated in the town but actually the temple of the Lahun pyramid complex), and documents from the houses which included wills and other legal documents as well as veterinary and medical papyri. The famous Kahun Medical Papyrus is the first known treatise on gynaecology from the ancient world, and deals not only with the treatment of diseases but also provides details of pregnancy testing and contraception. As one of his greatest achievements, the scholar F. Ll. Griffith deciphered and translated these papyri.

The artifacts from the town, today housed mainly in museum collections in London and Manchester, have been re-examined and re-evaluated in recent years, using various scientific techniques, and they provide unparalleled information about living conditions in Dynasty 12. Standing at a crossroads in metal-working techniques, the tools and other equipment are of great interest for the history of technological development. Petrie held the opinion that a proportion of the workforce at Kahun were of non-Egyptian origin. The temple documents and other papyri, as well as providing information about the working conditions, also indicate that some of the labourers, domestic servants and even temple personnel were 'Aamu (Asiatics) and other evidence suggests that people from the Aegean islands and perhaps Cyprus were resident in the town, possibly as merchants and metal-workers. Petrie believed that the 'foreign element' at Kahun was made up of the descendants of prisoners-of-war brought back from the conflicts of earlier years, but although some may have come to Egypt this way, it is more likely that many entered the country as traders or with special skills to offer, seeking employment as part of the king's workforce. The discovery of this site, the first example of a purpose-built town to be uncovered in Egypt, has been followed by the excavation of other towns, built specifically for the royal workforce, at Deir el-Medina near Thebes, Amarna, and Giza.

However, the royal burials of Dynasty 12 are only one aspect of the funerary wealth of this period. Before Sesostris III effectively terminated the power of the provincial nobles and their great tombs ceased to be built, there is ample evidence that magnificent non-royal tombs were constructed at various sites, particularly in Middle Egypt. Choosing to be buried in their own local centres of power instead of at the base of the king's pyramid, these men and their families had fine rock-cut tombs at centres in Upper and Middle Egypt including Beni-Hasan, Deir Rifeh, Assiut, Deir Bersha, Meir and Aswan. Cut in rows in the cliffs near to the provincial capitals, each tomb had a columned portico or terraced courtyard which led into a columned hall; a small room or niche leading off this contained the tomb-owner's funerary statue to which offerings were brought and presented. Beyond the chapel lay the burial chamber, usually reached through an opening cut into the floor of the columned hall. This hall was decorated with registers of painted wall scenes which continued the Old Kingdom custom of representing aspects of daily life which the owner

Above: Domestic items found at Kahun included a fibre brush (left) and plaited rush sandals (example, right); leather shoes were also found. The almost intact rush basket (centre) was discovered in the corner of a room in one of the houses. It contained metal tools belonging to a workman.

Below: At Kahun, Petrie found agricultural tools used to grow the town's food. Similar to implements shown in tomb scenes, these include a hoe (centre), rake (top right), scoop for winnowing (top left), grain scoop (bottom centre), and sickle for reaping (bottom right).

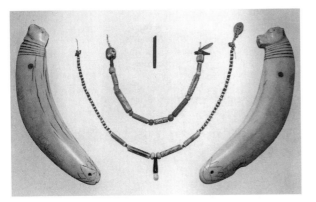

Jewellery from Kahun displays a variety of beads. The ivory clappers were found with other items in one of the houses. They probably belonged to a magician whose face mask was also discovered in an adjoining room. These may have been used in magical rites.

wished to experience and enjoy in the next world. Although the general content of the wall-decoration was repeated in tombs throughout Egypt, any centralization of art (as at Memphis in the Old Kingdom) had long since disappeared. The Memphite traditions enjoyed a revival in Dynasty 12, but there was still a strong Theban influence that had been introduced in Dynasty 11 and also the variations provided by local craftsmen who were now employed in the different districts.

Growth of non-royal tombs and tomb goods was a direct result of the popularity of Osiris, god of the dead. With the fall of the Old Kingdom, reliance on the king and Re, his patron deity, had been replaced by almost universal worship of Osiris, and this democratization of religious and funerary beliefs continued throughout the Middle Kingdom. Osiris, whose mythology is later recounted by Classical writers (most notably Plutarch), was described as a human king who had brought civilization and agriculture to Egypt at an early date. Murdered by his jealous brother Seth, his body was dismembered and scattered throughout Egypt, but Osiris still overcame his enemy and experienced resurrection and eternal life. His beloved wife Isis gathered the parts of his body together and reunited them with her magical skills. She then posthumously conceived her husband's son, Horus, and brought him up in the

marshes of the Delta, away from the evil machinations of Seth, but when Horus was grown he sought to avenge his father's death and entered into a bloody conflict with Seth. The combatants finally came before a tribunal of divine judges who found in favour of Osiris and Horus, with the result that Osiris became the god of the underworld and the dead, while every king on his accession became the divine earthly embodiment of Horus and, at death, became Osiris. It was also decided that Seth should be banished as the personification of all evil.

This story of the classic conflict between good and evil with the ultimate triumph of good had considerable influence on Egyptian belief and custom from the Middle Kingdom onwards. Some people equipped their tombs with goods to reflect aspects of Osiris' cult but others, too poor to aspire to lavish material possessions, at least now had the hope of an individual hereafter if, in life, they had worshipped Osiris and performed good deeds. At death, the deceased, whether rich or poor, was now believed to follow Osiris' example and face a tribunal of forty-two gods. Defended by Thoth, the ibis-headed god of writing, the man or woman would be required to recite the Negative Confession; this denied to each of the gods in turn that the person was guilty of any serious crime during his lifetime. Knowledge of magic or special spells might assist at first in deceiving the gods, but further interrogation followed in the presence of Thoth and also Ma'at, the goddess of truth, and Anubis, the god of embalming. The deceased stood before a large balance and his heart was placed in one pan and a feather (symbol of truth) in the other. Anxiously he awaited the gods' verdict of his character, after the goddesses of fate and destiny had given their testimonies; if he was declared innocent, his heart (the supposed seat of the intellect and emotions) would balance the feather in the scales, and Thoth would then declare him 'free from sin'. After the gods accepted this verdict, he could join his soul and they would pass together into the realm of Osiris. The deceased could now have 'Osiris' written in front of his own name and the phrase 'true of voice' or 'justified' placed afterwards, to indicate the successful outcome of his trial. However, these terms soon came to be a formality in inscriptions, simply indicating whether a person was alive or 'deceased'.

If a person was found guilty at his trial, it was believed that his heart was thrown to a mythical animal, the Devourer, which was depicted as a creature composed of parts belonging to different animals. Once his heart was destroyed, the person faced the dreadful fate of 'second death' or annihilation. Moral virtue was thus now essential for eternal life, and Osiris could offer resurrection to his followers because he had personally passed through this trial. Now neither personal wealth nor mere knowledge of magic could guarantee survival if sins had been committed in this life.

The land of Osiris to which all could aspire was idealized as a place of abundant vegetation and great happiness, situated below the western horizon or on a group of islands. Here, unfailing harvests and eternal springtime ensured that the joys of life could be continued without attendant pain or suffering. This paradise mirrored Egypt itself, but the land was democratically divided up into small plots, to be cultivated by rich and poor alike. Not surprisingly, the wealthy did not wish to engage in such agricultural pursuits throughout eternity, preferring the luxuries represented in the wall scenes and by the goods placed in their tombs, and so gradually three concepts of eternity emerged, closely linked to earthly status and material wealth. The kings, as in the Old Kingdom, continued to join the gods in the heavens; the nobility and aspiring middle-classes expected to pass time in the tomb, enjoying their luxurious provisions; and the poor tilled the land in Osiris' kingdom. There were attempts to rationalize these concepts and link them together, and they were to some extent interchangeable, but basically there remained three distinct and socially based ideas of the afterlife.

Model boats were placed in tombs from the Middle Kingdom onwards. Intended to allow the deceased to travel to Abydos, the centre of Osiris' worship, some were very elaborate, with sails and rigging. This model (c.1900 BC) incorporates the owner's mummy, mourners and sailors.

Before his rise to prominence as god of the dead, Osiris was a vegetation deity, personifying the annual rebirth of the land and its crops after the flood-waters had revived the soil. This role as a life-giver and source of fertility was readily associated with his secondary function as a god-king who had died but then triumphed over evil, to be resurrected as the ruler and judge of the dead. He may have had some connections with the other Near Eastern deities – Adonis, Dionysus and Tammuz – who were also shepherd gods, each bewailed and buried by a goddess. However, they differed from Osiris in other respects, and it is not possible to prove any common origin for these deities.

Osiris was also a moon-god and a corn-deity, and his great cult-centres were situated at Busiris in the Delta and at Abydos. An annual pilgrimage and great festival were held at Abydos in the last month of inundation to celebrate the god's resurrection and renewal of the vegetation, when the most sacred rites were held in the innermost area of the temple. The Temple of Sethos I was the last to be built at this site, although earlier monuments would have been constructed there because the place was so holy. In the set of rooms in this temple which are known today as the Osiris Complex, the wall scenes depict the rites once performed there; these were closely associated with a unique monument, the Osireion, found at the rear of the temple. This was probably regarded as the burial place of Osiris. Some other ceremonies took place outside the temple, watched by pilgrims known as the Followers of Thoth, and in these Mystery Plays, which were performed from Dynasty 12 onwards, priests probably wore masks and enacted events to celebrate highlights in the mythology of Osiris.

Abydos was Egypt's greatest centre of pilgrimage, and by the Middle Kingdom Osiris held the special position once enjoyed by the kings of the Old Kingdom because he was able to offer immortality to others. Thus, since the earliest kings had tombs there and it was also the burial place of Osiris, people made special arrangements to be buried at Abydos so that they could participate in the god's resurrection and have the personal hope of a greater chance of eternity. Even if burial at Abydos was too expensive, some had their mummies taken there briefly before returning to their own local cemeteries, but others had to content themselves with setting up inscribed stones (stelae) there, or placing model boats in their tombs which they could use after death to reach Abydos.

Tomb equipment was now a major feature of non-royal tombs and it became increasingly elaborate. In addition to model boats to sail to Abydos, other craft were often included for fishing on the river, travelling long distances, or transporting the deceased from his home to the necropolis. They are often beautifully made, complete with oars, deck cabins and crew members, and as with other models, the Egyptians believed that they could be made full-size by means of magic, to serve the owner's needs in the next world. There were also models of servants and soldiers. In the Old Kingdom, there had been single servant figures, each engaged in food production or presentation, but these now became complete groups, working in granaries, breweries and slaughter-houses or engaged in ploughing, fishing, or textile production. There are also complete models of the great landowners' houses, estates and herds, and in many cases the content of the scenes found on the walls of Old Kingdom tombs was now recreated in these wooden models. There are also 'concubine-figures', harpists and dwarves to entertain the tomb-owner, and a variety of animal models; some of these were perhaps intended as pets, and others as a food-source for the owner, who may also have hoped to take possession of the strength of some of these animals.

A named statue of the deceased (and sometimes also of members of his family) was usually provided in the tomb; this could be used by his returning spirit if his mummified body had been destroyed. Most non-royal statues are not life-size and there is great variation in the standard of craftsmanship. However, the magnificent sculptured heads of kings of this dynasty, with their grimly determined expressions, achieved a new level of excellence in portraiture.

Figurines of agricultural workers (known as ushabtis) were a special type of model. Introduced in Dynasties 9 and 10, they continued to

In early predynastic times the body was buried in matting or a skin, but later the burial chamber was lined with wooden planks or the body was placed in a wooden coffin. This coffin (c.2500 BC) from Tarkhan represents a house for the dead.

be produced, with some superficial variations, down to the last dynasties and were included in the tomb to undertake labours in the land of Osiris which the affluent tomb-owners wished to avoid. Each tomb-set consisted of up to 365 figures (perhaps intended to cover every day in a year) and a number of 'overseer' figures. At first they were made in wood but in Dynasty 18 faience was introduced and this continued to be the material most widely used for their production. Each figure is mummiform and has a set of agriculture tools painted or carved on its surface; an inscription identifies the owner's name, while the accompanying spell indicates that the ushabti (the word is probably derived from the Egyptian verb meaning 'to answer') will respond to the owner's call and perform all the irksome tasks in the afterlife.

Tomb equipment now also included the soul-house. These had developed from circular stone offering tables or rectangular slabs or platters placed in earlier tombs for food offerings, but the open courtyard at the front of these model pottery soul-houses was now used as the offering tray. Soul-houses show some variation in detail but they provide unique information about domestic architecture at that period. In addition to the cooking area in the front courtyard where the offerings were placed, most houses also have a two-storeyed portico and staircase leading up to a flat rooftop.

Other possessions placed in the tombs of the affluent included fine linen clothing, mirrors and cosmetics, and toys and games; these all provide evidence of the high standard of living which the Egyptians expected to enjoy in the next world. Some items were obviously favourite possessions they used in life, but they also prepared goods specially for the tomb. For example, some jewellery, heavier and more traditional in design, was made for the burial, but they also took the treasured pieces that they had worn every day. In

addition, pottery vessels and dishes were supplied for the meals the deceased hoped to enjoy throughout eternity.

The coffins that housed the body were now very elaborate. It became customary to have two coffins – an outer rectangular one and an anthropoid or body coffin which was placed inside. Royalty and the great nobles were sometimes provided with finely carved stone coffins but wooden coffins were widely used for the other classes. Rectangular coffins had either flat or vaulted lids, and their decoration of brightly painted geometric designs represented the façade of a palace or house, perhaps because they were regarded as dwelling places for the deceased. The design also incorporated a pair of eyes on the east or left side of the coffin so that the body inside, facing in this direction, was able to 'look out' and gain sustenance from the food offerings placed in the tomb. An eternal food supply was often ensured by painting offerings and lines of inscriptions on the coffin. Known today as the Coffin Texts, these were spells derived and adapted from the Old Kingdom Pyramid Texts and now made available to benefit non-royal persons. As with the Pyramid Texts, they included spells to deny death and to ensure that the deceased owner successfully overcame any dangers or perils he might meet in his passage from this world to the next. These spells, written in cursive Hieroglyphs, only appear in the Middle Kingdom but they were briefly reintroduced in Dynasty 26.

The body coffin placed inside the rectangular coffin took the form of a mummy; this had probably developed from the cartonnage cover placed over the head of the deceased during the Old Kingdom, when it was intended to act as a substitute for the owner if his body was destroyed. Some of the earliest anthropoid coffins were made of cartonnage (a combination of papyrus and gum), but later examples were carved from wood. Clients would select their coffins from the stock which was mass-produced by the workshops; these had painted stylized facial features and formalized inscriptions, but each would eventually be personalized by the addition of the owner's name. The eyes were often made of obsidian and alabaster inlays, and a false wooden beard and uraeus (serpent) on the forehead (both symbols of kingship and divinity) were added to emphasize that the deceased, having successfully faced the divine tribunal, was now an Osiris. The wide collar, girdle, bandaging and jewellery painted on the outside of the coffin depicted objects which sometimes actually adorned the mummy inside.

By the Middle Kingdom, the practice of mummification had become more widespread than in the Old Kingdom when it was first devised to preserve the bodies of the royal family and the great nobles. Very few examples have survived from the Middle Kingdom, but they suggest that poor preservation was the result of inadequate desiccation of the body and the application of resin to the skin surface before the drying process was complete. This hastened decomposition because it encouraged moisture to remain in the tissues. Even in the group of royal mummies of Dynasty 11 which were found in the pyramid-temple of Mentuhotep at Deir el-Bahri, the bodies had not been eviscerated, and although natron was used as the drying agent, dehydration was incomplete when the bodies were wrapped.

The increased range of funerary items found in non-royal tombs now included a wooden canopic chest which was customarily placed in a niche in the east wall of the tomb where it could be seen by the deceased. These chests, brightly painted with lines of inscription, geometric doors, and a pair of eyes, housed canopic jars which contained the deceased's viscera, removed during mummification. Canopic jars, four to a set, were usually made of pottery and had stoppers in the form of human heads. They were dedicated to the deities known as the Four Sons of Horus who protected the deceased's viscera: Qebhsennuef (the liver and gall bladder), Hapy (the small intestine), Duamutef (the lungs), and Imset (the stomach and large intestine). By Dynasty 18, the jar stoppers had changed to represent the specific heads associated with these

By the Middle Kingdom, wealthy people supplied themselves with fine tomb goods including nests of wooden coffins. These had developed from the earlier 'house-style' coffins. This body coffin from the Tomb of Two Brothers at Rifeh (c.1900 BC) is decorated with a painted 'broad-collar' and geometric designs.

deities – hawk, ape, jackal and human. The Four Sons of Horus were in turn protected by the goddesses Serket, Nephthys, Neith and Isis.

The increasing democratization of funerary goods in Dynasty 12 also brought about the large-scale production of private (non-royal) stelae. The stela developed from two features found in Old Kingdom non-royal tombs, namely the Offering List and the Autobiography, which were both designed to benefit the tomb-owner. The Autobiography gave a summary of the life and characteristics of the owner, emphasizing his virtues and worthiness but omitting any reference to his failures or sins. It also included his official rank and titles, and was intended to justify his claim to an eternity in which he would hold high office. In addition, it provides us with information about members of his family and their ranks and titles. The Offering List was a formal inscription that requested benefits (particularly food and drink) for the deceased in the next world, and also asked that he should be well received there. It employed a basic formula by which the offerings were presented either through the agency of Anubis, god of cemeteries and mummification, or through the king's own bounty (the phrase 'A-boon-which-the king-gives' is customarily used here). By Dynasty 5, the Offering List and Autobiography had become standard features of the tomb, and they reached their most complete form in Dynasty 6. They survived the upheaval of the early First Intermediate Period and emerged later, combined together in the form of the stela. This stone block, often round-topped, was carved with a scene showing the deceased owner offering to deities and it also displayed an inscription with the owner's name and title, and those of his family. It included prayers in praise of the king and the gods, and sometimes a fuller autobiography was given, recording in bombastic terms details of the owner's virtues and the major events of his life. Many stelae were set up by ordinary people as personal memorials and, since stone is a durable material, relatively large numbers have survived, although the stereotyped inscriptions usually provide little information about the owner or his lifestyle.

In general, the Middle Kingdom was the golden period of Egyptian literature when, apart from the funerary inscriptions, many other genres were developed. The classical form of Hieroglyphs, known today as Middle Egyptian, emerged during this period and literature reached its highest level so that later generations of school children were trained to copy the Middle Kingdom compositions as models for their style and content. The Instructions in Wisdom first produced in the Old Kingdom now developed new forms which incorporated political propaganda to emphasize the king's power, not so much as a god but as a human ruler and leader of a great nation, whose firm action had restored and unified Egypt. Two of the sacred dramas, composed to be performed by the priests at the great religious festivals, have survived; these are known as the Coronation Drama and the Memphite Drama.

The Execration Texts are also of great interest; they were intended to deal with the enemies of the king or the tomb-owner, and the inscriptions mention either a named evil (such as an Egyptian enemy or a foreign foe) or a generalized threat to the owner's well-being. Some were written on small tablets of clay or stone and placed in the tombs, and others were inscribed on small pottery bowls which were smashed to defeat the enemy and then buried near the tomb.

The concept of the short story also emerged at this time. Such tales may have had propagandist undertones, or been designed to promote a moral viewpoint (perhaps emphasizing the piety and legitimacy of a particular king), but primarily they tried to attract the listener's interest by entertaining him. The most famous of these, the Story of Sinuhe, tells how Sinuhe fled from Egypt and achieved recognition in Palestine. Finally, wishing to return home so that he could die and be buried in Egypt, he wrote with this request to the new ruler, Sesostris I, who granted him a free pardon and treated him with great courtesy and kindness on his return, thus proving himself to be a great and worthy ruler.

However, the literary and artistic excellence of the Middle Kingdom could not stem the arrival of a new period of decline and disintegration. The last rulers of Dynasty 12, Ammenemes IV and Sobekneferu (one of Egypt's few queens regnant), faced many problems and few remains of their reigns have survived; it has proved impossible to identify their burial places, although two ruined pyramids at Mazghuna, south of Dahshur, may have belonged to them.

The Second Intermediate Period

This second period of decline had much in common with the First Intermediate Period and, again, there was political decentralization when several parallel dynasties of weak rulers came to power. According to Manetho's account, Dynasty 13 was based at Thebes and consisted of 60 kings, while Dynasty 14, with 76 kings, had seceded at the end of Dynasty 12 and now ruled contemporaneously at Xois in the Delta. Internal chaos permitted foreigners to infiltrate from the north-eastern frontier, and they (the so-called 'Hyksos') ruled Egypt in Dynasties 15 and 16. Finally, Egyptian rulership was again restored by the Theban princes of Dynasty 17 who by their military prowess managed to subdue the Hyksos and drive them out of Egypt. They then established themselves in Dynasty 18 as the kings of a united land and became founders of the New Kingdom.

As with the First Intermediate Period, the sources of evidence are limited, but Manetho's account, preserved in Africanus and Eusebius, is augmented by the Jewish historian Josephus in *Against Apion* which is supposedly a verbatim extract from Manetho. He claims that the Hyksos invasion of Egypt took place under 'King Tutimaios' as a 'blast of God' when the conquerors came unexpectedly from the East and took Egypt without a battle. Their treatment of the Egyptians was vicious: they burnt the cities and overthrew the gods, razing their temples to the ground; some of the native population were killed while others were made slaves. Then they raised one of their own number – Salitis – to be king; he ruled from Memphis and took tribute from the whole of Egypt. He then established a new centre, rebuilding the Delta city of Avaris on the east of the Bubastite (east) arm of the Nile, fortifying it with massive walls and garrisoning it with 240,000 men. The account goes on to name the next six kings, the first Hyksos rulers, and says that their whole race was called Hyksos, meaning 'shepherd kings'; the derivation given is that: '*hyk* in the sacred language means "king" and *sos* in common speech is "shepherd"'. Another explanation claims that Hyksos meant 'captive shepherds', from the derivation of *hyk* as the Egyptian word for captive.

Josephus and others believed that the Hyksos invasion and their later expulsion from Egypt provided the basis for the biblical story of the sojourn in Egypt and the Exodus, but there is no conclusive evidence to support this. The name Hyksos in fact came from the Egyptian words *hekau* (meaning rulers) and *khaswt* (meaning 'foreign hill-countries') and had been used since the Middle Kingdom to describe the nomadic chieftains on Egypt's north-eastern border. The Hyksos were undoubtedly just a group of nomadic rulers who now entered Egypt, and not a race or ethnic group who went on to conquer the Delta and Nile Valley after subduing Syria and Palestine, although some scholars have continued to support the idea of some kind of mass invasion. Groups of Palestinians (who were probably mainly Semitic in origin but may also have included Indo-Aryan elements) were pushed forward by a people known as Hurrians who exerted pressure from the Caspian area down into Syria. It was these nomadic groups who now infiltrated and settled in Egypt.

The ease with which Egypt was taken by these foreigners may be explained in part by a document of Dynasty 13. The Brooklyn Papyrus lists forty-five men, women and children of Asiatic origin who were members of the household of an official of Upper Egypt and may indicate a widespread foreign population in the country prior to the Hyksos infiltrations which might have lessened resistance to the new foreign overlords.

Certainly, Josephus' account of the Hyksos' intimidation of the native population seems unduly harsh and is probably based on later propagandist accounts which sought to glorify the Theban restoration of Egyptian rule. In fact, evidence indicates that the Hyksos did not bring or seek to impose their own traditions on the Egyptians, but rather tried to adopt existing methods and customs (again suggesting that they were not a cohesive group with their own established culture). They appointed Egyptian bureaucrats to administer the land, and although they imposed taxes and took tribute from the southern vassal regions, they were merely continuing practices the native rulers had always employed. The Hyksos became Pharaohs, and took on royal powers and traditions; they supported the arts and crafts, temples continued to be built, and the traditions of literary composition were allowed to continue.

A new royal patron god, Seth, was adopted from the Egyptian pantheon. This may seem an unfortunate choice, since Seth had previously featured as the evil god in Egyptian mythology, but in fact this Hyksos deity probably had more in common with one of the Asiatic gods. A cult-centre was established for him at Avaris, and Re, the old royal god, was restored as another royal patron and protector.

Monumental evidence from this period is scanty, partly because the capital was in the Delta, with its less favourable environmental conditions. At one site, Tell el-Yahudiyeh, interest has focused on the massive enclosure walls which are without parallel elsewhere in Egypt, and some scholars have attributed them to the Hyksos. Identification of the site of Avaris has also given rise to much speculation. Tanis and Qantir have both been suggested as possibilities, but evidence of a large influx of foreigners at the beginning of Dynasty 15 at Tell el-Dab'a in the Delta has indicated that this was probably the site of ancient Avaris.

Despite the later critical view of Hyksos rule, it was clearly a time of innovation and development in technology. There were new building techniques, metal-working skills, and advances in weaponry, and at some point the horse and chariot were introduced into Egypt in addition to hump-backed cattle, the use of the vertical (as opposed to the horizontal) loom, and the lyre and lute.

However, for reasons which are not clear, relations between the Egyptians and the Hyksos rulers deteriorated. In Dynasty 17, a line of princes ruled from Thebes as vassals of the Hyksos, and it was they who now spearheaded the native rebellion. Part of a story has survived which relates how the conflict emerged between the Theban ruler Seqenenre and the Hyksos king Apophis who resided in the north at Avaris. Apophis needed to find a reason to complain about Seqenenre and his pretext was that the hippopotami at Thebes were causing such a commotion at night that they kept him awake (although he was some twelve hundred kilometres further north!).

In 1954 a great stela was discovered at Karnak which provides a detailed account of military actions taken by the Thebans, and augments information given in a Hieratic inscription on a tablet discovered almost fifty years earlier at Lord Carnarvon's excavations. It describes the earlier stages of the contest that Kamose, Seqenenre's successor, now fought against the Hyksos. He was apparently finally able to return to his capital after a successful campaign, and the people greeted him with great joy.

The last stages in the overthrow of the Hyksos were carried out by Kamose's successor who became Amosis I, the founder of Dynasty 18 and of the New Kingdom. An inscription on the wall of a tomb at el-Kab tells how the owner, Ahmose son of Ebana, pursued his military career under Amosis, taking part in campaigns against the Hyksos. By this time, they had been pushed back into Palestine where the Egyptians finally subdued them. A younger relative from el-Kab, Ahmose Pennekheb, also left an account of his military endeavours when he served as a soldier and courtier throughout the course of five reigns.

In later times, the Egyptians glorified the Theban rulers of Dynasty 17 who kept the native traditions alive in the south and finally drove out the foreign dynasts. The Hyksos Period was significant in the country's history because it profoundly changed the Egyptians' attitude to the outside world. Previously isolated from the direct threat of invasion, the Egyptians had engaged their neighbours in trading ventures and occasional military forays but had not pursued direct expansionist policies. Now, however, they were forced to recognize that, unless they were active and aggressive conquerors, others would be attracted by Egypt's wealth and would try to invade their country. In future, it would be necessary for the Egyptians not only to ensure that they had commercial access to resources in other areas, but also to establish a professional army and begin to build the foundations of the world's first empire.

The New Kingdom
••••••••••••••••••••••

The Theban princes who had driven away the Hyksos set out to establish their own line as kings of Dynasty 18 and founders of the New Kingdom. Particularly in the early years, great emphasis was placed on close dynastic marriages and the role of the royal wives in transmitting the kingship. Seqenenre Ta'o II and Ahhotpe, the parents of the first king of the dynasty, Amosis I, were brother and sister. Queen Ahhotpe was highly regarded: in a stela found at Karnak, dedicated by Amosis I, it was recalled that she had rallied the army and terminated a rebellion, although no further details are known. Her tomb was discovered by locals in 1858, where the mummy, adorned with treasure, still survived; this jewellery, given to her by her son Amosis, is now in the Cairo Museum. Amosis I married Ahmose-Nefertari who was probably his niece, and she became the most powerful of these queens influencing the reigns of both her husband and their son, Amenophis I, with whom she probably shared a tomb and a funerary temple.

The reign of Amenophis I saw the development of various policies which established the pattern of Dynasty 18. First, the capital city was now based at Thebes, the local centre of this royal family, although undoubtedly substantial cities and military bases continued to exist in the north at Memphis, Heliopolis and other Delta sites. The Theban rulers attributed their ascendancy over the Hyksos to the powerful support of their chief local god who had been worshipped at Thebes since Dynasty 12. They also credited their deity with the great successes they continued to enjoy in Asia where they were able to lay the foundation of the Egyptian Empire and augment the country's wealth. Originally, Amun had been regarded as a god of the air but

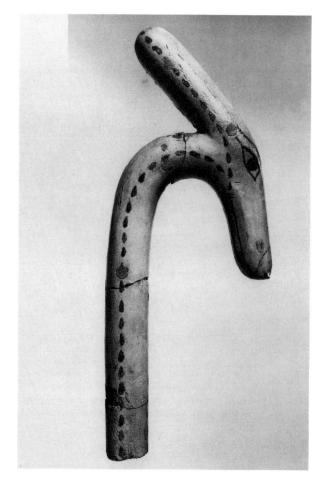

Gods are often shown with sceptres which had special powers. This was sceptre (believed to give its owner dominion) is made of faience and represents a gazelle head. It is from Nagada (c.1450 BC) and was probably used in temple rituals.

he soon acquired powers as god of fertility and warfare; to ensure that their god had no rival, the Theban kings also now associated him with the old northern sun-god Re, creating the all-powerful deity Amen-Re. By the middle of Dynasty 18, when Egypt's foreign conquests had reached their peak, Amun's universality as a creator and ruler of all peoples was emphasized, and his great temple and priesthood at Karnak in Thebes wielded unprecedented power.

The priesthood sought to promote Thebes as the original site of creation and added a new cosmogony to the earlier myths. This claimed that

147

Cosmopolitan influences were strong in Egypt during the New Kingdom. This blue glaze flask (c.1450 BC) from the royal residence town of Gurob imitates some foreign features by copying the 'pilgrim vessel' shape. Birds and lotus flowers are outlined in black paint.

achieved not only religious but also considerable political and economic power. This was the direct result of royal policy towards the god in the earliest years of the New Kingdom when, in Nubia and more especially in Asia, the Egyptians achieved great military success. They returned from their campaigns in Asia with booty and prisoners-of-war and subordinate rulers of other areas also presented Pharaoh with gifts. In gratitude to Amen-Re for their successes, the early rulers of Dynasty 18 made donations to Amun's temple at Karnak; great estates were established to feed and support the temple personnel, raw materials were assigned to the temple, and prisoners-of-war were employed there in the god's service. However, the priesthood's increased wealth and power were to have disastrous results for the kings as the dynasty progressed. As in the Old Kingdom, the king's own generosity built up the priests' influence so that they became his arch-rivals. The god, as the king's divine father, selected and supported a particular candidate to rule Egypt and when the succession was disputed or there was a weak candidate, the priests could exercise unchallenged power by expressing or withholding divine approval. By the end of Dynasty 18, it became essential for the kings to attempt to curtail the priests' control, but their success was short-lived and the problem recurred in later dynasties.

Most of the rulers of the New Kingdom added to the magnificent but confusing temple complex of Amun at Karnak, but major building projects were also undertaken on the west bank opposite the city of Thebes (which was on the east bank). From the beginning of Dynasty 18, the kings selected a new burial site hidden in the bleak western hills. In this barren, narrow valley (known today as the Valley of the Kings), they abandoned their earlier custom of building pyramids, perhaps because of their vulnerability to tomb-robbers, and opted instead for deep, rock-cut tombs. Above the valley, the natural formation of the Theban cliffs, resembling a pyramid both in shape and colour, may have prompted the Egyptians to select this as the royal burial area. The highest point of the mountain, called the Peak, was personified as a goddess who protected the burials below. Isolated and relatively easy to

Amun had begotten himself in secret on the Island of Creation and that all other gods and creation myths came into existence from this first act of creation. As the supreme state-god, he was regarded as 'King of Gods' and he absorbed the powers and qualities of other deities such as Re, Min and Ptah. His consort was Mut, the vulture-goddess who with their son Khonsu (the moon-god) was worshipped at Karnak but also possessed her own temple near by (the Southern Harem, now known as the Temple of Luxor).

Amen-Re thus became the royal god, protecting the kings and supporting their claims to rule Egypt. His cult-centre at Thebes became the most important religious and political city in Egypt and the empire, where the king's main residence was situated and the royal necropolis was now developed.

The god's greatest temple – Karnak at Thebes – was extended and embellished and his priesthood, who came to control the royal succession, guard but also close to the city of Thebes, these barren valleys were regarded as an ideal location to develop as a royal necropolis. Here the tombs, consisting of a series of stairwells, corridors and chambers cut out of the mountainside, were designed to defeat the tomb-robbers but, with the exception of Tutankhamun's burial, all the known royal tombs in the Valley of the Kings were massively plundered in antiquity. These tombs, however, are still magnificently impressive: most retain the finely carved sarcophagus in the burial chamber and the walls are decorated with carved and painted scenes taken from the various funerary books and designed to assist the king to use magic to defeat the dangers he would encounter in passing from this world to the next. The Valley of the Kings was apparently used almost exclusively for the pharaohs. However, Queen Tiye received the unusual honour of burial there in her husband's tomb and the Valley also accommodated her parents despite the fact that they were commoners. During Dynasty 18, most of the queens were buried in tombs scattered across the necropolis area but in later times favourite wives and royal sons were interred in the so-called Valley of the Queens. Here, rock-cut tombs only slightly less elaborate than those of the kings are decorated with beautiful wall scenes which concentrate on the relationship between the gods and the deceased and the final journey to the next world.

As in earlier times, when the tombs of nobles and officials had clustered around the king's pyramid, now they were cut into the mountainside and arranged in a number of major groups near to the royal valleys. Directly evolved from the portico-tombs built by the provincial nobility of the Middle Kingdom, these tombs of Dynasty 18 consist of a rectangular courtyard behind which there is an inverted T-shaped chapel cut into the rock. A hidden shaft located in the floor at the rear or in a corner of the chapel descends to the subterranean chambers where the burial and the funerary possessions were housed. These tombs are also decorated with wall scenes; however, unlike the Old Kingdom cemeteries in the north, there was no ready access to a good supply of local stone and so most scenes were painted but not carved. After the

This doughnut-shaped alabaster vessel of the New Kingdom (c.1450 BC) from Abydos was probably used as a container for perfumed oil; alabaster was particularly suitable for this, as it would have kept the oil cool. The vessel's shape shows a foreign influence.

walls were coated with stucco and mud-plaster, they were painted directly on to the prepared wall-surface; sometimes, walls in the burial chamber were also decorated with inscriptions taken from the funerary books but more usually only the tomb-chapel was painted. Here, in the front hall, events and daily activities once enjoyed by the owner were depicted; usually scenes on the rear wall illustrated his career or profession and his duties for the king while others showed his family and estate, social events, sports and recreation, and his worship of the gods. From the centre of this transverse hall, a passage ran back into the mountain; at the far end was a small sanctuary with a niche to hold statues of the tomb-owner and his wife, and sometimes also a false door for the owner's spirit to enter the tomb and enjoy the food-offerings. In these areas, scenes illustrated the funeral preparations, the burial procession and ceremonies, the presentation of the funerary offerings, and the funerary banquet. The owner was also shown in the next world, meeting the gods and undertaking the sacred duty of a pilgrimage to Abydos. This wall-decoration was intended to provide the deceased with a world that he could enter by magic and continue to enjoy throughout eternity. However, it also provides us with a wealth of information about the religious beliefs and customs and the agriculture, crafts and living conditions of the New Kingdom.

The west bank was the location for another major New Kingdom religious and architectural development. Traditional temples (such as those at Karnak and Luxor) known as cultus temples had developed in purpose, function, and architectural form from the earliest reed shrines built in predynastic villages. Each cultus temple, regarded as the Island of Creation where gods

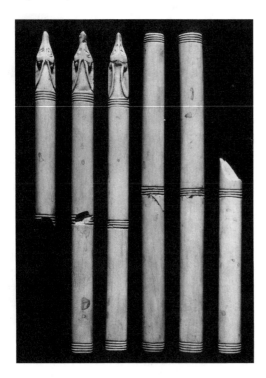

These ivory sticks from a New Kingdom tomb (c.1450 BC) were used for playing games. Three have finely carved jackal heads and are a good example of skill in working ivory which was imported from the south. Furniture was sometimes elaborately inlaid with ivory and ebony.

and mankind had first come into existence, was the owner-deity's earthly residence. Here, the god's statue, housed in the sanctuary, was approached through regular rituals by the king (or his delegate, the high-priest) to establish a relationship from which both the god and the king, as representative of Egypt, could derive mutual benefits.

However, the mortuary or funerary temple had also evolved from the earliest reed-shrines. Originally attached to the pyramid, this was the place for the performance of the burial rites and of the perpetual rituals which ensured that the king was received in heaven as a god and could derive spiritual sustenance from his food-offerings. However, when in the New Kingdom the tombs were built in the Valley of the Kings, there was no adjoining place for the attached mortuary temples or tomb-chapels, and so it became the custom, from the reign of Amenophis I onwards, to construct separate mortuary temples. Most were located on the flat, cultivated plain which lies between the river and the necropolis area. Some of these impressive temples belonging to Sethos I at Qurna, Ramesses II (the Ramesseum), Hatshepsut at Deir el-Bahri, and Ramesses III and Tuthmosis III at Medinet Habu survive today. Others have left little trace and at Amenophis III's temple, only the two great statues (the Colossi of Memnon) which once flanked the temple's entrance can be seen, indicating the size and magnificence of the complete building.

New Kingdom mortuary temples served the same purpose as the earlier ones attached to pyramids; they provided a place where worship of the dead, deified ruler could continue, by means of rituals which presented him with food-offerings. They also accommodated the cult of the chief local god and so, whereas a cultus temple provided only for the needs of a god, mortuary temple rituals were performed for both the god and the kings. The ruling king sought the god's blessing and the acceptance of his reign by all the previous legitimate rulers (known as the Ancestors) and, in order to gain mutual benefit for the king and his forebears, the Ritual of Amenophis I (more generally known as the Ritual of the Royal Ancestors) was performed. If the temple

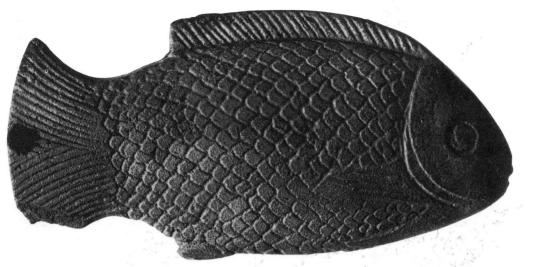

A glazed cosmetic dish in the shape of a fish (New Kingdom, c.1450 BC). Egypt had a flourishing cosmetic industry: some preparations tried to arrest the ageing process and others were used to colour the face. This dish was probably used to mix eye paint.

was completed before the king died, the rituals were apparently performed even in his lifetime to benefit the future deified form he would eventually assume.

Mortuary and cultus temples had distinct functions but they shared close ritual and architectural associations. Since the mythology and ritual requirements dictated their basic form, there are only minor variations in detail and even those built in the Graeco-Roman Period have the same essential features as the New Kingdom buildings. Temples throughout Egypt, dedicated to different gods and to the kings who built them, vary only slightly with regard to the figures represented in the wall scenes and the accompanying inscriptions, but in general each cultus or mortuary temple had the same role and function.

On the west bank there was also a village for the workmen engaged on the construction and decoration of the royal tombs. They and their families were housed near to the workplace in isolation from the general community, to prevent them from broadcasting the secret locations and details of the royal tombs. It was Amenophis I, the first king with a tomb in the Valley of the Kings, who founded this community; they later

deified and worshipped him, although the construction of their village (known today as Deir el-Medina) was probably started by a successor, Tuthmosis I. In this remote village, isolation was a greater factor than the availability of water, which had to be brought up from the river, and it was occupied almost continuously for some four hundred years throughout Dynasties 18, 19 and 20 by the men who built the tombs in the Valley of the Kings. They worshipped in the local temple, and eventually they were buried in nearby tombs which bear witness to their own expertise and skills. There are colourful wall scenes and the adjoining tomb-chapels often incorporate miniature pyramids. Archaeological and documentary evidence from the village, its rubbish heaps, and the tombs have enabled Egyptologists to gain considerable insight into the life of this comfortable and relatively affluent community.

Once the king's tomb was completed, the workforce were delegated to decorate the tombs of queens, princes and high-ranking officials; in their spare time, they could undertake private work for clients, preparing funerary goods and equipment for use in life. The community flourished and prospered and when its size increased some families had to build homes outside the brick enclosure wall that surrounded the original village of seventy houses. Skills and trades were passed down in families and every workman sought to obtain a coveted place for his son on the Royal Gang, if necessary resorting to bribery of the officials (which was not always successful).

Surviving evidence provides details of working conditions, hours of labour, equipment, payment, and also industrial action. In Dynasty 20, the men ceased work on the royal tomb because of a delay in their food rations but this 'strike' (in the last years of Ramesses III's reign, c.1165 BC) was only the first of several, and such actions may well have occurred in earlier times. The authorities, fearful of delay in completing the royal tomb, were forced to take action and the vizier finally obtained food rations from outside the area, thus persuading the men to continue their work.

An independent attitude is also evident in the degree of legal and religious autonomy that the villagers enjoyed. They organized and ran the local law court and could pass judgement on their peers; they were only required to submit a case to the vizier's court if it carried the death penalty. They also performed duties as priests and regulated the community's religious life. The gods worshipped at Deir el-Medina included the most popular 'household' deities such as Bes, the dwarf-god of love and marriage, and Tauert, his hippopotamus-wife who was responsible for fecundity and childbirth. However, the villagers also had a special cult for Amenophis I, as the founder of their community, and his mother Ahmose-Nefertari, and they worshipped Amun, the great state-god of Egypt, as a personal deity who championed the weak and supported them in their daily lives.

Perhaps nowhere is the spirit of these people – humorous, independent, and sure of their own importance – better illustrated than in the sketches they drew on limestone flakes for their own entertainment. These were thrown away in the rubbish heaps but they provide a wealth of detail, depicting women at work in the village, hares playing together, and the contortions of the village dancer. One series shows caricatures of the nobility represented as mice receiving the attentions of their servants in the guise of cats, who prepare their meals, dress their hair, and undertake a range of household tasks.

The community of Deir el-Medina undoubtedly played an important role in the king's burial preparations but the momentous events that moulded Egypt's foreign policy and foundation of empire were enacted far away from Thebes. Early in Dynasty 18, Egypt's rulers restored control over Nubia and then began to try to control the areas to the north, turning their attention to the small independent states which made up Palestine. They tried to gain their allegiance but soon found themselves fighting the two other great powers, Mitanni and later the Hittites, who had their own ambitions in this area. However, the Egyptians, under the able rulers of Dynasties 18 and 19, achieved a considerable degree of success, establishing the first empire in the Near East which at its peak stretched from Nubia in the south to the region of the River Euphrates in Asia.

Egypt pursued different policies in these regions: whereas in Nubia, colonization produced extensive Egyptianization of the area during the New Kingdom, in the north they gained the allegiance of the many semi-independent rulers of small states. This produced a loose association of loyal, native princelings rather than a system of direct control administered from Egypt.

The earlier pharaohs of Dynasty 18 prided themselves on their military valour and prowess. The inscription of Ahmose in his tomb at el-Kab recounts his bravery when he accompanied Tuthmosis I's campaigns in Nubia and the kingdom of Mitanni beyond the Euphrates. This king's achievements were only surpassed by those of his grandson, Tuthmosis III, who must rank as one of the world's greatest military commanders. During the reign of his stepmother, Hatshepsut, the princes of Palestine and Syria had seized the opportunity to regain their independence from Egypt, and Tuthmosis III's first task was to march on the rebellion leader, the prince of the great city of Kadesh on the River Orontes. Texts on the walls in the Temple of Karnak, and two stelae (one at Napata (Gebel Barkal) in Nubia and one at Armant) summarize the king's great military achievements; the highlight, and indeed the foundation of his future military achievements, was the capture of the fortified town of Megiddo in Year 23 of his reign.

The inscriptions describe his tactics in some detail: having routed the protective enemy forces who fled back to Megiddo, Tuthmosis III laid siege to the town for seven months; after the fall of Megiddo, the coalition of over three hundred princes who had opposed the Egyptians was punished, and the Egyptian king selected new native rulers whose allegiance was assured by the removal of their brothers and children to Egypt where they were educated and held as hostages. During the siege, some neighbouring orchards and crops were destroyed, but the Egyptian troops were also allowed to increase their rations by cultivating the land, and a wealth of booty and many prisoners were ultimately taken back to Egypt. However, the area remained volatile, and it was necessary for Tuthmosis III to pursue fourteen campaigns in sixteen years to control the area fully.

In his eighth campaign in Year 33 of the reign, he crossed the River Euphrates and defeated the Mitannians, recalling this achievement in detail on the Napata stela. In a later campaign in the same area, he emulated his grandfather Tuthmosis I when he hunted elephants on the return journey. In the last twelve years of his reign, when there is no record of any expeditions to Syria, the king had probably fully established his power in the area and could concentrate instead on his building projects at home.

His son Amenophis II continued to express pride in physical strength and military valour, recounting his own achievements on a stela found near the Great Sphinx at Giza. An expert oarsman and horseman, he also excelled in all the arts of warfare at an early age. He had inscribed on a stela in the temple built at Amada in Lower Nubia an account of his first campaign of victory in Syria and another stela inscription, this time from Karnak, augmented by a more complete version from Memphis, provides further details of his Syrian adventures. It is also clear that Assyria, Babylonia and the Hittites were anxious to vie with each other in presenting the Egyptian king with gifts and seeking his support. However, in the final two decades of Amenophis II's reign, there are no surviving records of further military undertakings and in the later years of Dynasty 18,

Ushabti figures were placed in tombs to help the owner with agricultural tasks in the next world. This one, belonging to a man named Paser, was found in his tomb at Rifeh (c.1400 BC). A scented wax cone is represented on the figure's head; these were worn to banquets.

the Egyptian kings resorted to diplomacy and alliances rather than warfare.

Development of Tuthmosis III's military genius had almost been prevented by the machinations of his stepmother, Hatshepsut. When Tuthmosis I died, the throne was inherited by Tuthmosis II, his son by a lesser wife, Mutnefert; according to the custom, he had been married to the Great Royal Daughter Hatshepsut, the offspring of Tuthmosis I and his Great Royal Wife Ahmose, to confirm his claim to rule. However, his reign was relatively short – perhaps less than ten years – and Hatshepsut bore him only daughters. Tuthmosis III, his young heir by a concubine, was vulnerable when he succeeded to the throne and his stepmother Hatshepsut (who, had she been a man, would have had a strong claim to the throne through her parentage) now seized her opportunity.

Presumably supported by one of the strong factions in the kingdom, she usurped the throne from Tuthmosis III and became one of Egypt's few queens regnant. In formal scenes she assumed male dress, and in the royal inscriptions she is referred to in the masculine form. Amongst her officials, Senenmut was the most powerful; he became Royal Tutor to Hatshepsut's daughter and claimed responsibility for all the queen's Theban monuments, including her magnificent funerary temple at Deir el-Bahri which was excavated by Naville. Here, scenes show the famous expedition to Punt to obtain incense and also depict the divine procreation of Hatshepsut as the daughter of the god Amun and her earthly mother Queen Ahmose, in an attempt to justify her claim to rule Egypt. In another small temple at Beni Hasan, known as Speos Artemidos, an inscription states that she refurbished the neglected sanctuaries of Middle Egypt.

The cause of her death is unknown but she prepared a tomb for herself in the Valley of the Kings (discovered by Howard Carter in 1903), which had an additional sarcophagus for the body of her father Tuthmosis I (which she presumably intended to remove from his own tomb). Soon after her death, Tuthmosis III began to obliterate her name and inscriptions from the monuments and as a fully grown man

he now started to make his own considerable contribution to Egypt's history.

However, this dynastic upheaval was of minor importance compared with the tumultuous events that occurred towards the end of Dynasty 18. When Amenophis III, son of Tuthmosis IV and Mutemweya (who was possibly a Mitannian princess), came to the throne, Egypt had reached its height of power and prosperity. Diplomatic alliances and subsidies of gold now replaced the military campaigns that earlier kings had waged, and in terms of wealth and power, Egypt was acclaimed the greatest nation in the area. Amenophis III pursued an active and extensive building programme and his Court enjoyed a lavish, cosmopolitan lifestyle at the palace at Malkata on the west bank at Thebes. His Great Royal Wife was a woman named Tiye whose father Yuya held the titles of 'god's father', 'Prophet of Min at Akhmim' and 'Overseer of the Royal Stables'; her mother Thuya was 'Chief Lady of Amun's Harem'.

Thus Amenophis III again broke with tradition, as his father had done, by not marrying the royal heiress, and this may have been a deliberate attempt to prevent the priests of Amen-Re from interfering in the royal succession. He certainly emphasized his wife's non-royal origins, stressing her parentage on commemorative scarabs that were issued to honour their marriage.

Although Amenophis III married many other wives, including two royal princesses who were sent to Egypt by the kings of Mitanni, it was Tiye's son Amenophis IV who became the next king. The possibility of a co-regency between Amenophis III and IV has been the subject of much controversy; the evidence is inconclusive and some scholars discount the idea entirely, but others support the possibility of either a twelve-year co-regency or one that lasted only a few months. Amenophis IV had not been trained for the kingship, but became royal heir because his elder brother Thutmose died prematurely. A period of co-regency would have strengthened his claim and minimized the powers of the Amen-Re priests in attempting to support a rival.

Amenophis IV spent the early years of his reign at Thebes. His queen was Nefertiti, a woman whose portrait heads have convinced the modern world of her great beauty but whose origins and family background remain obscure. It has been suggested that she was one of the Mitannian princesses who came to Egypt to marry Amenophis III. More probably she was a non-royal Egyptian, perhaps the daughter of a powerful courtier who may have been a member of Queen Tiye's own family. At Thebes, Amenophis IV now began to promote the cult of the Aten, a hitherto unimportant deity represented by the sun's disc. The Aten was known to exist as a facet of the sun-god Re as early as the Middle Kingdom, but in the reign of Tuthmosis IV it was identified as a separate god; it came to receive increasing support under Amenophis III who established and promoted the god's cult. The Aten, now envisaged as a creative force, acquired universal powers so that the deity could be worshipped beyond Egypt; indeed, Amenophis III may have had the conscious aim of developing a convincing rival to threaten the omnipotent Amen-Re. However, he did not neglect the many cults of the other gods and made no attempt to promote the Aten as an exclusive deity.

It was Amenophis IV who imposed radical changes on Egypt's religious beliefs and customs; the cult of the Aten was turned into a form of solar monotheism based on the worship of the life-force present in the sun, whereas previously the Egyptians had directed their devotions towards the material body of the sun. Never before had monotheism been promoted; although each period and line of kings had favoured a supreme state-god, there had always been toleration of the multitude of deities in Egypt's pantheon.

Amenophis IV took his first moves while he was still at Thebes. At first the traditional deities were allowed to continue, but alongside the cult-centre of Amen-Re the king now erected a number of buildings which included temples to the Aten. In the 1960s and 1970s, a study of these buildings (the Akhenaten Temple Project) enabled a re-evaluation of the earliest years of the reign to be made. The Aten buildings had been dismantled by later rulers and the material used as infill in new constructions in the Temples of Kar-

nak and Luxor; with the dismantling of these later structures in modern times, some 36,000 decorated blocks from the Aten buildings were revealed and, with the aid of a computer, a team of scholars was able to piece together many elements of the relief scenes and inscriptions which covered these blocks. The material probably originated from at least two Aten temples at Karnak and at Luxor, and also possibly from a palace. Until this discovery, scholars had not realized the importance of the Aten cult so early in the reign, nor that the king had been able to promote the new god in the city devoted to Amen-Re and his powerful priesthood. Additional tantalizing evidence has indicated that Nefertiti held a position of unprecedented power in this divine cult which perhaps gave her equal status with the king.

However, undoubtedly the relationship between Amenophis IV and the Amen-Re priesthood deteriorated at Thebes, and in the fifth year of his reign the king decided to take several radical steps which would establish Atenism as an exclusive monotheistic cult. The priesthoods of all other gods were disbanded, the deities' names were obliterated from the monuments, and the income was diverted from these cults to support the Aten. The king emphasized his total allegiance by changing his name from Amenophis to Akhenaten ('Servant of the Aten') and Nefertiti added the new name of Nefernefruaten ('Fair is the goddess of the Aten'). Finally, a site far from Thebes was selected for the new royal residence and religious capital, and the king, his Court, and a nucleus of professionals and craftsmen required to establish this city moved from Thebes to the new site.

Apparently chosen by the king at the god's behest, the city was built on a virgin site so that there would be no association with any of the traditional deities. It covered some eight miles of land on the east bank of the river, about midway between Thebes and the Delta; on the west bank, land was also set aside to provide crops for the city. Akhenaten encircled this whole area with fourteen large boundary stelae which were inscribed with the conditions of establishing the city. Given the name of Akhetaten ('Horizon of the Aten'), the capital was hastily constructed; temples to the Aten were a major feature, and there were palaces, a records office, administrative headquarters, military barracks, and houses for the officials and craftsmen.

In the eastern cliffs behind the city, a series of rock-cut tombs were prepared for the royal family and their courtiers and officials, in a complete break with the tradition of locating the necropolis on the west bank. The site, more often known by its modern name of Tell el-Amarna (from the name of a local tribe, the Beni Amran, and the nearby modern village of el-Till), has provided most of the evidence and information available about this period, and the general term Amarna is often used with reference to the religious beliefs, art, and literature of these years.

At Akhetaten, the royal family (which now included the six daughters of Akhenaten and Nefertiti) continued to develop the cult, although it probably gained little support or acceptance outside the immediate Court circle. The royal couple produced no sons to inherit the throne and continue the religious innovations, and the king made two new marriages to his own first and third daughters, presumably in an attempt to beget heirs. These were no more successful, and ultimately the succession passed to two young princes, Smenkhkare and Tutankhamun, whose parentage remains uncertain. Some claim that Amenophis III was their father; their mother was perhaps (although not very probably) Tiye, or another royal wife, or even Sitamun (the daughter of Amenophis III and Tiye) but Akhenaten and perhaps his minor wife Kiya may have been their parents. A relatively recent study of the mummies of Tutankhamun and the body found in Tomb 55 (now believed to be that of Smenkhkare) included an anatomical survey and the use of radiological and serological techniques. Because of the similarity of the bodies which these studies demonstrated, it is thought likely that they belonged to brothers; Smenkhkare may have died when he was about twenty while Tutankhamun was about nineteen, although the specific causes of death have not been discovered.

Identification of the body found in Tomb 55 in the Valley of the Kings with the young ruler Smenkhkare is only the most recent theory regarding ownership of the tomb and its contents. The tomb was unfinished at the time of the hastily prepared burial. Since some of the funerary equipment was inscribed with the name of Queen Tiye, this initially led to the conclusion that the body belonged to a woman, most probably Tiye herself. However, subsequent examination identified the body as a male aged between twenty-three and twenty-five years, and it was then suggested that it could belong to Akhenaten and had perhaps been brought back to Thebes for burial after the failure of his revolution at Amarna. However, the chronology of his reign dictates that he must have been much older at the time of his death, and so it was then proposed that it could be the body of his young co-regent and heir, Smenkhkare. Another argument against an identification of this body with Akhenaten was provided by the skull: although unusual in shape, it showed none of the peculiar features found in artistic representations of Akhenaten.

Amarna art is unique in its characterization of the human figure. It may be based on Akhenaten's own physical abnormalities but, since the bodies of the king, his queen and daughters have never been found, this remains speculation based only on sculptured or painted representations of the king which show him with physical peculiarities exaggerated almost to the point of caricature. However, although the elongated face and head, slanting eyes, and malformed body with its emaciated neck, pronounced breasts and ample hips and thighs may be a true likeness, perhaps indicative of a disorder of the endocrine glands, these features may simply express a new art form. They were soon extended to the representation of all human figures in Amarna art, perhaps to emphasize that the king's physique, as the embodiment of the god, was in fact the accepted norm to which all lesser individuals aspired.

Early in the reign, the art was more traditional with no abnormal exaggerations, but when the Court moved to Amarna the conventional artists remained at Thebes. Akhenaten took new craftsmen with him, and encouraged them to break new ground by representing physical 'reality' rather than producing idealized portraits; they depicted the royal family in informal situations and poses, and painted the natural beauties of plants and animals, reflecting the creative force of the Aten. The distinctive art of this period provides the only known major break with tradition and illustrates how closely state art was interwoven with religious beliefs. It also demonstrates how a determined ruler could overturn concepts and practices which had existed for thousands of years.

Until Akhetaten city was discovered in modern times, this whole period of history had been obscured since the New Kingdom. Scholars immediately tried to assess the character and motives of this most enigmatic pharaoh Akhenaten. First he was regarded as a 'failed Messiah', a man who had tried to introduce monotheism to the Egyptians but whose death and lack of a strong heir had brought his vision to an abrupt end. More recently he has been considered a political opportunist who tried to restore the status and influence of the kingship by introducing a new, omnipotent deity to destroy the power base of Amen-Re's priesthood. He was perhaps responsible for carrying to a logical conclusion the trends and reforms begun by his father and grandfather. There may be elements of both the visionary ruler and the calculating politician in Akhenaten's nature, and he continues to intrigue the modern world.

Scholars have also speculated about the origin of such beliefs, seeking an explanation in possible foreign influences exerted either through the women in the Court of Amenophis III where Akhenaten grew up, or through general concepts found in the Near East at that time. For example, in the famous *Hymn to the Aten,* a major source for the doctrine of Atenism, there are close parallels between some passages and verses found here and in Psalm 104 in the Bible.

It is most probable that the worship of the Aten was in fact a development of the old solar cult of Re, with Akhenaten's single radical departure being the establishment of exclusive monotheism. He may have wished to restore the supreme power of the kingship as it had existed in the early Old Kingdom, and to achieve this aim he found it necessary at the end of Dynasty 18 to introduce new concepts. The priesthoods which had always undermined royal power were now removed, and the Aten received a new role

as a universal creator-god so that he could successfully challenge Amen-Re. However, most of the Aten's 'new' aspects – his universal force as the creator of mankind, animals, birds and plants; his fatherhood of foreign peoples as well as Egyptians; and his unique nature – had previously been applied to Amen-Re.

No single source has been recovered to provide evidence for the cult's beliefs and doctrines, but scenes and inscriptions in the tombs and city at Amarna provide some information. The most famous text, the Hymn to the Aten, found inscribed on some of the tomb walls, is a composition of great beauty, describing the god's nature and role as creator of all living things. Nevertheless, it contains little that does not occur in the earlier hymns to Amen-Re and the sun-god Re.

From the source material, it is clear that the Aten or sun-disc was merely the symbol of the deity, visible in the heavens, but the god's real essence was the beneficent and universal creative force which was expressed through the warmth and light of the sun. The third element was the king who, as the divine agent on earth, acted for the god and was virtually interchangeable with the deity. Akhenaten, as the god's sole representative on earth, had a divine nature, and thus the role and power of the king which had existed in earliest times were now fully restored. Scenes show the king with his family basking in the glory of the rays descending from the sun's disc; each ray ends in a hand which gives all bounty to the royal couple in return for their devotion and worship.

However, this royal idyll was not shared by the rest of the population. The Aten had no moral philosophy or attractive mythology which could inspire the general worshipper; the temples of the many gods had employed large numbers of people besides the priests and they were now presumably displaced by the closures; and the sun-disc was an abstract symbol to which most people could not relate. However, and perhaps most importantly, the evidence of the Amarna tombs suggests that the non-royal dead now expected to attain eternity through the king's bounty rather than with the help of the traditional gods of the dead, particularly Osiris. The cult of Osiris had offered comfort and support to people of all classes with its clearly defined moral values and conditions for entry to the afterlife, and the new beliefs provided no convincing alternative.

Later generations certainly regarded Akhenaten as a heretic who ruled without the traditional gods' approval. Even if the hostility shown to him and his immediate successors was partly the result of propaganda generated by the counter-revolution and the reinstated priesthoods, there was nevertheless discontent at the course of his 'revolution'. The economy and prosperity of Egypt was probably affected not only by the temple closures but also by the expense involved in constructing a new capital city at Amarna. Again, in foreign policy, it appears that the king neglected his duties although the extent of his lack of interest in the empire remains unclear. One theory casts him as a pacifist ruler engrossed in his religious duties at Amarna while Egypt's possessions abroad were allowed to fall away, and certainly the correspondence discovered in the Records Office at Amarna (the so-called Amarna Letters) indicates that Egypt had become a less reliable overlord. The rulers of foreign and vassal states wrote to Akhenaten in vain, begging for military aid against the other great powers who sought to take them over. However, although he did not pursue an active military policy abroad, Akhenaten was possibly only continuing his father's custom of replacing full-scale expeditions with other means of influence, and he may not have consciously decided against intervention in the area.

More recently, the idea that Akhenaten was a pacifist has been treated with some caution since he is represented in some scenes as a warrior-king. In others, troops of soldiers appear prominently at the Amarna Court, leading to speculation that a military presence was required there to protect the king.

However, the religious experiment was apparently not terminated by problems abroad nor by any popular revolt at home. Akhenaten's own courtiers seem to have realized the dangers inherent in this revolution and to have taken action to change its course. When Akhenaten died, probably in Year 17 of his reign, his heir (and perhaps co-regent) was Smenkhkare who

had been married to Akhenaten's eldest daughter Meritaten in order to consolidate his claim to the throne. Smenkhkare probably ruled alone for only a few months, and because of his untimely death and the lack of a direct heir, the throne passed to his younger brother, Tutankhaten. This nine-year-old child was now married to Akhenaten's third daughter, Ankhesenpaaten, since presumably the eldest daughter Meritaten and the second daughter Maketaten had both died. Ankhesenpaaten was also the widow of her own father, Akhenaten.

Tutankhaten's immaturity enabled the courtiers and officials to direct political and religious events, and they began to promote a counter-revolution, gradually reinstating the many traditional deities and unravelling Akhenaten's policies. The two most significant advisers who acted were Ay, a courtier who had supported Akhenaten's changes, and Horemheb, an army commander originally loyal to Atenist beliefs. It remains unclear whether their change of heart was dictated by long-held personal doubts or by the final realization that the Aten policies were disastrous for Egypt.

As the Court moved back to Thebes, the royal couple changed their names to Tutankhamun and Ankhesenamun, demonstrating their renewed allegiance to Amen-Re. The king restored the old temples of the many gods, and reinstated the priesthoods. The break with the Aten was not complete (the sun's disc still predominates on the golden throne found in Tutankhamun's tomb), and there was probably no widespread destruction of buildings at Amarna or obliteration of the Aten's name and titles. However, Tutankhamun under his courtiers' influence certainly abandoned exclusive monotheism.

With his early death, the smooth return to traditionalism was threatened again, particularly as he left no heir. Interred in a tomb prepared for someone else in the Valley of the Kings, the boy achieved his greatest fame because his burial remained virtually undisturbed until rediscovery in the 20th century. An internal conflict probably now arose about the succession: a letter was sent from an Egyptian queen (probably Ankhesenamun, the royal widow) to the king of the Hittites, Egypt's great enemy, in which she begged him to send his son to become her husband. This effectively gave the prince the right to become ruler of Egypt. With understandable reluctance, the Hittite king cautiously delayed, but a further request persuaded him to send his son; however, the prince was murdered on his journey, presumably by the agents of those who were determined to prevent such an alliance.

Ay then married Ankhesenamun; as a commoner, such an alliance with the royal heiress was essential to give him the right to rule. For four years, he continued as king to promote the return to traditionalism, and at his death the throne was inherited by the army general Horemheb. He had no close marriage ties with the royal family, although it is possible that his wife Mutnefert was the sister of Queen Nefertiti.

Horemheb ruled for twenty-seven years and completed the destruction of the Aten cult, ordering the city of Akhetaten to be levelled and the stone taken elsewhere for other building projects. There was unprecedented determination in his desecration of the Amarna tombs, and the erasure of Akhenaten's name from the inscriptions; the cult-centres of the god were similarly treated, and the Great Temple to the Aten at Amarna was razed to the ground and its sacred furniture destroyed while the Aten temples at Thebes were dismantled. His aim was obviously to expunge all trace of Akhenaten and his cult and to obliterate the city of Amarna from people's memory.

Horemheb is remembered as the king who restored traditional beliefs; he placed men loyal to him in the powerful priesthoods who once again served all the gods, and he re-established a strong army. His actions, undertaken to rehabilitate the old systems, are detailed in his restoration decree, a copy of which is preserved on a stela in the Temple of Karnak. When he was finally buried in the Valley of the Kings, Horemheb was able to pass on to his heir a stable and prosperous country which at least superficially carried no traces of the brief Amarna interlude. The new king, founder of Dynasty 19, was Horemheb's old army comrade, Pa-Ramesses, who now ruled briefly as Ramesses I. Horemheb had doubtless entrusted the kingship to this man because of his proven military prowess and his ability to found a new dynasty. Later generations obviously

regarded his son Sethos I, who was destined to re-establish the greatness of Egypt, as the inaugurator of a new era.

The family had come from the northern Delta and had no royal lineage; also, the shadow of the Amarna period could not be entirely forgotten, and it was essential that the new dynasty restored Egypt's traditional glories at home and abroad. Sethos I embarked on an ambitious building programme; not only did he construct a mortuary temple for himself at Qurna on the west bank at Thebes, but also built another magnificent mortuary temple at Abydos, the home of the god Osiris. This was a national shrine, located near to the Osireion or cenotaph of Osiris, and it emphasized the new dynasty's allegiance to traditional deities. The sanctuary provided chapels for six gods and one for the king in his future deified form (usually there was only one sanctuary for the sole resident deity of each temple). Further information about this temple is preserved in a decree inscribed on a rock at Nauri near the Third Cataract which gives details of the privileges of the temple and the sources of its wealth.

In the temple of Amun at Karnak, Sethos I began the great Hypostyle Hall which still commands the awe of modern visitors. Here, on the exterior north walls, there are scenes of Sethos' military campaigns undertaken to re-establish Egypt's empire. The main objective was again northern Syria where he reached the city of Kadesh on the Orontes. Another register shows him in conflict with the Hittites who were gradually gaining power, and a battle against the Libyans is also recorded. Egypt's Asiatic empire, restored during the early years of Dynasty 19, was once again administered through local princes. To the south, in Nubia, punitive action was required against one of the tribes, but here the administration was differently organized and an Egyptian governor known as the King's Son of Kush ruled Nubia directly as the royal delegate.

After a long and successful reign, Sethos I was buried in the most impressive tomb in the Valley of the Kings, which was discovered and recorded by Belzoni. His alabaster sarcophagus was eventually brought to London where it now forms the centrepiece of Sir John Soane's Museum.

This early photograph shows massive columns in the hypostyle hall area of the Temple of Amun at Karnak. Extensive excavation and restoration have been undertaken here since 1895 by the Department of Antiquities, and many columns have been reinstated in their original locations.

Sethos I's son and successor Ramesses II enjoyed a long reign, and he ensured his immortality by producing an extensive family and an ambitious military programme, as well as a range of impressive monuments. Sethos I had provided his son with a harem while he was still his co-regent, and he fathered many children; however, his reign was so long that it was his thirteenth son, Merneptah, who finally succeeded him.

Some of his Great Wives were accorded considerable honours: Queen Nefertari was provided with the most beautiful tomb in the Valley of the Queens and also with the smaller temple at Abu Simbel. The king also took as his consort Bint-Enat (his daughter by his Great Wife Isinofre who was also the mother of Merneptah) and, as part of his peace negotiations with the Hittites, he married a Hittite princess.

His extensive building programme included the completion of the Hypostyle Hall at Karnak, the construction of his mortuary temple at Thebes (the Ramesseum), a temple at Abydos, and two magnificent temples at Abu Simbel, designed to impress the Nubian population with

A colossal statue of Ramesses II flanking the entrance to the Temple of Luxor. Several early writers studied these statues of the king in whose reign much of this temple was completed.

An avenue of sphinxes leading to the Temple of Amun at Karnak. This temple complex, dedicated to Amun, Mut and Khonsu, was Egypt's most important shrine during the New Kingdom.

A view of the Temple of Luxor, floodlit so that modern tourists can visit it at night. Originally linked with the Temple of Karnak by a sphinx-lined avenue, the Luxor temple was the 'southern harem' of the god Amun.

A wall scene in the tomb of Horemheb in the Valley of the Kings, Thebes. This tomb was prepared for him when he became king, but he had also built a tomb at Sakkara when he was Commander of the Army.

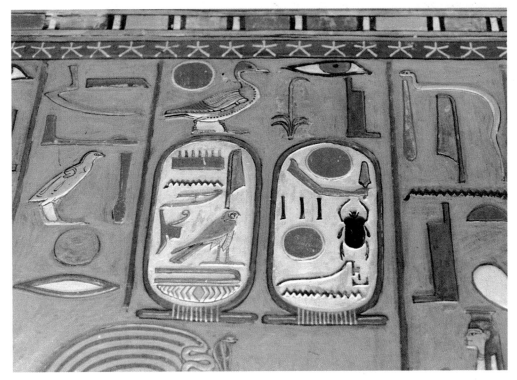

A detail of the wall scene in the same tomb, showing the king's two names. Royal names were always enclosed in the cartouches (ovals) shown here.

The colossal Osiris pillars representing
Ramesses II in the first hypostyle hall of his
temple at Abu Simbel are shown here in a
lithograph from David Roberts' *Egypt and
Nubia* (1846).

A sphinx in the Temple of Luxor. Egyptian sphinxes usually had human heads and lion bodies, and symbolized strength and power. The name probably comes from the two Egyptian words meaning 'living image'.

A stone statue of Horus wearing the Double Crown in front of his temple at Edfu. Many early travellers visited the temple, including Napoleon's savants, and it was cleared of sand by Mariette.

A colossal figure of Nefertari, favourite queen of Ramesses II, as the goddess Hathor. This decorates the façade of her rock-cut temple at Abu Simbel. With the Great Temple, this was rescued by the UNESCO salvage campaign.

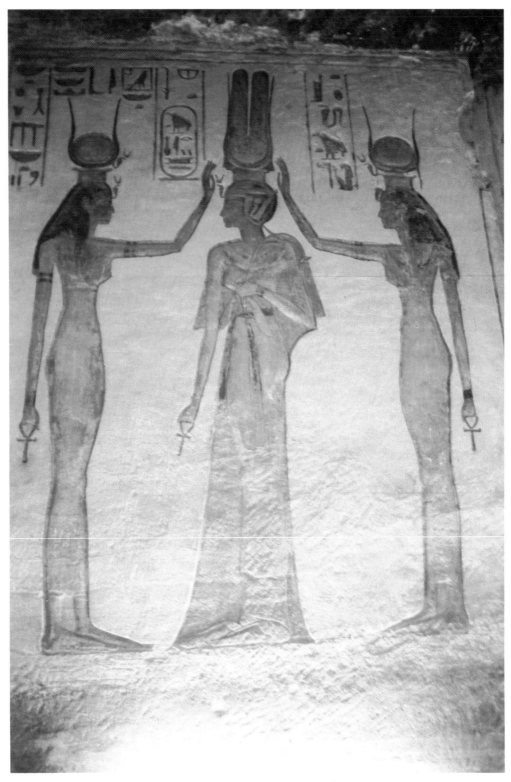

A temple scene from Abu Simbel, showing goddesses giving life to the queen. The monuments were cut from the rock.

Pharaoh's might. Less well-preserved remains in the north were also undoubtedly extensive in antiquity, and there was major construction at Memphis and various Delta sites. Two of the most intriguing Delta cities of this dynasty are named in the Bible as Pithom and Ramses, and although there is no conclusive evidence, it has been suggested that it was Ramesses II who was king during the Hebrews' captivity in Egypt.

Nevertheless, it was the conflict with the Hittites which dominated Ramesses II's foreign policy. In Year 4 of his reign, Ramesses led a large-scale campaign against the Hittite king Muwatallis, reaching the Dog-river in Palestine, and in the next year, the struggle reached its climax when Ramesses was able to exhibit great personal valour. The narrative of this is preserved in two accounts – the so-called Poem inscribed in eight duplicate copies in the Temples of Karnak, Luxor, Abydos and the Ramesseum, and the shorter Report which occurs at Luxor, Abydos, Abu Simbel and the Ramesseum. His main objective was Kadesh, which had been captured by Sethos I but subsequently taken by the Hittites, and this conflict is often known as the Battle of Kadesh. The narratives tell how Ramesses II routed the enemy single-handed, but this is a supreme example of the exaggeration generally found in Egyptian 'historical' texts; it was the arrival of new troops at the crucial moment that doubtless carried the day.

However, the Egyptian records are offset by tablets found in the Hittite capital of Boghazkoy which indicate that the Egyptian success was not quite so overwhelming, and it obviously became essential for both sides to end a conflict which neither could ultimately win. Therefore, in Year 21 of his reign, Ramesses concluded a treaty with Muwatallis' brother Khattusilis who was now king of the Hittites. The Egyptian version is recorded on a stela in the Temple of Karnak, while the Hittite one is preserved on two inscribed clay tablets found at Boghazkoy. This

A stone ushabti figure (c.1350 BC) which, according to the inscription, belonged to Met-Mehy, Governor of the Southern Oasis. The figure holds agricultural tools to undertake work on behalf of the deceased in the next world. Some tombs were equipped with as many as 365 ushabtis.

important discovery provides the first evidence of such a treaty; the terms prevented encroachment on each other's land and committed the allies to support each other against another attacker, while conditions were also set for the extradition of refugees from both sides, and these were to be well treated on return to their own countries.

The conclusion of peace formalities opened up the possibility of friendship between the Egyptian and Hittite Royal Courts, and cordial letters were exchanged between Ramesses and the Hittite king and queen in which the matter of a proposed royal marriage was discussed. Finally in Year 34 a Hittite princess arrived in Egypt for her marriage to Ramesses II, and this was recorded in a great inscription, duplicated for public information and placed in the temples of Karnak, Amara, Abu Simbel, and at Elephantine. The Hittite princess was given the Egyptian name of Manefrure and the marriage was well favoured, for the king soon elevated her to become one of his Great Royal Wives.

In his sixties when he came to the throne, Ramesses II's heir had already assisted in managing state affairs in Pi-Ramesse and the Delta and he ruled as prince regent for the last twelve years of his father's reign. However, as a new king, Merneptah faced several military crises: first, he sent expeditions to Canaan and southern Syria to re-establish Egyptian power there; and then in Year 5 he faced a conflict which is described in several Egyptian sources, inscribed in the Temple of Karnak, on a stela from Athribis, and on a granite stela discovered by Petrie in Merneptah's funerary temple. This latter source not only recounts the defeat of the enemy but also provides the only reference to Israel known from Egyptian texts; this proves that Israel was already established in Palestine by Year 5 of the reign, although, until this stela was found, scholars had believed that the Exodus should be placed in Merneptah's time. Now, it is considered more likely that it occurred during the reign of Ramesses II.

A wooden face from a New Kingdom coffin (c.1300 BC) is crudely painted, with a lotus flower shown on the front of the wig. Such stylized representations of the human face were traditional in Pharaonic Egypt. Coffins were mostly mass-produced in workshops and clients selected from stock.

The enemy Egypt faced in Year 5 was a coalition of the Libyan tribes who lived to the west of the Delta, and a group of migrants – the Sea Peoples – who now approached Egypt from the eastern Mediterranean and the Aegean Islands. This association, led by a Libyan prince and spurred on by famine, hoped to settle in the fertile lands of the Delta. The Sea Peoples brought their wives and children, their cattle and other possessions, and obviously had long-term plans to remain in Egypt. However, Merneptah mobilized his army and dealt severely with the coalition; over six thousand of the enemy were killed, their Libyan leader fled, and the Egyptians took many prisoners and much booty. However, the problems did not end with this defeat; the Libyans next attempted to unsettle Egypt's southern border, causing problems in Nubia which Merneptah had to send an expedition to subdue.

After a ten-year reign, Merneptah died; he had held out against the gathering enemies but the danger posed by the Sea Peoples did not disappear and had to be faced again by a successor. In the years following Merneptah, there was apparently confusion over the succession; a usurper Amenmesse appears to have seized the throne during the absence of the Crown Prince Sethos who seems nevertheless to have regained the throne to become King Sethos II. His successor, Siptah, was probably only a young boy who ruled for a few years; he may have been placed on the throne through the influence of Bay, a powerful courtier who was possibly of Syrian origin. However, on Siptah's death, Queen Twosret, the wife of Sethos II, was apparently sufficiently powerful to seize the throne herself and rule Egypt as Hatshepsut had done. Twosret's reign marked the end of Dynasty 19, and her tomb was usurped by Setnakhte, the founder of Dynasty 20. His son Ramesses III was perhaps the last great king of Egypt, and he again had to contend with the threat of the Sea Peoples.

The first conflict of the reign came in Year 5 when the Libyans, having recovered from their defeat by Merneptah, again looked for land in the Delta. The scenes and inscriptions on the walls of Ramesses III's funerary temple at

Medinet Habu are the main source for these events, and this campaign was fought against three tribes known as the Libyans, Sped and Meshwesh. They had entered hostilities with Egypt on the pretext that they disliked the new ruler Ramesses III had imposed on them. However, the Egyptians resoundingly defeated them, and took many prisoners who were forced to become their labourers.

A greater threat emerged in Year 8 when the Sea Peoples again approached Egypt. They may have come originally from a number of different homelands, but hunger and possibly displacement united them at this time; they first attacked the Hittites, Cyprus and the coast of Syria and then moved southwards through Palestine, bringing their families and possessions on ox-carts. To realize their ambition of settling in Egypt, they joined cause with the Libyans to attack the Delta from the west. As they marched by land, they were accompanied offshore by a considerable fleet, so that Ramesses III had to face them on two fronts, mobilizing his forces in Palestine and preparing the troops in Egypt. He managed to block land entry into Egypt with the Palestine garrisons, and in a successful sea battle in one of the mouths of the Nile, the enemy fleet was trapped and destroyed.

This association of Sea Peoples included the Sheklesh, Sherden (who had been known and had fought in Egypt as mercenaries since the reign of Amenophis III), Weshwesh, and three new groups – the Peleset, Tjekker and Denen. Some of the Sea Peoples fought both for and against the Egyptians in these battles. Eventually, the Peleset and Tjekker remained behind in Palestine as settlers (the word Palestine is derived from Peleset) while others took up residence in Egypt, first as soldiers and then as landowners. The descendants of this stock ultimately became the kings of Dynasty 22. However, most of the Sea Peoples, repulsed by the Egyptians, travelled on to settle in other places throughout the Mediterranean countries and islands. They are of great historical interest since some of their names show a similarity to later names of particular areas. This may indicate that some Sea Peoples now settled down in these localities, and particular attention has been drawn to possible associ-

ations between the Shardan and Sardinia, and the Sheklesh and Sicily.

A final attack by the Libyans in Year 11 was also repulsed before Ramesses III, who attempted to emulate the style and achievements of Ramesses II, was able to enjoy a peaceful and prosperous reign. His funerary temple at Medinet Habu stands as the ultimate indication of his achievements, but he also built at Karnak and prepared a fine tomb in the Valley of the Kings.

The Great Papyrus Harris (now in the British Museum collection) was doubtless part of the funerary temple archive; it was probably compiled in the reign of his son, Ramesses IV, but it lists the benefactions that Ramesses III bestowed on the temples and also provides information about the events of these two reigns. This great state archive shows that expeditions to Punt for incense and to Sinai for turquoise and copper still continued to provide Egypt with a wealth of materials.

However, seeds of discontent were already present: in Year 29 the first strike by the royal workmen at Deir el-Medina was held because of a delay in supplying food rations and at some time there was also an unsuccessful attempt to assassinate the king and to replace him with the son of a secondary wife. The details are preserved in the state record of the would-be assassins' trials which are documented in the Conspiracy Papyri now kept in the Turin Museum. The secondary wife, named Tiy, had persuaded the royal harem women and some of the officials to join her in a plan to cause a rebellion and overthrow the king. Measures included the use of magic involving spells and waxen images, but the plotters were discovered and duly brought to trial. However, five of the judges chosen to hear the cases were also arrested and tried since they had caroused with the accused women. In the end, justice prevailed and the defendants were found guilty; some were put to death but those from prominent families were, according to the custom, permitted to take their own lives.

Other fascinating documents dating to the later Ramesside period also provide invaluable insight. The Turin Papyrus (a list of accusations against several people, but particularly a priest in the Temple of Khnum at Elephantine) gives details of crimes – theft, embezzlement and religious offences – which occurred in the reigns from Ramesses III until Ramesses V. The Abbott, Amherst and Mayer A. Papyri supply detailed information about the tomb-robberies and great state trials which began under Ramesses IX and lasted for many years. Further problems are related in the Deir el-Medina records of the same reign when the workforce was apparently terrorized at Thebes by groups of foreigners. Generally, the end of the New Kingdom was a time of economic hardship, and strikes, tomb-robberies and administrative laxity were all symptomatic of this decline.

The *Story of Wenamun,* a Theban envoy sent on a mission to Syria to obtain timber, clearly illustrates the conditions that an Egyptian faced abroad at the end of Dynasty 20. Together with two other literary papyri, this document was bought in Cairo in 1891 and it provides a unique view of Egypt's declining power. Wenamun, meeting foreign princes on his journey, can no longer rely on his own country's prestige to facilitate his arrangements. It is a sad comment on the decline which Egypt was experiencing and the story also confirms that the pharaoh, Ramesses XI, had become an almost nominal ruler. The real power was now divided between north and south, and exercised by Nesbanebded (Smendes) from the city of Tanis in the Delta (he subsequently became the first king of Dynasty 21) and by the high-priest of Amun, Herihor, from Thebes in the south.

With Ramesses XI's death, the New Kingdom drew to a close. By now, the empire in Syria/Palestine had been lost and finally in this reign Nubia broke away from Egypt and continued as a separate political entity. In the next dynasty, the royal capital city moved to Tanis; Ramesses XI was probably the last king to be buried at Thebes in the Valley of the Kings, since the royal necropolis was now also transferred to the north, and the royal workforce, no longer required at Thebes, abandoned their village at Deir el-Medina.

Third Intermediate Period

From Dynasties 21 to 25, Egypt continued on a course of gradual decline, and there were periods under the rulership of foreign dynasties.

With the death of Ramesses XI at the end of Dynasty 20, Nesbenebded (who had effectively ruled the north while the high-priest of Amun concurrently controlled the south) now took the name Smendes and became the founder and first king of Dynasty 21. The kings of this dynasty chose Tanis as their main residence and here in 1940 the French archaeologist Pierre Montet discovered several royal tombs. Their construction could not equal the earlier Theban burials, and the environmental conditions of the Delta have not preserved the Tanis mummies and organic remains, but Montet nevertheless uncovered a superb royal treasure with gold and silver vessels, jewellery, a solid silver coffin and solid gold face mask, which belonged to King Psusennes I and others and recalled the contents of Tutankhamun's tomb at Thebes.

The sequence of the seven kings who, according to Manetho's list, ruled during Dynasty 21 remains uncertain; however, although they are recorded as the only legitimate kings of this period, they exercised their rulership only in the north. The south was dominated by a powerful line of high-priests of Amun who descended from a priest named Herihor who had established the Theban power base in Dynasty 20. One of the most famous of this line, Pinudjem I, had recognized Smendes as pharaoh and in return Smendes agreed to accept Pinudjem as the effective ruler in the south. Both acknowledged mutual rights of succession in the north and in the south; the two families remained on good terms and there were even marriage ties between Tanite princesses and Theban high-priests so that, from the time of Pinudjem I, the Theban high-priests became the legitimate descendants of the Tanite pharaohs, through their mothers.

A far-reaching decision taken by the Theban high-priests of Dynasty 21 involved the rescue and reburial of some of the desecrated mummies of the kings and queens of the New Kingdom, to provide them with another chance of immortality.

Pinudjem I had ordered this to be carried out, but his successor Pinudjem II was personally responsible for the removal and reburial of the mummies and their surviving funerary goods. They were placed in a tomb belonging to Queen Inha'pi, situated to the south of Deir el-Bahri, and a few years later the necropolis officials added other mummies belonging to priests and members of the royal family, including Pinudjem II's own body. This cache, discovered by the villagers of Qurna, was eventually investigated in 1881 by Maspero, the Director of Antiquities, and the mummies and tomb goods were taken to Cairo Museum.

Other royal mummies reburied in the tomb of Amenophis II in the Valley of the Kings were discovered by Loret in 1898. In 1891, the villager from Qurna who had indicated the whereabouts of the Deir el-Bahri cache identified another important tomb, just north of the temple at Deir el-Bahri. When Daressy, the archaeologist placed in charge of the excavation for the Antiquities Service, entered the tomb's extensive galleries, he found many coffins, statuettes, ushabti-figures and other objects belonging to the family of the high-priest Menkheperre and to the priests of Amen-Re. Women – mostly temple musicians – were also included, and the inscriptional evidence associated with these funerary items has provided us with a major source for the history of Dynasty 21.

When the last ruler of the dynasty, Psusennes II, died, there was no male heir and the throne passed to his son-in-law Shoshenk, a powerful chief and army commander. As Shoshenk I, he and his descendants formed Dynasty 22, which is sometimes known as the Bubastite Dynasty since Bubastis was Shoshenk's home city. In fact, the family was of foreign origin and had first called themselves Chiefs of the Meshwesh. However, they were not invaders but had descended from the Libyans who fought against Merneptah and Ramesses III; subsequently, they settled in the Delta where they became numerous and powerful.

Few historical sources exist for this period but generally the same trends continue as in the preceding dynasty. This dearth of information is partly because the dynastic capital was now situated in the north, either at Bubastis or Tanis, where archaeological evidence is less abundant or well preserved than at sites in Middle or Upper Egypt. However, Thebes still continued as the great religious centre in the south, and relations between the north and the south continued to present difficulties. Shoshenk I had his second son Iuput appointed as high-priest at Thebes and this brought the southern centre under the king's control, but generally the country remained unsettled.

Two of the main historical sources for this period are the Serapeum at Sakkara and the Bubastite Portal in the Temple of Karnak. Auguste Mariette, a young French archaeologist destined to become one of the greatest figures in Egyptology, discovered the Serapeum in 1850. Here, in huge sarcophagi, the sacred Apis-bulls were buried in vast subterranean chambers; the earliest burial dated to the reign of Amenophis III (Dynasty 18) but the inscriptional evidence is most informative for Dynasty 22 and the later period. The dates of birth and death of several Apis-bulls are given and also their lifespans, which assists particularly with the chronology towards the end of the dynasty; in addition, the discovery of the stela of Harpson provided further useful information about the period, since Harpson, a priest who held the title of Prophet of Neith, was the descendant of four kings, the earliest of whom was Shoshenk I.

The Bubastite Portal – an entrance into the main temple at Karnak erected by Shoshenk I – was decorated with important inscriptions including an autobiographical record placed there by Osorkon, a high-priest and son of King Takelot II. The significance of this inscription is that it describes the internal conflicts in Egypt at this time when the rulers in the north were attempting to maintain their control.

Despite some political troubles, these kings built extensively at Tanis and Bubastis: Osorkon II removed and used stone from Ramesses II's city at Pi-Ramesse to make additions to these cities, and at Bubastis the archaeologist Naville revealed a great granite doorway that was decorated with reliefs depicting royal events, particularly Osorkon II's jubilee festival. Most kings of this dynasty, like those of Dynasty 21, were buried with magnificent treasure in tombs at Tanis discovered by the archaeologist Montet.

From Maspero's Histoire Ancienne des Peuples de l'Oriente
Classique *(1899), this drawing is based on Naville's restoration of the
granite gate in the Festival Hall at Bubastis. This was decorated with
scenes of royal events, particularly Osorkon II's jubilee festival. Kings
of Dynasty 22 built extensively at Bubastis and Tanis.*

General view of Gebel Barkal taken from Cailliaud's Voyage à Méroé au Fleuve Blanc *(1823); his expedition is shown in the foreground. The god Amun was believed to live in this table mountain (Gebel Barkal) and here, in the ancient capital of Napata, temples were built to him.*

In foreign policy, perhaps only Shoshenk I is of interest. As the ablest ruler since early Ramesside times, he set out to take action abroad once he had consolidated his kingdom, and trade with Nubia and Byblos flourished again. He also attempted to intervene in Palestine, and when, in 930 BC, the realm was divided into the two kingdoms of Judah and Israel, Shoshenk used the excuse of a border skirmish to lead a campaign in Palestine. The biblical account refers to him as King Shishak and states that he took away a large amount of tribute from the temple and palace in Jerusalem, returning home in triumph. However, his foreign ambitions seem to have been limited to this action for there is no record that he sought to extend Egypt's power by marching on into Syria.

The history of the succeeding dynasties becomes increasingly obscure. Dynasty 23, according to Manetho, consisted of only four kings and was centred at Tanis. Some evidence indicates that this line of kings may have been contemporary with some rulers of Dynasty 22, and perhaps this situation represented a breakdown of centralized government and its replacement by local rulers. Certainly, Manetho's scanty entry for Dynasty 24 indicates that the power of these rulers was limited to only one area, and he supplies the name of one king – Bochchoris of Sais (a Delta town) – in whose reign one notable event is recorded: 'in his time a lamb spoke'. From other evidence, it appears that the lamb used a human voice to foretell the Assyrian conquest of Egypt which actually came to pass in Dynasty 25.

The rulers of Dynasty 24 were the descendants of Tefnakhte, a prince of Sais who had tried to expand his influence southwards as far as the city of Lisht. However, this ambition was thwarted by the emergence of Piankhy, the ruler of a kingdom that had developed to the south of Egypt. Its capital was at Napata where the population worshipped the god Amen-Re and retained many aspects of the Egyptian culture of Dynasty 18. Their origins remain obscure, although they may have been partly descended from a group of priests of Amen-Re who perhaps left Egypt at an earlier date; now combined with local elements, they formed a vibrant society whose leader was determined to impose some order in the homeland of his deity, Amen-Re.

Napata was situated near the Fourth Cataract, in the shadow of the great rocky mountain of Gebel Barkal where Mariette discovered the great stela dating to Year 21 of Piankhy's reign. This provides details of his campaign against the Libyan rulers of Egypt in *c.*730 BC, when cities and prisoners were taken and there was a great slaughter of people. Egypt was now obviously segmented and ruled by several factions, but Piankhy subdued the south and forced submission from the north. Nevertheless, he did not remain in Egypt but returned to his Nubian kingdom where he was buried in a pyramid at Kurru.

In Egypt, the various princes continued to rule but Piankhy's brother and successor Shabako returned to Egypt to defeat Bochchoris, Tefnakhte's successor at Sais, and to found Dynasty 25 which is sometimes known as the Kushite or Ethiopian Dynasty. This first Nubian pharaoh chose Thebes, the home of the god Amen-Re, as his Egyptian capital, but few monuments have survived from his reign. He was also eventually buried in a pyramid at Kurru far to the south, and rulership of Egypt passed to his successors Shebitku and Taharka.

Taharka, the ablest ruler of the dynasty, was crowned at Memphis. At first, his reign was prosperous and peaceful and he was able to undertake building programmes in Egypt and Nubia. However, his foreign policy brought him into conflict with the Assyrians. The old Hittite power which had once dominated Egyptian policy abroad had been swept away by the Assyrians who began to emerge as a considerable force around 900 BC. Their empire, the greatest to that date, was conceived of as a single nation which was supported by a sophisticated army and weaponry, rather than as a loose confederation of vassal city-states and spheres of influence, as the Egyptian empire had been. One of their great rulers, Sennacherib, came into conflict with Egypt when the King of Judah, Hezekiah, appealed to the latter for help against the Assyrians. The Assyrians defeated the Egyptian forces at el-Tekeh, and although Sennacherib was finally assassinated in his own capital of Nineveh, the struggle with Egypt

continued under his successors, Esarhaddon and Ashurbanipal.

A key aim of the Assyrians' ruthless expansion policy was to gain control of the small states in Syria/Palestine which continued to ask their old overlord, Egypt, for help against the new enemy. The new Assyrian ruler Esarhaddon pursued this policy in Syria/Palestine even more vigorously and, becoming resentful of Egypt's intervention there, he decided to take the fight into Egypt. In 674 BC his first attempt to invade Egypt was defeated by Taharka, but in a second attack in 671 BC he drove the Egyptian king out of Memphis and back down to the south. Records of this campaign preserved in cuneiform texts on stelae and tablets report that he destroyed Memphis and removed booty and people from Egypt. A new policy was now introduced: Esarhaddon appointed different rulers to control Egypt, drawn from native governors and officials whose loyalty could be assured; amongst these was Necho, a prince of Sais, who would eventually become the founder of the next dynasty.

Further troubles in Egypt drew Esarhaddon south again a couple of years later, but he fell ill en route and died at Haran. The Egyptian king Taharka now took this opportunity to reinstall himself at Memphis but his triumph was short-lived; Ashurbanipal, who would become Assyria's greatest ruler, attacked Egypt and regained Memphis in 662 BC. He installed new governors and princes in the towns, to replace Esarhaddon's men who had fled, and Taharka was driven south, first to Thebes and then to Napata where he finally died and was buried in a pyramid at Nuri.

The local princes were poor allies for the Assyrians, and began to intrigue again with Taharka at Napata; when this was discovered, the Assyrians removed them to Nineveh, although Necho of Sais and his son Psammetichus were subsequently returned to Egypt by Ashurbanipal and installed again as petty rulers in the Delta.

With no firm local control, it was possible for Taharka's nephew and successor Tanuatamun to return to Egypt and establish himself again at Memphis. However, Ashurbanipal quickly returned from Nineveh and drove Tanuatamun from Thebes back to Napata where he eventually died; meanwhile, Ashurbanipal ransacked the Temple of Amun at Thebes and carried large amounts of booty back to Nineveh. His record of events, preserved in a cuneiform text on the Rassam cylinder, gives an account of an overwhelming victory but the Egyptians told another story in their version, which was inscribed on the Dream Stela found at Gebel Barkal; this claims that Tanuatamun had in fact overthrown the Assyrians.

The Nubian kingdom now shrank back to its earlier boundaries and the rulers soon ceased to claim any jurisdiction over Egypt. The kingdom's northern boundary was probably fixed south of the Third Cataract and a new capital was established at Meroë. Apart from trading contacts between Egypt and this Meroitic kingdom, no political ties continued, although Egyptian culture survived there for many years, with the construction of Egyptian-style temples and the burial of royalty in pyramids. They also continued to write in hieroglyphs, developing two distinctive scripts which are known today as Meroitic. Egyptian culture actually continued to exist here long after it had died out in the homeland, and only came to an end when Aeizanes, ruler of Axum, destroyed Meroë in AD 350.

Meanwhile, the emergence of Dynasty 26 and its line of native rulers brought about many changes in Egypt; and in the wider sphere of foreign politics there were also new forces to be considered. A Scythian invasion and the growth of a new empire of Medes in north-western Iran threatened Assyria's power, and in 626 BC the Babylonians under their ruler Nabopolassar succeeded in defeating the Assyrians. A dangerous new alliance now emerged between the Medes and the Babylonians which persuaded the Egyptians to join forces with the Assyrians. Such were the entanglements of this final period of Pharaonic history, but in Egypt an important political development now occurred which would affect the power balance there throughout most of the later dynastic period.

In the New Kingdom, the king's chief wife carried the title Divine Wife of Amun and took part in the state festivals as the god's consort. However, from Dynasty 21 the king's daughter was accorded this title and she became a priestess with extensive political and religious powers as well as considerable wealth and possessions. She had her own house, land and officials at Thebes where, as the consecrated wife of Amun, she made offerings to the gods. Most importantly, she was obliged to lead a life of chastity, and this was also imposed on the women of her Theban court who were the concubines of Amun. As she was not allowed to marry, the Divine Wife had to adopt the daughter of the next king as her own 'daughter' and successor. Thus Amenardis I, daughter of King Kashta who founded Dynasty 25, was adopted as the divine heiress by Shepenopet I, daughter of Osorkon III of Dynasty 23, and Amenardis I in turn adopted Shepenopet II, daughter of King Piankhy of Dynasty 25.

This development was of considerable significance because it ensured that each king secured control over Thebes through his daughter's unrivalled position there (she was of equal status to the king but her power was limited to Thebes). It also ensured that no male rival to the king could seize power at Thebes and, since the Divine Wife could not marry, neither her husband nor her sons could threaten the king's control of Egypt. Finally, the adoption of the next king's daughter as successor at Thebes ensured a smooth, uninterrupted passage of this process from one dynasty to the next. The Egyptians had witnessed the disruption which had been caused by the division of the country into northern and southern factions in Dynasties 20 and 21, and by Dynasty 25 the role of the Divine Wife of Amun had become a vital means of ensuring the unity of the kingdom.

The Late Period

There was a brief resurgence of national pride and power in Dynasty 26, but the old glories were never truly regained and Egypt's decline continued on its inevitable course during these final years.

Esarhaddon had given limited authority to native princes in Egypt to govern during his absence, and Necho, prince of Sais, became the most powerful of these, establishing a substantial kingdom in the western Delta. He probably began to rule as a local king at Sais in 672 BC. Despite their disloyalty to the Assyrians and subsequent removal to Nineveh, the leadership qualities of Necho I and his son Psammetichus were obviously recognized, and Ashurbanipal reinstated them. However, Necho I was killed by the Nubian ruler Tanuatamun who briefly regained Egypt and reached Memphis, but his son soon regained control and, as founder of Dynasty 26, claimed the kingship of Egypt.

In these later dynasties, Egypt's destiny was closely interwoven with those of other countries who were either allies, trading contacts or conquerors, and contemporary non-Egyptian historical documents rather than native monuments or inscriptions provide the most extensive evidence for this period. The most important are the Babylonian chronicles, the biblical Old Testament, the writings of the Jewish historian Josephus, and the *Histories* of Herodotus, who provides particularly interesting information about this dynasty.

He refers to the Dodecarchy of Egyptian princes led by the Saite prince Psammetichus I whose first few years were spent establishing control over the Delta. At this time, he probably ruled in the north while Tanuatamun remained king over the south, but once Tanuatamun left Egypt for his own Nubian kingdom, Psammetichus was ready to take over the rulership of the whole country. He followed the tradition of earlier rulers in placing his daughter Nitocris in the line of succession at Thebes to become the Divine Wife of Amun.

According to Herodotus, it was Psammetichus I's alliance with Greek mercenaries which enabled him to become leader of the Delta princes and the dynasty came to rely on the fighting ability and naval skills of foreign soldiers and on foreign merchants. The Saite kings continued to encourage foreigners to settle in Egypt and doubtless came to regard them as a safety measure against the potential power of other local princes, but the indigenous population became unhappy about their presence. Eventually, it became necessary to establish certain districts where the

Wooden figures (c.600 BC) of Osiris, god of the dead, and his wife Isis who is shown protecting him with her wings. According to mythology, she used magic to reassemble his dismembered body. The cult of these deities was important for over two thousand years.

foreigners could live and continue their own traditions, and Naucratis, the Delta city founded by Psammetichus I and finally discovered and excavated by Petrie, was specially built to accommodate a Greek population.

Perhaps as a reaction to the unprecedented number of foreigners – Greeks, Carians, Jews and Syrians amongst them – who now took up residence in Egypt, the native population increasingly tried to revive their own traditions in art and religion. National spirit enjoyed a brief resurgence and there was an increased interest in the animal cults which were so distinctively Egyptian. There was also a tendency towards archaism in literature and art, and forms which had existed as long ago as the Old Kingdom (particularly relating to funerary customs) were now revived. Dynasty 26 was the last period when Egyptian objects of the finest quality were produced, and in particular, the ushabti figures have survived well enough to demonstrate the excellence of the craftsmanship.

When Assyrian power declined, Psammetichus I was in a strong enough position to stop paying tribute, but the new alliance of Medes and Babylonians now persuaded him to form an alliance with Assyria in 616 BC. The danger posed by the Medes and Babylonians was soon demonstrated when in 612 BC, the Babylonians sacked the Assyrian capital of Nineveh. Psammetichus I's son and successor, Necho II was obviously interested in exploration and trade, and to increase commerce he initiated the construction of a canal to re-establish a waterway between the Nile and the Red Sea. He also set up a fleet of triremes and his Phoenician sailors made a three-year voyage around Africa, going from the Red Sea round the Cape and then returning by Gibraltar.

However, foreign concerns dictated the most important events of his reign and, in the tradition of many earlier Egyptian kings, he interfered in the politics of Syria/Palestine. He fought against Josiah, the king of Judah, and when the latter was killed Necho II ensured that he approved of the new ruler at Jerusalem. However, any international ambitions he cherished were terminated by the Babylonians, who were now the leaders of the area. Their ruler, Nabopolassar, regarded Necho II as his prime enemy and, despite some initial Egyptian successes at various places on the River Euphrates, it is recorded in the Babylonian chronicles that Nebuchadrezzar, Nabopolassar's son, inflicted a resounding defeat on them at the Battle of Carchemish in 605 BC. The Babylonians pursued the Egyptians in the district of Hamath and caused them to flee, and eventually they were able to seize all Egypt's territorial possessions.

With Nabopolassar's death shortly after the Battle of Carchemish, Nebuchadrezzar II became ruler of the Babylonian Empire; in 601 BC, he embarked on a new campaign against the Egyptians but he suffered great losses and returned to Babylon. His showdown with the Egyptians would wait for several years.

The reign of Psammetichus II, the son and heir of Necho II, was brief, and he concentrated his energies on domestic policies and building programmes and did not come into conflict with the Babylonians. However, when he died in 589 BC, Apries (his son and successor) was again drawn into foreign affairs when King Zedekiah of Judah rebelled against Nebuchadrezzar. In 587 BC the Babylonians captured and destroyed Jerusalem and took Zedekiah away as a prisoner. A large proportion of the population of Jerusalem was removed to Babylon, but some of those who remained behind went with the prophet Jeremiah to Egypt. However, the actions of Apries (who is referred to in the biblical record as the Pharaoh Hophra) and the exact role he played against the Babylonians on this occasion remain unclear.

The downfall of Apries was brought about because of other foreign involvement, and centred around an extensive and prosperous colony that the Greeks had established at Cyrene on the North African coast. The native Libyan population greatly disliked this colony and in 570 BC their chief, Adicran, asked the Egyptians for help. An army was dispatched but was severely defeated, and the Egyptian people blamed Apries for this outcome. He was deposed and the people chose an army general named Amasis to rule in his stead. At first, Apries was kept alive and given a place at the capital Sais, but later he was handed over to the masses, who killed him.

Herodotus, again the best source for information about these tumultuous events, provides details of the background and life of Amasis, depicting him as a drunken but popular and shrewd ruler. His military engagements with the Babylonians remain obscure, although it is recalled in a cuneiform tablet in the British Museum that he and Nebuchadrezzar II engaged in further hostilities in 568–7 BC. At home, he continued the policy of using Greek mercenaries but he was fully aware that he owed his kingship to the native Egyptian population, and he checked the growth of Greek merchants in Egypt by confining their trading activities to the exclusively Greek city of Naucratis.

Amasis' son Psammetichus III briefly inherited the throne in 526 BC but the reign lasted only a few months and was brought to an end by the Persians. This new power had already subdued Media, Lydia and the cities of the Ionian coast when, in 539 BC, Cyrus II (the Achaemenid ruler who founded the Persian empire) overthrew the last Babylonian king, Nabonidus, as he entered Babylon. Cambyses, the son of Cyrus II, was sent to conquer Egypt and bring it within the Persian fold and, having subdued the Phoenicians and acquired their fleet, he proceeded to rout the Egyptians at the Battle of Pelusium in 525 BC. After a final siege at Memphis, Psammetichus III was put to death and the Persians annexed Egypt; this first period of Persian domination – Manetho's Dynasty 27 – lasted until 404 BC.

Egypt now became a satrapy of the Persian Empire, ruled by a governor (satrap) on behalf of the Persian kings, who seem to have regarded themselves as pharaohs and to have undertaken some of the religious duties associated with the position. Some Persian kings even showed interest in Egypt's institutions and traditions, and there is no evidence that their rule was excessively oppressive. Numbers of foreigners now resided in Egypt, Egyptian artists and officials were taken to work in the Persian cities (where their influence can be seen in the art and architecture), and Egyptians were accustomed to fighting in Persian campaigns, but the Persian domination, like the Assyrian interlude, had little long-term effect upon Egypt's civilization.

Cambyses is characterized by Herodotus (whose visit to Egypt took place in this dynasty) as a cruel tyrant who neglected the gods of Egypt and killed one of the Apis-bulls worshipped at Sakkara. However, here the archaeological evidence does not support Herodotus' story, since on the sarcophagus of an Apis-bull discovered in the Serapeum at Sakkara there is a dedicatory inscription by Cambyses, suggesting that in fact he honoured the bulls' cult. The final years of his reign after he conquered Egypt were fraught with difficulties: on one occasion, a complete army he sent to the Siwa oasis disappeared in a sandstorm, and Herodotus speculated that perhaps his misfortunes made him slightly mad. A pretender to his throne

forced him to return to Persia, and he left Egypt under the control of the satrap Aryandes.

Darius I became the next Achaemenid ruler and the great Persian Empire flourished under his influence. In Egypt, he acted differently from other Persian rulers and took a positive interest in the country's civilization and traditions. He gave his support to several important schemes, and is remembered in the writings of Diodorus Siculus as an Egyptian law-giver. Information written on the back of a later papyrus (known as the Demotic Chronicle) records that he sent a satrap with instructions to form a group of the wisest soldiers, sailors and priests to write down and preserve the laws of Egypt down to Year 44 of Amasis' reign.

Darius regarded himself as a pharaoh and did not entirely delegate the government of the country to a satrap; he was also pious to Egypt's gods, supporting their cults and making additions to the traditional temples. In practical matters, too, he was active: Herodotus records that the project to link the Nile and the Red Sea by means of a canal, started in Necho II's reign and subsequently abandoned, was now completed (in 518 BC), and a number of stelae were set up along the banks of the canal to record this achievement in hieroglyphic and cuneiform inscriptions. The scheme improved communications and facilitated transport between Egypt and Persia.

In 486 BC, Darius' son Xerxes succeeded him, but he made no attempt to emulate his father and neglected his duties as pharaoh. A series of uprisings in Egypt in 486 BC were promptly put down by the new emperor, who seems to have exploited the country and its people. Herodotus claimed that he was a cruel tyrant to the Egyptians.

Xerxes was murdered and succeeded by Artaxerxes I in 465 BC. Local disturbances in the north-western Delta now developed and the Egyptian leader Inaros asked for Athenian help against the Persians. Such conflicts continued until the Persians and Athenians concluded peace in 449–8 BC, and a local chieftain, Amyrtaeus, carried on his independent stance against the Persians in the extreme western area of the Delta. It was apparently one of his family – the similarly named Amyrtaeus of Sais – who is recorded in Manetho's List as the only king of Dynasty 28.

This brief resurgence of native rulership continued in Dynasty 29 when, according to Manetho, four kings from the town of Mendes became rulers; for Dynasty 30, he gives three kings of Sebennytus, the most important of whom was Nectanebo. However, Artaxerxes II was determined to re-establish Persian control over Egypt and he began to make his preparations. In 373 BC, the Persian forces under the satrap Pharnabazus set out to take Egypt, but when he reached there, local circumstances including the Nile inundation enabled the native forces to repel the enemy. With the accession of Artaxerxes III Ochus as emperor in 358 BC, the Empire was revived and reorganized; finally in 343 BC, he led a great campaign against Egypt when he succeeded in driving King Nectanebo II southwards and once again was able to establish Persian power in Egypt. The walls of the most important cities were destroyed, vast quantities of treasure and inscribed records were removed from the temples, and a new satrap was installed before Artaxerxes and his army finally left for Babylon.

This second period of Persian domination was known as Dynasty 31 and this was later added to the thirty dynasties given by Manetho; it included the reigns of Artaxerxes III, his son Arses, and Darius III. However, the arrival of Alexander the Great of Macedon in Egypt in 332 BC brought Persia's power to an end and introduced the final phase of the country's ancient history, which is often called the Graeco-Roman Period.

The Graeco-Roman Period
....

Many changes occurred between the end of the Pharaonic civilization and the start of medieval times, in the period when the country was occupied and ruled by the Greeks and then the Romans. Although some of the national institutions survived, almost every aspect of life was profoundly affected by the new rulers and their customs. In addition, the arrival of Christianity finally obliterated old beliefs and practices and influenced most aspects of life in which religion played a major role.

The kings of Dynasty 26 had been the first to introduce Greeks into Egypt in large numbers when they came as mercenaries to assist the Saite rulers in their fight for freedom against the Persians. Later rulers also employed their services, and they were responsible for modernizing the Egyptian army and introducing new fighting techniques. Greek merchants had also settled in Egypt in large numbers and were established in their own great city of Naucratis. In addition, travellers and tourists – including writers such as Herodotus – visited Egypt to marvel at the ancient monuments and quaint customs.

When Alexander the Great conquered the country in 332 BC, he was welcomed as the man who saved the people from the yoke of Persian domination and the effects of an increasingly segmented and ineffectual native rulership. The son of Phillip II, King of Macedon, Alexander had been trained as the king's Deputy, and by the age of twenty he was an able administrator who also showed prowess in hunting and warfare. When his father was assassinated, supporters helped him gain the throne of Macedon, and he set out to achieve his destiny of conquering the known world.

The Persian Empire was ripe for conquest, and Alexander's brilliant leadership now brought its provinces under his control. He claimed the land owned by the Persian king for himself and for Macedon, and the tribute formerly paid by the subject peoples to the Persian ruler now came to him. However, even as his armies moved forward in conquest, he introduced changes which would produce long-term benefits for the peoples of his new Empire. Native inhabitants were now allowed to practise their own religions and customs whereas the Persians had often suppressed any individuality, but Alexander also sought to unify diverse peoples by providing them with common social and economic interests, so that they regarded themselves as fortunate to be part of his Empire. New opportunities for trade existed, with increased travel and co-operation between Greek and Oriental merchants, and further stimulation was provided by the issue of Alexander's own coinage (which was produced from the Persian treasure) and by his foundation of new cities to spread Greek culture, especially in the areas of economics and education, throughout the Empire. He was regarded as a benign and tolerant conqueror, and his unprecedentedly vast conquests gave him the inspiration and power to create a new type of empire. This was based on the ideals of religious freedom, toleration of different races and their legal and social customs, and general economic prosperity. He hoped to allow national traits to flourish, but also to provide some common ideals which would bind the empire together and ensure that certain Greek concepts would be generally accepted. If he had lived longer and had enjoyed the opportunity to develop this new world, the results would doubtless have benefited many people.

After the conquest of Syria/Palestine and the siege of Tyre, Alexander proceeded to attack Gaza before he arrived in Egypt in the autumn of 332 BC, when the Persian satrap surrendered without a fight and the people welcomed him as their liberator. In November he was invested by the priests as pharaoh, and was determined that the Egyptians' religious freedom should be maintained.

Although he remained in Egypt for only six months, Alexander made some important arrangements for the future government of the country. A Greek system of control was established over military matters and finance: a viceroy was appointed (Cleomenes of Naucratis) and given the title of satrap, and a group of six governors – two Macedonians with military powers, and two Greeks and two Egyptians with civil powers – was established to limit the danger of a *coup d'état*. Garrisons were placed at Pelusium and Memphis, and the Nile fleet was put under the control of Macedonian commanders. Arrangements were also made for the imposition and collection of taxes.

Although Alexander travelled as far south as the First Cataract on the Nile, his major building activities were concentrated in the north. According to Plutarch's *Life of Alexander,* he had a prophetic dream which confirmed where the new city of Alexandria should be built, situated near the ancient village of Rhakotes and opposite the island of Pharos. This location on the west mouth of the Nile and on the Mediterranean coast ensured that Alexandria, with two harbours, would become the great centre of commerce for the whole area. Planned by a Greek architect, the city had temples to Greek gods, a Council-house, an Agora, and all the major institutions of a Greek city. Tradition relates that the foundation of Alexandria took place on 7 April 331 BC and, as Egypt's new capital, it not only provided a link with the rest of the empire but its location enabled the country's wealth and commodities to be more readily exported. Before long, it became a great centre of Hellenistic learning and knowledge, attracting scholars from many parts of the empire.

As soon as he arrived in the country, Alexander had given the ancient gods his special attention and sacrificed to the deities of Egypt and Greece at the old capital of Memphis, where he was probably crowned as pharaoh in a traditional ceremony held in the Temple of Ptah. As pharaoh, he was acclaimed as 'son of Re', and he built a temple at Rhakotes to Isis, the supreme Egyptian mother-goddess.

However, while he was in Egypt, he apparently felt a strong desire to visit the famous oracle of Jupiter Amun at Siwa, Egypt's most westerly oasis in the Libyan desert. The legend later persisted that when he entered the shrine, the god recognized him as his son and promised him dominion over the whole world. As Pharaoh, he was the Son of Re, and it was traditional that a ruler of Egypt should receive this form of recognition from the priests who were the god's mouthpiece. However, on this occasion, their address appears to have been interpreted as a form of personal deification for Alexander which led to rumours that he was more than a mere mortal. The Egyptians interpreted this oracle to mean that Alexander had received the god's special recognition and that therefore his successors, although foreign, were to be accepted as the legitimate rulers of Egypt. However, there is really no evidence that Alexander himself regarded this 'deification' as anything other than the usual political convention in Egypt, nor that he used this to establish his divine autocracy in the rest of the empire.

In the spring of 331 BC, he left Egypt to pursue further conquests in the East; he finally reached India, but became ill on the return journey and died in Babylon in 323 BC. Legend says that his body was taken to Egypt and kept first at Memphis before being buried in a tomb at Alexandria; the last recorded visit to this tomb was made by the Roman emperor Caracalla in AD 215 but, despite repeated attempts to discover the burial place, it has never been found.

Alexander's empire was now divided between his generals; his Macedonian general in charge of troops in Egypt – Ptolemy, son of Lagos – became satrap of Egypt first under Philip Arrhidaeus, Alexander's half-brother, and then under his son, Alexander IV. However, in 305 BC, Ptolemy assumed the independent rulership of Egypt and as King Ptolemy I Soter ('Saviour'), he founded the Ptolemaic or Macedonian dynasty. He regarded himself as the regenerator of Egypt, and ensured the continuation of the dynastic line by appointing his son as co-regent and also re-establishing the old Egyptian tradition of royal brother-sister marriages. The country was reorganized, and there was an extensive programme to build and restore the Egyptian temples. Ptolemy I also introduced the cult of a new hybrid deity, Serapis, who combined the features of the Egyptian god Osiris with those of several Greek deities, and he founded a cult of Alexander the Great at Alexandria which set a precedent for the official worship of the later rulers of this dynasty (eventually, Ptolemy I was himself worshipped in a temple built at Koptos).

The Ptolemaic dynasty now began to establish its basic principles of government. The kings adopted the role of Pharaoh to give themselves the religious right to rule Egypt and to lay claim to the country's resources and the right to impose heavy taxes. For the first time, foreign dynasts went to extreme lengths to enhance their own power and to gain control of the people, but although the kingdom became wealthy, the native population enjoyed few benefits and there were frequent rebellions. To uphold the traditional role of Pharaoh, the Ptolemies built great temples to the Egyptian gods such as those at Edfu, Denderah, Philae, Esna and Kom Ombo where the wall scenes show them performing divine rituals.

Ptolemy I and his successors imposed Hellenistic culture on Egypt and changed old traditions to an extent never attempted by previous foreign rulers. Large numbers of Greeks now came to set-

tle in Egypt, taking up residence not only in cities such as Alexandria, Naucratis and Ptolemais, but also in country districts like the Fayoum which was noted for its natural beauty. At Alexandria, Ptolemy I founded the Museum and the Great Library in the palace quarter and, in addition to these embellishments, he must receive credit for establishing a prosperous kingdom.

Greek language and Greek customs now became predominant although the old traditions survived amongst the native population. Greek cities, with their theatres, gymnasia and chapels, exerted a strong Hellenistic influence but in the countryside, new settlers who were more exposed to Egyptian traditions sometimes adopted the old customs. There was also a degree of hybridization in some areas of religion, art, and architecture.

The process of Hellenization was most actively pursued under Ptolemy II Philadelphus, Ptolemy I's son. Certain policies inaugurated by Ptolemy I were now consolidated; for example, Ptolemy II married his sister Arsinoe and took the name Philadelphus, and dynastic state-worship of the ruler became established with an official cult for the king and queen. During this most prosperous of the Ptolemies' reigns, Greek farming communities were set up in the Fayoum and a detailed system of financial administration was organized throughout the country, in which new Revenue Laws monitored industries such as papyrus manufacture and oil production. In order to encourage better communication and trade, the canal between the Red Sea and the Nile was also restored.

The abolition of the old Egyptian aristocracy enhanced the status of Greeks in Egypt, who now formed the new upper classes. Greek culture also flourished because Ptolemy II actively promoted Hellenism by patronizing the arts; he enlarged the Great Library at Alexandria and encouraged seventy scholars from Jerusalem to come to the city to translate the Pentateuch into Greek. Alexandria was enhanced with new

This mask (Ptolemaic Period, c.200 BC) was placed over the face of a mummy. Made of cartonnage (a mixture of papyrus and gum), the face is gilded, and decorations and figures of gods are painted on the headpiece and chest cover. Such masks were produced in large numbers for wealthy clients.

buildings which included the Pharos, and Ptolemy II was also responsible for introducing magnificent processions and games to the city.

His son, Ptolemy III Euergetes I, continued to make great donations to the temples and cults and began to build a great temple to Horus at Edfu, although the native rebellions in the area around Thebes delayed its completion. These problems continued in the reign of his son, Ptolemy IV Philopator, who had to contend with nationalistic riots which began in the same area in 207–6 BC. The rebels even succeeded in establishing some degree of control over this district, and ruled as a line of native 'pharaohs' for nineteen years before Ptolemy V Epiphanes finally managed to subdue them in 186 BC. However, the problem was not resolved and riots occurred again later in the dynasty.

The Ptolemies gained some military successes abroad: Ptolemy III advanced on Babylonia, but the original ruler Seleucus managed to regain most of his territory; and Ptolemy IV achieved some success in defeating Antiochus III of Syria at the Battle of Raphia in 217 BC. However, under Ptolemy V most Egyptian possessions in Asia Minor, Palestine and the Aegean were lost, with the exception of Cyprus and Cyrene.

In the later years of the dynasty, the government and administration faced many problems including dynastic conflicts. The violent and ruthless Ptolemy VIII Euergetes II (nicknamed 'Physcon' or 'Pot-bellied') fought his brother Ptolemy VI Philometor and briefly seized the throne, but his sister and niece (who both became his wives) continued the struggle until they issued an Amnesty Decree in 118 BC.

One inscription, famous for its role in the decipherment of Hieroglyphs, dates to this later Ptolemaic period. Known today as the Rosetta Stone, this Decree (issued on 27 March 196 BC) commemorated the religious ceremonies performed at the coronation of Ptolemy V at Memphis.

The Ptolemaic dynasty drew to a close with the life and death of one of Egypt's most famous queens, Cleopatra VII. In 51 BC she became joint ruler with her father, Ptolemy XII Auletes, and then ruled successively with her brothers Ptolemy XIII and XIV (she was also married to both of them). The wealth of Egypt had already attracted Rome's attention, and the Roman Consul Pompey had been involved with the internal and financial affairs of Ptolemy XII. When the latter died, the Roman Senate appointed Pompey as guardian of Cleopatra and her brother. Conflict with Gaius Julius Caesar, Roman Dictator from 49 until 44 BC, ended with Pompey's defeat in 47 BC at the Battle of Pharsalia, and he fled to Egypt where he was killed by some Egyptian courtiers. Caesar pursued him to Egypt where Cleopatra VII, who had been ousted from the joint rulership in favour of her brother, now appealed to him to restore her to the throne.

Caesar spent some time in Egypt and accompanied Cleopatra on a Nile voyage in 47 BC. She regained her royal powers, her brother was drowned in the Nile, and the child of Caesar's liaison with Cleopatra – Ptolemy XV Caesarion – was adopted as her co-regent and ruled jointly with her from 36 BC. Cleopatra and her son are shown in the southern exterior wall reliefs at the Temple of Hathor at Denderah where they accompany the goddess Hathor, her husband Horus of Edfu, and their son, Ihy.

Cleopatra was a woman noted for her great intellect and her ambition to preserve her country's position in an increasingly threatening world. She now turned her attention to Marcus Antonius, a Roman Consul and Triumvir. In his early career, he had risen at Rome as a supporter of Julius Caesar whom he had accompanied on the conquest of Gaul, and marriage to Octavia, the sister of Octavian (Augustus), had also enhanced his standing.

Both Cleopatra and Mark Antony were ambitious and astute and each hoped to gain prestige and benefits from their alliance. The queen sought to use this marriage to gain Rome's support for Egypt and to acquire her share of eastern territorial possessions. For his part, Antony probably hoped at first that this association with Egypt would bring him power, prestige and wealth, but ultimately he seems to have identified himself with the Hellenistic East and to have preferred its customs to his own Roman traditions.

His first meeting with Cleopatra was hardly auspicious: Antony summoned her to Cilicia to account for her conduct of military matters at Philippi, and he may have planned to turn Egypt

The hypostyle hall in the Temple of Hathor at Denderah. The columns are placed close together as in earlier temples, but instead of plant-form capitals, these Hathor capitals represent the goddess' cow-eared, human face. She was worshipped here with her son and husband.

into a client-state of Rome. However, Cleopatra, a remarkable and formidable woman, came to the meeting in a spectacular gilded barge. With her intelligence (she was the only Ptolemaic ruler who learned to speak Egyptian), wit, and legendary beauty (although coins of the period do not confirm her physical charm), she seems to have persuaded Mark Antony to embark on an obsessive and ultimately destructive relationship.

The couple spent time together at Alexandria, and Antony showered the queen with gifts. He presented her with the contents of the library of the kings of Pergamum for the Library at Alexandria, and at a great ceremony known as the Donations of Alexandria which was held in 34 BC, Cleopatra and her children (born from her liaisons with Caesar and with Mark Antony) were assigned some of Rome's eastern provinces and anticipated conquests. However, the Roman Senate was not pleased with this disposal of property, and Mark Antony had to justify his decision by explaining that he was simply presenting Roman territory to Rome's client-state.

However, Mark Antony's brother-in-law Octavius had both personal and professional reasons to detest this eastern association. He obviously regarded Antony's courtship of Cleopatra as an insult to his sister Octavia (Antony's wife), and he was probably fearful of Antony's power-base in Egypt and regarded it as a threat to Rome. He began to denounce Antony in a propaganda campaign, persuading the Senate and people of Rome that Antony had spent his time in drunken debauchery at the Alexandrian court. He was denounced as a traitor of Rome, and Octavian's verbal hostilities were followed by a personal declaration of war on Antony and Cleopatra.

Gaius Julius Octavianus was the first emperor of Rome and when he became its sole ruler in 27 BC, he took the title of Augustus. An outstanding political and military leader, he was determined to put an end to Egypt's ambitions and to humiliate its queen, and Antony and Cleopatra saw their troops defeated in the Battle of Actium in western Greece in 31 BC. For some reason, Cleopatra ordered her squadron to withdraw at the height of the battle and, followed by Mark Antony, she fled to Alexandria where they spent their final ten months awaiting the arrival

of Augustus. When Alexandria was taken, the couple could not face the defeat and humiliation which Augustus would impose on them and they chose instead to commit suicide. The legend has persisted that the queen ended her life on 12 August 30 BC by submitting to a snake bite.

Augustus had Caesarion (Cleopatra's son by Caesar) put to death immediately, but her children by Mark Antony carried on the succession, ruling Egypt nominally for eighteen days before Augustus was declared Pharaoh on 31 August 30 BC. Egypt now became a Roman province and lost all its independence. Augustus created a special status for the country, so that, unlike other major Roman provinces which were governed by the Roman Senate, it became the emperor's personal property. He appointed a Prefect (viceregal governor) to administer it, with direct responsibility to the emperor, and the first, named Cornelius Gallus, ruled there from 30 to 29 BC.

Changes were now introduced in the government and the administration. Egypt no longer had its own king or capital city but was regarded as a district to be administered for the benefit of the Empire, and its main function was to supply grain for Rome. Augustus established a system which would remain in place for three hundred years; essentially, it retained the administration used by the Ptolemies and kept the same principal officials in their posts, but it also included some important new measures such as the introduction of Roman law.

The new government's main function was to collect taxes, but there was no real attempt to invest in Egypt in return for this tribute and, although at first the people would have noticed few obvious changes, the country was nevertheless now headed on a downward path. The economy actually flourished against the background of political stability provided by the Roman Empire, but the emphasis was on the production of goods (such as corn, papyrus and glass) which were required for Rome, and Egypt's own population enjoyed few benefits from this prosperity.

Augustus followed the example of the Ptolemies in adopting the role and titles of Pharaoh as the divine son, and his successors also

On the southern rear outer wall of the Temple of Hathor at Denderah, this scene shows (on the left) Cleopatra VII and her son Caesarion (the child of Julius Caesar), in the presence of the gods of Denderah: Hathor, her son Ihy, and husband Horus.

found it politically expedient to preserve this fiction since it gave them legitimacy to rule. They interpreted this rulership as the power to exploit the land's resources and its people. Augustus made offerings to the Apis-bull, and later emperors continued the tradition of temple-building, adding to Denderah, Esna, Philae and Kom Ombo where wall scenes depict them as pharaohs performing the divine rituals. Augustus established his power as far south as possible, and Cornelius Gallus led an expedition on his behalf to bring under Roman control the ever-fractious district around Thebes, while in Nubia the emperor founded temples at Dendur and to the local god Mandulis at Kalabsha.

Augustus left Egypt as a well-established province of the Roman Empire. Respect for Alexander the Great and admiration for the city's beauty had fortunately persuaded him not to destroy Alexandria.

He even enlarged and enhanced it, adding the suburb of Nicopolis with an amphitheatre and racecourse and completing the Caesareum, a temple which had been started by Cleopatra as a mark of honour to Mark Antony but which the Romans now established as a centre for the divine cult of the Caesars. Greek remained the official language and Hellenistic culture continued to flourish in the Greek cities of Egypt, but the Roman Period was soon to witness some dramatic changes.

Several of the emperors visited Egypt; its vast monuments and ancient civilization attracted many travellers, and some of the emperors were obviously keen to see the country. Hadrian (AD 117–38) travelled more extensively than any previous emperor and he spent several months in Egypt in AD 130. His activities apparently included lion-hunting in the desert west of the Delta and taking part in discussions with scholars at the Museum in Alexandria. He also visited the Colossi of Memnon at Thebes to hear the 'singing statue'.

However, he was overtaken by personal tragedy when his friend and lover, a young man named Antinous, drowned himself in the Nile

A plaster head of a woman from the cemetery at Mallawi (near Beni Suef), the location of a Roman garrison. The head, originally placed over a mummy, dates to the Roman Period (2nd century AD). Such representations seem to have been in use here for only about eighty years.

Another emperor, Septimius Severus (AD 193–211), visited Egypt on his way to Syria. At Alexandria he established a municipal constitution and issued a series of judgements in cases which the people of the city and surrounding countryside had brought to court.

By this time, the Romans were confronting the growth of Christianity, and Septimius Severus' Edict of AD 204 prohibited Roman subjects from embracing Christianity. In AD 50 Decius accelerated this process and ordered severe persecutions of Christians at Alexandria. He appears as Pharaoh in a scene in the temple at Esna where the accompanying inscription provides one of the last surviving texts in Hieroglyphs. Diocletian (AD 284–305), the last reigning Roman emperor to visit Egypt, was responsible for removing the country's southern border from Nubia and re-establishing it at Philae in c.AD 298. He was also in Alexandria in AD 302, just before the Christians were persecuted; he was despised as the instigator of these events, which continued to take place in Egypt for another ten years.

Constantine I (the son of Saint Helena), the first emperor to support the growth of Christianity, put an end to the persecutions started under Diocletian. He issued the Edict of Toleration in AD 311, and further measures included the Edict of Milan (AD 313) which restored the property of the churches; additional grants to churches were made available, and public funds were used for church building and restoration programmes. In AD 324–30, Constantine founded Constantinople, which became the first Christian city and acted as a counterbalance to Rome; it had some impact on Egypt because it lessened Alexandria's importance as a great city in the East and also partly replaced Rome as the major recipient of Egypt's grain supplies.

During Constantine's reign, Christianity spread throughout Egypt; the famed Caesareum at Alexandria was converted from a temple with a cult to the Roman emperors into a church dedicated to St Michael, and it later became the seat of the Patriarch of Alexandria. Far to the south at Thebes, an altar was dedicated to Constantine and erected in the Temple of Luxor.

to fulfil a prophecy that Hadrian would suffer a great loss. By killing himself, Antinous hoped to prevent a worse outcome befalling the emperor, and Hadrian rewarded his loyalty and preserved his memory by founding the city of Antinoupolis at the place of his death.

Hadrian's reign is also recalled at several other sites: a temple was erected in his honour at Armant, his gateway adorns the Temple of Isis at Philae, important texts have survived on the walls of the hypostyle hall at Esna and, with the Emperor Trajan, he was responsible for the addition of the wall reliefs on the birth house built by Augustus at Denderah.

The government was now reorganized, and Egypt became a diocese divided into six provinces. As problems emerged in the Church, they were addressed at a series of councils of which the most famous was held at Nicaea, and these attempts to unite the various religious opponents had long-term effects on the general development of Christianity.

When Theodosius I (AD 379–95) was baptized a Christian soon after his accession, Christianity was set to become the religion of the empire. His Edict (AD 384) formally declared this and also ordered the closure of temples dedicated to the old gods. Persecution of heretics and pagans now became widespread, and systematic destruction of temples and monuments in Egypt and Syria succeeded in obliterating most of the ancient faiths. However, although Christianity was now adopted as Egypt's official religion, it was not until the reign of Justinian (c.AD 540) that the last remnants of the old faith were swept away and the temples on the island of Philae at Egypt's southern border were finally closed.

In AD 305, the territories of the Roman Empire had been divided into eastern and western portions, ruled from Constantinople and Rome, and Egypt now came under the control of the Eastern Empire. The long period of Roman rule in Egypt was only finally brought to an end when, in AD 641, the Arabs conquered the country. The Graeco-Roman Period provides a unique opportunity to study the final stages of the Pharaonic civilization and the changes in religion, art, architecture, language and documentary sources which resulted from the interaction of the native culture with the newly imposed Hellenism.

As Pharaohs, the Roman emperors were obliged to promote the Egyptian temples and they built these at a number of sites. Many are still well preserved and justify considerable study and investigation, but most of the Greek-style temples which the Ptolemies erected in Egypt have not survived. Egyptian temples of the Graeco-Roman Period are the best-preserved examples and, with only minor variations, they continue the traditions of Pharaonic temple building. At first, the Ptolemies made additions and restorations to existing monuments such as

This plaster head of a woman from the cemetery at Mallawi (2nd century AD) depicts the contemporary hairstyle and jewellery of that period, when tomb robbery had led to the custom of representing jewellery on the mask instead of placing it in the tomb.

Luxor, Karnak and the Theban funerary temples, but from the reign of Ptolemy III they began to construct new temples (although apparently on older sites) at Edfu, Esna, Denderah, Kom Ombo and Philae. Like the earlier examples, these were based on a single plan and all had the same major architectural and decorative features. Each consisted of a series of courts, halls and the sanctuary, all approached through the main pylon, but certain innovations were added: screen walls now separated inner areas from the forecourts, roof apertures replaced clerestory lighting, and there was a birth-house (Mammisi) where the god's birth was celebrated. There were also new forms of columns which were not Greek but were based on earlier Egyptian designs. Like the original Pharaonic temples, these Graeco-Roman

buildings also copied the plan of a house, and had reception and living quarters for the deity.

The tombs were the only great architectural development of the period, and here again the Greeks and Egyptians followed separate customs. There is one particularly interesting example of Greek influence on an Egyptian tomb situated at Tuna el-Gebel in Middle Egypt in the necropolis of the ancient city of Hermopolis where the ibis-god Thoth was worshipped. Here, Egyptian and Greek art and religion seem to have fused to some extent from the 3rd century BC to the 3rd century AD. Funerary houses of sun-baked bricks, dating to the Roman period but decorated with scenes from both Greek and Egyptian mythology, have been excavated, as well as the family tomb of Petosiris, an important citizen of Hermopolis. He was High-priest of the Temple of Thoth and lived during the reign of Ptolemy I. His family tomb, excavated by Lefébure in 1920, consists of a pronaos with the façade of an Egyptian temple, a chapel, and a shaft with several sections which contained the sarcophagi of Petosiris, his wife and younger son. However, it is the decoration of the tomb as well as its architecture which is of particular interest. The general theme of all the scenes remains true to the Egyptian tradition, but the clothes, hairstyles and personal adornment of the figures is Hellenistic, and the hieroglyphic wall inscriptions include sentiments such as personal piety which are not usually found in traditional Egyptian texts. This fusion of styles is rare, partly because the underlying concepts of Egyptian and Greek art and sculpture were so different, and generally it was customary to maintain two distinct styles.

The last major religious development in Egypt during this period was the arrival and spread of Christianity. Egyptians eagerly adopted this new religion, which reached them as early as the 1st century AD. There is no conclusive evidence about the beginnings of the Christian community there, but the religion had several concepts which

A mummy of a child (2nd century AD) excavated by Petrie at Hawara. It has a cartonnage cover with separate gilded pieces for the head, chest and feet. The eyes are inlaid and the moulded imitations of jewellery are set with glass to represent semi-precious stones.

were already familiar to Egyptian thought. It was introduced to Egypt through Alexandria, to which relatives and friends of the Jewish community had brought it from Jerusalem, and the new faith produced ideas, such as disinterest in worldly goods and mutual support, which were immediately popular to the masses. These concepts soon spread amongst the poor even while the wealthy retained their old religions.

Although many people were converted to Islam after the Arab conquest of Egypt in the 7th century, strong Christian communities still survived, particularly in the south and around Thebes. The name Copt (derived from the Greek Aigyptios, which became Qibt after the Arabs arrived) was first used in Europe in the 16th century as a term to distinguish the Christians in Egypt. Today, the Copts have their own Patriarch and they form a substantial and important minority in Egypt.

The change of religion and language profoundly affected other aspects of Egypt's culture. Until then, it had drawn its inspiration from the Pharaonic and Hellenistic traditions, but new and distinctive art forms now emerged. Although at first non-Christian themes tended to predominate, by the 4th and 5th centuries Christian concepts began to be the inspiration for the paintings, sculpture and textiles found in monasteries, churches and houses. Decorative and ornamental frescos were used on the walls, and woollen and linen textiles that have also survived well in Egypt's climate provide fine examples of religious vestments, burial garments and wrappings, and secular tunics and domestic furnishings.

With the arrival of Islam, the country again underwent radical changes but the native genius continued to flourish, producing some of the finest masterpieces of Islamic architecture and art. The discovery over the past few centuries of Egypt's earliest history has provided a view, as yet incomplete, of one of the world's most magnificent civilizations. Many monuments and a wealth of texts written by the Egyptians and their neighbours (who both envied and admired them) have survived, and these enable us to understand something of the scope and stature of Egypt's achievements. They make us aware of the Egyptians' wisdom and humour, their constant search for excellence, and their appreciation of style and elegance in literature and the visual arts. Perhaps most of all, the buildings, artifacts and inscriptions provide a magnificent record of their unfailing determination to defeat death on a vastly conceived and unprecedented scale; and by winning the admiration of the modern world, they have indeed ensured their own immortality.

A Chronological Table of Egyptian History

PERIOD	DATE	DYNASTY
Predynastic Period	c.5000–c.3100 BC	
Archaic Period	c.3100–c.2890 BC	I
	c.2890–c.2686 BC	II
Old Kingdom	c.2686–c.2613 BC	III
	c.2613–c.2494 BC	IV
	c.2494–c.2345 BC	V
	c.2345–c.2181 BC	VI
First Intermediate Period	c.2181–c.2173 BC	VII ⎫
	c.2173–c.2160 BC	VIII ⎬ (Memphite)
	c.2160–c.2130 BC	IX ⎫
	c.2130–c.2040 BC	X ⎬ (Heracleopolitan)
	c.2133–c.1991 BC	XI (Theban)
Middle Kingdom	1991–1786 BC	XII
Second Intermediate Period	1786–1633 BC	XIII
	1786–c.1603 BC	XIV (Xois)
	1674–1567 BC	XV (Hyksos)
	c.1684–1567 BC	XVI (Hyksos)
	c.1650–1567 BC	XVII (Theban)
New Kingdom	1567–1320 BC	XVIII
	1320–1200 BC	XIX
	1200–1085 BC	XX
Third Intermediate Period	1085–945 BC	XXI
	945–730 BC	XXII (Bubastis)
	817(?)–730 BC	XXIII (Tanis)
	720–715 BC	XXIV (Sais)
	715–668 BC	XXV (Ethiopian)
Late Period	664–525 BC	XXVI (Sais)
	525–404 BC	XXVII (Persian)
	404–399 BC	XXVIII (Sais)
	399–380 BC	XXIX (Mendes)
	380–343 BC	XXX (Sebennytos)
	343–332 BC	XXXI (Persian)
Conquest by Alexander the Great	332 BC	⎫
Ptolemaic Period	332 BC–30 BC	⎬ Graeco-Roman Period
Conquest by Romans	30 BC	⎪
Roman Period	30 BC–4th century AD	⎭

Further Reading

BAINES, J. and MALEK, J., *Atlas of Ancient Egypt* (Oxford, 1980)

CARTER, H. and MACE, A. C. *The Tomb of Tut-Ankh-Amen* (London, 1923–33)

CLAYTON, P. A., *The Rediscovery of Ancient Egypt: Artists and Travellers in the 19th Century* (London, 1982)

DAWSON, W. R. and UPHILL, E., *Who Was Who in Egyptology* (London, 1972)

DENON, V. *Travels in Upper and Lower Egypt* (London, 1803)

DROWER, M. S., *Flinders Petrie: A Life in Archaeology* (London, 1985)

EDWARDS, AMELIA B., *A Thousand Miles up the Nile* (London, 1877)

EDWARDS, I. E. S., *The Pyramids of Egypt* (Harmondsworth, rev. ed. 1985)

FAGAN, B. M., *The Rape of the Nile: Tomb Robbers, Tourists, and Archaeologists in Egypt* (London, 1977)

GREENER, L., *High Dam over Nubia* (New York, 1962)

GREENER, L., *The Discovery of Egypt* (London, 1966)

IVERSEN, E., *The Myth of Egypt and its Hieroglyphs in European Tradition* (Copenhagen, 1961)

JAMES, T. G. H. (ed.), *Excavating in Egypt: The Egypt Exploration Society 1882–1982* (London, 1982)

KEMP, B. J., *Ancient Egypt: Anatomy of a Civilisation* (London, 1989)

MAYES, S., *The Great Belzoni* (New York, 1961)

PETRIE, W. M. F., *Ten Years Digging in Egypt, 1881–1891* (London, 1892)

PETRIE, W. M. F., *Seventy Years in Archaeology* (London, 1931)

TILLETT, S., *Egypt Itself: The Career of Robert Hay* (London, 1984)

WILKINSON, J. G., *Manners and Customs of the Ancient Egyptians,* 3 vols. (London, 1837); 2nd ed. rev. by S. Birch (London, 1878)

WORTHAM, J. D., *British Egyptology 1549–1906* (Newton Abbot, 1972)

Illustration Acknowledgments

The Publishers are grateful to the following for permission to reproduce copyright photographs.

Manchester Museum: pp. 38, 41, 42, 43, 47, 56, 57, 70, 77, 79, 80, 83, 85, 94, 98, 103, 104, 105, 106, 136, 137, 138, 139, 141, 142, 147, 148, 149, 150, 151, 153, 160, 161, 162, 171, 177, 179, 181, 182, 183, 184.
Plate section: plates 6a, 6b, 8, 9a, 9b, 12

By courtesy of the Director and University Librarian, The John Rylands University Library of Manchester: pp. 17, 19, 21, 22, 23, 27, 39, 55, 63, 64, 86, 100, 112, 127, 129, 167, 168.
Plate section: plates 1b, 2/3, 4, 10b, 15b, 20/21

The following photographs in the plate section are taken by Geoff Thompson and reproduced by his permission: plates 1a, 3, 5, 6/7, 10a, 11, 13a, 13b, 14a, 14b, 15a, 16, 17, 18a, 18b, 19a, 19b, 21, 22, 23, 24

Index